The[re]
You Are

Marion Woodman:
Biography of a Friendship
Jill Mellick

CHIRON PUBLICATIONS • ASHEVILLE, NORTH CAROLINA

www.ChironPublications.com

Front Cover Photo © Jeanne Shutes
Cover design Jennifer Wilkerson
Interior design by Danijela Mijailovic
Printed primarily in the United States of America.

ISBN 978-1-63051-996-4 paperback
ISBN 978-1-63051-997-1 hardcover
ISBN 978-1-63051-998-8 electronic
ISBN 978-1-63051-999-5 limited edition paperback

Library of Congress Cataloging-in-Publication Data Pending

For

Ellen

Eleanora

Dorit

Foreword

"No matter how many hours, days, months, or years pass between certain people, the rhythm of their conversation remains the same as when they first spoke."[1] This "quiet linguistic fact" was reflected in the deep and enduring relationship between Jill Mellick and Marion Woodman. It also has been true of my relationship with Jill Mellick.

I met Jill in the early 1990s. She has been a quiet and powerful presence in my life ever since. Jill, herself an introvert, is the one who helped me recognize my own introversion and the importance of allowing time and space for silence, especially in the context of my own public-facing work and my life as the mother of four children. One of the many pearls of wisdom Jill imparted was that for an introvert, emptiness can serve as the vehicle for finding presence; silence can be the context in which voice is heard. Her life has served as a beautiful example, even a form of permission: taking time for silence and cultivating a creative practice in one's private space can generate greater contributions for the wider world.

This book, *THERE YOU ARE Marion Woodman: Biography of a Friendship*, is but one of many gifts Jill has brought into the world. Not surprisingly, it also manifests the unique alchemy of Jill's own creative process. Every project she undertakes manifests a strange combination of freedom and interconnectivity, in both form and content. This may be the most important aspect of Jill's legacy.

Marion Woodman has also been an important voice of wisdom for me over the past three decades. I started reading and listening to Marion Woodman, no doubt at Jill's suggestion, during a period when I was hit hard by a dawning recognition of the damage done by patriarchy, especially within my own Catholic spiritual tradition. I remember listening to a now well-known recording of an event described in this book, wherein Marion

---

[1] From Introduction to this book.

recounted a dream in which she had lost her pearls, jewels that symbolized her feminine wisdom, buried in the dirt. In Marion's dream, the responsibility for uncovering the jewels of feminine consciousness rested with the dreamer herself. But unexpectedly, Marion tied the dream to a line from the New Testament: *"Don't cast your pearls before swine, lest they trample them under their feet."* (Matthew 7:6). That paradoxical linkage between the wisdom of the dream and the wisdom of the scripture was signature Marion Woodman. Her singular voice continues to reverberate through this extraordinary biography of her friendship with Jill.

In an instance of synchronicity of the sort often noticed and highlighted by Jill, the day she contacted me to write a few lines as a foreword to this book, a flash of Marion had already come to mind. That day I had a public presentation that was significant to me, but where I knew that there would be some unspoken pressure to perform in a way that might feel inauthentic. Before the event, Marion's memorable words, "I am a woman greatly loved, capable of great loving," crossed my mind, reminding me to literally listen to the timbre of my voice as I was speaking, to stay connected with the meaning and ideas I had come to share.

Not surprisingly, the living, embodied wisdom manifest by both Jill and Marion is a significant feature running through this unique biography of their friendship. But this book also captures dimensions of their relationship of which I was previously unaware. While I knew that Jill and Marion had been close friends and professional colleagues for decades, I did not know until I read this manuscript that Jill and Marion were soul mates. There was a mysterious dynamic between them from the moment they met. The fearlessness and openness with which they approached their relationship over the following decades allowed them to tap into previously uncharted wells and release a wealth of feminine wisdom. The trust and intimacy they cultivated fueled new forms of creativity in both of their remarkable lives. This recounting of their friendship will be incalculably beneficial to others, as it unlocks more of their shared wisdom.

Eileen Donahoe, J.D., Ph. D.
U.S. Ambassador, United Nations Human Rights Council, 2010 - 2013
Executive Director, Global Digital Policy Incubator, Stanford University

August 2021

Preface

To sustain close friendships across decades and oceans is a grace, particularly if one is an introvert. One may walk through the front door, sit down to tea, and talk as though months or years have not passed. Of course, circumstances change, usually not mentioned by those in my generation and culture; siblings, parents, and children might have had troubles, turmoil, and triumphs, sensed in an unfinished sentence or a year deftly omitted from the conversation.

Why do I refer to some close friendships as deep and others as warm and wonderful? Am I using language that puts something elusive yet substantive at risk of death by hyperbole? I ponder the enduring, remarkable friends in my life. Each friendship has evolved uniquely, and I treasure each: its uncanniness, the commonalities and complementarities, the synchronicities that preexisted and influence the relationship. Too, what often characterizes deep, abiding friendships is not what one says to the other but what does *not* need to be said—or, at times, what is intentionally left unsaid.

Why have I chosen Marion's and my experience, not another? My other deep friendships are very much alive; each is unique, precious, evolving. Too, I am still involved with my second of two passionate vocations as well as several passionate avocations. I have chosen my friendship with Marion because it has lived its arc and because we have left paw prints. I share a few of these on behalf of us both.

Marion had many special friendships, of which mine was but one. I mention particularly her friendship with Eleanora Woloy, M.D. Eleanora was closer in age to Marion than I. Marion and I were almost a generation apart, she the older. For Marion, both Eleanora the individual as well as her friendship with Marion held as steady, warm, and solid as sun-drenched rocks on an island in the sun. And their loving connection was as deep and clear as Georgian Bay, where the Woodmans spent so many summers.

Eleanora was one of those who gave *to* rather than sought something *from* Marion. Later, when Marion experienced increasingly critical medical storms, it was Eleanora who was again an island, one where Marion and Ross, her husband, could seek shelter, moor, and rest a while, receive unconditional love and help. She flew to Canada many times to be with them during prolonged crises, and it was from Eleanora I sought guidance about how best to support Marion as certain changes advanced.

Eleanora and I share a birthday. We also share deep appreciation for our own friendship. It holds steady for months as we live our lives on opposite coasts, then picks up with delight and a palpable sense of immediacy and presence as though we have been sharing a cup of tea daily. We also share deep appreciation of and respect for our separate friendships with Marion.

Marion's and my unexpected, profound friendship was and is still a mystery and a grace. I have recorded this not so that you can know either of us better but so that you, too, might recognize and consider the mystery of what sustains certain remarkable friendships. I reiterate: this is not a book about Marion, and it is not a book about me; neither is this really a book about Marion *and* me. It *is* about the experience of deep friendship. It surprised and nourished us. Neither of us understood our intense connection, but we stood under it at peace, with trust and gratitude. When I agreed to give my professional and some personal materials for archiving, I became aware that Marion and I had left prints in our field. Neither of us knew what the *animal* looked like, but when I reviewed the archival material, I saw some of its paw prints.

Most of our experiences took place in person or on frequent phone calls. We also wrote letters. Our friendship grew in an era of now-antiquated forms of correspondence: phone calls, letters, postcards from anywhere that wasn't "home," birthday cards, Christmas cards. Marion wrote the preface to my first and second books, *The Natural Artistry of Dreams* and *The Art of Dreaming*; we jointly published one book, *Coming Home to*

Myself; and Marion includes us throughout her book *Bone*. These—and many photographs—are some of the paw prints.

Beyond such paw prints, I cannot in fact describe our unexpected, intense, steady, uncanny friendship. I know what it felt like. So did Marion. She told me almost at once how she experienced it; I echoed her in that same startled conversation. One's heart senses and stands still when such a mystifying connection brushes low branches, strolls through ferns and twigs on the floor of one's inner forest. I share its presence so that you can sense its evanescent core for your own use, recognition, or receptivity.

I once attended a lecture on menopause by a respected ob-gyn. A woman in her thirties asked how she would know when she had hot flashes. The audience erupted into laughter. One doesn't ask; one knows. A deep friendship is like that. And it is just as all-encompassing and startling; I had to manage its impact, my doubt of self and other, my surprise, self-examination and clarity. Each person has to be willing to live into the twists and turns of such a friendship, to treat it with both curiosity and respect—especially when distance, family needs, health, and professional worlds challenge its steadiness.

When I joined some of the Jung family in 2019 to present *The Art of C.G. Jung*[2] at an event co-sponsored by Pacifica Graduate Institute and the University of California, Santa Barbara, the senior archivist showed me the OPUS Archives and Research Center, where my own archives would be. She thoughtfully added that, given how close Marion and I had been, she would be placing my archives next to Marion's. So, I reflected, we shall remain separate yet side by side in death as in life. Original copies of what is in this book will be available years after my demise. I want to write about our friendship myself. I want the inaccuracies, inferences, and errors to be mine, not someone else's after my death.

Another reason why this is wise to be attempted by me is that our friendship had an invisible cultural context, not evident to many. Marion grew up in Canada and I in Australia, both Commonwealth countries.

---

[2] JM was a contributing author for *The Art of C.G. Jung* by The Foundation of the Works of C.G. Jung (W.W. Norton & Co., 2018).

Although a generation apart, we were raised knowing that health, wealth, and achievement should rarely if ever be discussed. I once called a distant cousin, a medical specialist, not having spoken with him since a visit three months earlier. We reached the "How is Jane?" part of our warm conversation. He replied about his wife of decades, "She's had a spot of bother lately, but we hope to join John in England for Easter." I later learned that Jane had been in intensive care for six weeks with a life-threatening illness.

Successes were never discussed either by those who succeeded or by their family members. Oblique allusions were acceptable under complex, unspoken rules e.g., "Come in if you can make your way through. The place is a wreck. We've just flown back from a surprise do for Robert." The "do" could be anything from a surprise birthday party to a national award. Professions have wound their way into conversations as women have taken on more and varied professional roles. Marion and I were at ease mentioning facts such as a publication or a change in our academic work or our focus as therapists. Our worlds might change; the tea was the same.

Marion and I did cross invisible lines of colonial acculturation that ruled both her generation and mine. While we *never* would have dreamt of talking about wealth or the lack thereof, we did talk health. And when we were together and in our second vocations, in-depth psychology, we abandoned the greatest shibboleth—with relief and a good dose of asperity—by giving voice to the work of the psyche, the life of the soul, the role of the body, and creative expression in psychological and spiritual development.

These shibboleths are dwindling with time, new generations, and social media. Obliquity, bathos, irony, understatement, innuendo, and reserve are dying a fast death with the passing of time and the introduction of new technology.

What one cannot experience in social media is a quiet linguistic fact that someone has surely researched but whose explanation has passed me by: no matter how many hours, days, months or years pass between certain people, the rhythm of their conversation remains the same as when they first spoke—unless something medical intervenes. Whenever they re-engage, the melody, beat, and pauses in their conversation are still uncannily the same as they were before. Rhythm of conversation is the thrum of the heart of a friendship, and often what determines its quality and longevity. Too, it is often at the core of a successful analysis or therapeutic experience. A therapist and patient may like each other, but if the conversational rhythm is not synergistic, the work will not progress easily. Marion and I enjoyed a rhythm of conversation that was our own and that prevailed through grief and joy.

Other subtleties lost in friendships predominantly sustained through social media are the characteristics of someone's "hand," as graphologists and calligraphers call handwriting. Emojis hardly do the trick. Marion handwrote her communiqués—to me, to all. She doubtless never learned how to type. She and I grew up in eras when those headed to university were expected *not* to know how to type and expected *not* to type. Typing was reserved for those headed straight to a job or to other institutions. I didn't know how to type and wrote in Italic script with a fountain pen for years. I loved calligraphy and graphology. When I found myself immigrating to the United States, I quickly learned that my lack of typing skills was a deficit. I learned. Fast. Later, when a severe car accident left me still able to make art but unable to write, I resorted to typing for personal as well as professional work.

So the letters in this book were handwritten by Marion and typed by me. No emails. No texts. (Most students no longer learn cursive writing. I wonder if anybody will be able to read Marion's letters in her elongated, narrow, forward-leaning script twenty-five years from now.) What is missing from my transcription of Marion's letters is the unspoken emotional and energetic quality of each. I could sense before I read a word whether Marion was tired, pensive, hurried, harried, excited. How she wrote later in her life already told me much about her physiology, whether or not she had told me personally or mentioned it in the letter.

I have made careful decisions about what to include here. I use full names only when they are relevant to the onward movement of the material and/or the individuals are at ease with their names being mentioned. I add almost no material from Marion's and my private lives. Marion was extroverted, though she was sure she was a serious introvert; I pass as a socialized introvert, a fairly social animal, but am deeply introverted. Too, Marion was raised with—and I still have—a culturally determined, now outmoded sense of privacy. I choose to respect this; many things we shared were implicitly understood to be for the other alone.

This small biography assumes but doesn't detail all the August birthday cards, the Christmas cards, many of the modest gifts, each time she stayed with us, each of the innumerable phone calls. We saved intimate exchanges for when we were physically together and for the phone calls between us— Marion at home in Toronto or London, Ontario, or wherever she was working domestically or overseas, and me in my Palo Alto home, my natal Australia, second homes in New Mexico or Kaua`i, or traveling overseas.

I undertake this biography of a friendship knowing that I cannot and shall not include the deepest moments. These happened when we didn't speak at all or when we spoke of something once and never referred to it again; kairos looked favorably on a particular hour and not again, either on the telephone or in person. Moments walking on the beach, moments under a wet moon, moments late at night when things were said before sleep took us into our own realms. Perhaps you will sense some of the experience in the photographic images and paintings I have included.

I know that if I am to be honest and fair about Marion's experience of this friendship, I need to include her experience of me. I suspect that part of my spendthrift use of language is that I am not at ease in the spotlight. I overcompensate. However, an historian friend[3] specializing in Abigail Adams's friendships and correspondence said firmly, "You *can't* leave out Marion's experience of you. That's excising *her*." Oh. I hadn't thought of that.

This story has a chronology, but the friendship was not linear. Friendships don't evolve in a linear way, and I tire of being linear; I've put the correspondence in as linear a fashion as I can. Other letters I wrote to Marion might or might not be in her archives; I can only include ones that are in my own computer archives and those already formally archived in

---

[3] Edith Gelles, Ph.D., historian and author, Senior Scholar at the Clayman Institute for Gender Research at Stanford University.

Marion's materials. I also include, in minimal temporal order, moments that were the essence of our experience and characterized the friendship. Ours was not better than other deep friendships. Like all deep friendships, it had its own unique rhythm and intensity. Intense it was. It was a love affair without sex, emotional seduction, or propinquity.

Why this book? I didn't plan to write it—quite the opposite after a recent marathon effort on another project. But Marion is dead, and I have terminal cancer. Time is changing perspective on the history of our friendship. Knowing that my words will be inadequate, I still want to pay homage to it myself.

Minor notes: Spelling and punctuation are idiosyncratic. Marion's spelling and punctuation use Canadian English, which closely resembles British English (and which made my computer persistently unhappy). I am a bilingual speller and user of punctuation. When writing to someone who is not American, I usually spell and punctuate in British/Australian English. I learned American spelling and punctuation when I was a freelance textbook editor, generating money for doctoral classes. So in this book I use American English spelling and punctuation for my own notes and descriptions.

At first, for the sake of consistency, I tried to convert everything to American spelling and punctuation. It was then I learned about yet another subtle element that linked Marion and me: what frames and is the substrate for the written word. I became conscious that I felt a sense of comfort and "home" when I would read a letter from Marion and its spelling was almost exactly what I had been trained in since childhood. (My computer has been most unhappy about my choice to keep Marion's and my letters as they were spelled.)

I have taken editorial liberties for the sake of privacy with Marion's letters and liberties with my own letters for the sake of clarity, brevity, simplicity and privacy; once an English teacher and editor, always an English teacher and editor.

Jill Mellick
Palo Alto, CA, 2021

A hair clip brought Marion and me together.

We had met before, but it was the hair clip that did it.

Marion and I had met briefly at conferences. Conferences have long replaced shipboard romances for bringing people together for intimate, circumscribed periods: they are intense, usually located in places of beauty, limited in numbers and time, and removed from the rhythms of ordinary life. Two of my experiences of deep friendships started this way. One began at a conference in Palo Alto with the hair clip; the other began at a conference in Italy with mutual sartorial admiration across a crowded rooftop bar in Assisi, followed by an ice cream in the town square.

Marion was offering a workshop in Palo Alto. Colleague, coauthor, and soul mate Jeanne Shutes and I decided that we'd attend. The room was packed. Marion's deep voice was speaking about the feminine spirit and the importance of relating to one's body, her own life's ever-receding siren. The body-psyche connection was her special love as an analyst; she and others such as Arnie Mindell were actively bringing the role of the body into Jungian analysis.

"Her throwaway lines are almost better than her prepared material," my discerning companion whispered. She was right.

At Marion's behest, the whole room broke into pairs. Each member of a pair was to "sculpt" the other's body. We chose to sculpt Demeter and Persephone. Marion walked slowly through the mass of anonymous pairs silently absorbed in their sculpting. She watched intently. I was holding my position as Persephone just as Jeanne, steeped in Greek mythology, had sculpted me. I then sculpted her as Demeter. It was fun—living clay. The room was silent. As Marion walked by us the second time, she paused for a long time in front of us.

"Persephone … Demeter," she murmured. She looked a little longer and moved on.

Marion, Jeanne, and I found ourselves standing side by side during one of the breaks that weekend. My hair clip fell out. I picked it up and slipped it back in again.

"Jill! How did you do that? I want to do that! With *my* hair." I was surprised she remembered my name. Marion and I both had thick hair. Hers was wiry and rebellious; mine, wavy and fine. I turned my back to her, pulled out the clip, slid it back in and clipped it again. "I just do … this," I replied.

"Ohh!" She clapped her hands as though she'd won the lottery.

"I would've been a hairdresser, listening to similar stories to those I hear in my office, had my parents and others not had higher aspirations for me," I said.

"I want to find a clip like that in Canada."

"I'll send you one."

"Really? You can find another one?"

"This blessed one came from our travels in the south of France. But I've just found a local source. I'll send you one."

"You must tell me the cost, Jill," Marion said earnestly.

"Of course I shan't. It's my huge gift. They're ringing the bell. Go!"

∞

JM Notes

I sent Marion the hair clip and a note when she was back home in London, Ontario, writing another book. She would soon leave for ShaSha, the small island in Georgian Bay (off the northern edge of Lake Huron) that she and Ross owned. She had once described it as surrounded by morning mist, moss, rock, water, and silence.

∞

An evening in San Francisco. Marion was giving a lecture at the Unitarian church, where larger events associated with the C.G. Jung Institute in San Francisco were held at that time. The church was packed, and we were seated far back. Marion finally mounted the stage. She spoke first of her fear of speaking to us and told us what would become one of her signature stories.

"When I arrived here, I became so paralyzed with fear I felt as though I were passing out. I slipped out that side door to get some fresh air. I stood in the night air. I heard a stern inner voice saying reprovingly, 'You should never have left the church basement in Port Stanley, Marion!'" It was, indeed, a long way from her father's parsonage in rural Ontario to that stage in San Francisco. "I couldn't do it. I knew I couldn't do *this* without help. So I raised my arms up to the night and asked Sophia for help. Well, I've made it onto the stage. I'm still overwhelmed but I'm no longer passing out. I can stand here before you if I repeat to myself what a wise woman I knew used to tell herself: 'I am a woman who is greatly loved and capable of great loving.'"

The audience was already in love with Marion and what she seemed to represent for them. It did not occur to her to imagine the intensity of their feelings for her—something that later concerned more than one Jungian institute. The audience broke into applause.

Much later, Marion told me and others what had triggered this experience. She was driven to the venue by the warm, kind event organizer for the institute; they had passed a long line of people snaking around a block. Making small talk, Marion asked, "Who's in town?"

"Woodman," her host had replied calmly.

∞

May 19, 1988

Dear Marion,

Last night, after a day working with my Alzheimer's patients and families, I thought my heart couldn't get any bigger. I was wrong. Seeing your letter on the table,[4] I was deeply touched. Touched that you had responded, let alone so soon. I wasn't anticipating hearing from you, let alone during the summer. From what you said and what you did not, I sense that even responding was to draw on precious energies already stretched to transparency. Your letter nourishes with its clarity, honesty, and caring.

By way of partial thanks, I offer you this dream, which came a few hours after reading your letter. I knew at once it was a dream that wasn't just personal, but transpersonal. It didn't just belong to me. The dream: I'm with you. You have asked two women to act out parts of a dream I have had. I turn to the first, touch her bare and ample back and sense no conscious connection with her. Perhaps I'm even slightly repelled. I turn to the second woman, who is tall, slim, clothed. She begins to speak with authority, quiet finality, and barely suppressed indignation.

She calls me to task as might a woman who is finally claiming her equality with a chauvinistic husband. She lists incident after incident in which I failed to consult her, failed to ask her opinion, made unilateral decisions, insulted her by committing her to things she had no say in. I know as she speaks that you have asked her to play the role of, and that she is, my body.

I turn to the ample, undressed woman and ask, "Then who are you?" She smiles a quiet, small smile and leaves. There was more, but the rest is for me to work on personally. The above belongs to you as well as to me. May

---

[4] JM's original letter and MW's response are missing. It seems JM had written to thank MW for the positive impact her writing, workshops and talks had had on her and her patients.

the energy, insight, and loving support you have cast so wide return to you sevenfold during this transition time.

Again, my thanks with love,

Jill

∞

JM Notes
Friday, February 24, 1989 – Sunday, February 25, 1989

A weekend workshop with Marion at Esalen. Jeanne and I decided to attend. Hoping to invite Marion to give a workshop where I was teaching, I asked her if she could spare a few moments to discuss its feasibility at some point. She invited me over to the house that Esalen had provided Ross and her for their extended stay.

I walked over early so I could sit a little, just looking out to the Pacific and the mating monarch butterflies. Then I rose and walked over to the house. I could see Marion talking on the phone. Ross answered the door. He smiled down at me and was warm and friendly. His authoritative, nuanced voice had almost a Scottish lilt and a rich, kind timbre. He was handsome to my eye: a dapper, professorial type with trim, rusty beard and piercing blue eyes. His teeth were stained from cigarettes or a pipe—something comfortingly familiar to me that I'd not seen since I'd emigrated (unintentionally) from Australia. Ross reminded me of an eagle, coasting on an invisible wind. Then, spotting a prey, he would fold the wings of his attention close and plummet ergonomically down on a topic or person.

Until Marion got off the phone, Ross and I found ourselves chatting in a way that only colonials do, he being Canadian and I, Australian. We talked about the West Coast where we were perched, about west coasts in general—Ireland, Scotland, Iona—and about the gloriously clear, cool weather.

Marion was wearing a cream three-quarter coat over what she had been wearing that morning during the workshop. It imbued her with an odd air of formality and impermanence. She explained that they had just arrived at the house and hadn't settled in yet. Their suitcases stood unpacked.

"We can do this another time, Marion."

"No, no. Now is good. But we must find somewhere to sit." She looked around, perplexed.

"What about outside? It's a lovely day," I suggested.

Ross offered to move some wicker chairs out onto the patio, but Marion didn't want to take them outside. I sensed that she thought they shouldn't. Finally, she lighted on the sitting room, a large, cold room with big pillows thrown all over and a pair of high-backed chairs in front of an inactive fireplace. Ross vanished.

We sat. The chairs evoked a formality that was uncomfortable both physically and psychologically for me. However, Marion placed them on either side of the fireplace at angles to each other, which helped a little. We were seated close enough for the conversation to be warm and personal.

Before I could explore workshop possibilities, we just talked. We discovered uncanny parallels in our life experiences: we had each completed English Honours degrees, a British university system equivalent of Master of Arts in the U.S. The subjects and syllabi we had taken in high school and university had been almost the same, so we shared an inner library—from Shakespeare to Chaucer to Yeats to T.S. Eliot. Marion had been Ross's teaching assistant for a year; Ross taught Romantic Literature at the University of Western Ontario. My father taught English Literature at the University of Queensland.

As young colonials do, Marion and I had each traveled abroad after graduation. Both of us had taught high school English literature and language. Marion's first classroom experiences were during her pursuit of her teaching credential; she was interning at a government school and terrified. Her supervisor advised voice lessons, so she took them. She went on to teach high school English in London, Ontario, for more than twenty years. I had taught high school English at my "sister school,"[5] and my experiences were delightful except for the small matter of a fierce, unspoken pecking order among the faculty. I left after two years, sadly wiser about territorial politics if still in love with teaching and my students. I returned to teaching much later in the field of psychology and taught for decades at the graduate level.

Marion and I had each been raised with a strong Protestant affiliation. Each of us had moved from teaching to the practice of psychotherapy. Each had nurtured children of our hearts, not bodies, and agreed that, in retrospect, Fate had been wise. We were both writers; her first books— *The Owl Was a Baker's Daughter* and *Addiction to Perfection*—were far better known than my first two, which had been published in Australia to inspire elementary students in creative writing. We loved the ocean. We loved singing. We loved dancing. I mentioned last night's dream of dancing with a young man, "Sam," and the synchronicity of her telling a story about her dog, Sam, that morning in the workshop.

Both of us had had major car accidents that had changed the course of our lives. I spoke of my October 1988 accident in which, on my way to a meditation retreat in upstate New York, I had been hit by an old convent car driven by an elderly wimpled nun. The weight of her convent clunker struck my light rental car; I spun clockwise twice. Were it not for my genetic hypermobility, my neck would have snapped; instead, muscles and ligaments tore. It would take years to heal and leave me unable to write by hand. I didn't know then, but a rare condition, severe Ehlers Danlos Syndrome (including its even rarer vascular form), had saved my life while simultaneously making recovery long and always partial. Unlike others whose bodies take six weeks to mend and then six months for the tissue to mature, mine takes six months to mend and two years for tissue to mature. At the time of this Esalen workshop, I didn't know that I was only six months into an initial two-year partial recovery. Marion asked piercing questions diffidently. The accident had created jagged inner responses and

---

[5] A term used to describe independent girls' schools run by the same entity.

strong indications of life-changing directions; however, I only alluded to them briefly. Though Marion asked deep questions, I didn't want to change the tenor of our visit by intruding with my inner work. Marion paid disconcertingly deep attention to these brief statements.

She spoke about her own car accident. She said she had had a similar severe experience that resulted in prolonged paralysis of one side of her face and a slow return to full functioning. She temporarily lost the use of an arm and sat with a crystal subtly held against her paralyzed facial tissue during sessions with patients. She spoke of having slowly, slowly regained movement in that side of her face. Eventually, feeling in her face returned. She urged patience. "You've already learned remarkable things from this accident if that's what's taught you to be in your body the way I see you are."

"I am? Well, whatever it is I'm doing, it's a twenty-four-hour-a-day thing. It has to be."

Marion's energy soared. Her accident, too, had come at a crucial time in her life. She leaned forward in a way I would later learn was an iconic physical pose of rapt attention.[6] I stopped, "I'm sorry! You're kind to ask, and I'm happy to answer, but we were not meeting about this. You do *not* need to hear this!"

"No, Jill. I want to. I really *do* want to hear, Jill!"

During the two and a half hours we spent together, the energy in the room was electric. What was generated between us would have lit a fire had there been anything other than psychic wood. I finally commented on this. Marion strongly agreed: she felt it too. It wasn't just my imagination. We were each in our full strength, even though she was tired and my neck was weak.

We never did get around to exploring the workshop possibility.

---

[6] MW told JM that she realized much later that her father, the minister, would sit just like this, especially when he was visiting First Nation tribal members.

I finally insisted that I leave so they could unpack. We rose and walked toward the front door. Marion said diffidently that she would welcome my sending her—only if I wished—any dreams I had after our conversation. She also suggested I phone her when she was in Palo Alto in two weeks. I explained that I would be in Australia then, so we agreed that I would write to her. I walked back to our cabin and did dream that night. As promised, I wrote.

∞

March 2, 1989

Dear Marion:

Thank you for your gift of time, compassion and wisdom on Sunday afternoon. I have been exploring avenues in consciousness and too tired to find an angel with whom to wrestle. The unexpected numinosity of our time together is still nourishing me and giving grounded inspiration to my work with patients and students. Our time, I realised later, was, for me, like my experiences on Iona, in Jerusalem, at Epidaurus, at Delphi: a parenthesis in my spiritual and psychological journey.

Sunday night's dreams as promised:

—A group of women pass by a jewellery store. Jewellery has fallen on the floor. Two helpful women pick some up and put it back on the counter but the officious manager says it is *his* place to do that.
<u>Reflection</u>: Pretty obvious so I'll move on.

—You, Marion, write something about me which reads approximately: "Jill's work with her needlepoint/embroidery in no way indicates the presence of any underlying depression."
<u>Reflection</u>: ? but positive I think.

—I am in my paternal grandmother's bedroom, which is poorly lit. Despite her being ill, she has made up a sofa/bed for me. I thank her genuinely, while inwardly noting how uncomfortable it looks for my neck at present. I glance with longing out a window; outside, it is sunny and a cherry tree is in full bloom.

Reflection: I appreciate but cannot fit myself into the expected, the collective…. I am energised by a symbol of spiritual beauty…feminine beauty …. For some strange reason, it brings the image of one who gives [her] life for a cause… a short but beautiful career (!)… spring ….

—A beautiful, ivory-skinned young woman quietly distributes pamphlets. Backlit by the sun, her long, shining, intensely red hair creates an aura around her; her hair looks like flames. A conservative, well-dressed group of elderly women talk self-righteously about her amongst themselves.

I whisper crossly, "Old hags."

The young woman moves past me, oblivious, and disappears into the trees.

Reflection: It seems that the only goddess with hair of flames is Sridevi. In mild form, she is the common mother; in ferocious form, the protectress of the Dalai Lama and monks. She is usually accompanied by five Long-Life Sisters (old women in the dream?) and the Jewel goddesses (women in the first dream?). I sense I am connecting with my inner strength again as opposed to my current lack of outer strength. Unfettered, quietly passionate, contained. She's about her own business, unconcerned with others' judgment.

Marion, to me the dreams indicate we were touching on important themes in our conversation. Too, I have felt restored, energised, strong, exhausted, optimistic, sad, and joyful since we were together—inner experiences, yet ones on which some students and patients are commenting.

Of course, the inner work doesn't stop: I must continue to follow my soul's path and to be at peace about this long healing and where it takes me, and about finding my path so far from my natal home, so far from my immediate family whom I love and want to help.

Miniature pot carved from Iona stone. Jill gave one exactly like her own to Marion. ©Mellick

I am sending a tiny pot I bought on Iona. It is carved whole from local stone from the abbey. I bought it on my last visit there.[7] To me the pot is container, birth canal, a soul stone birthed. For a brief, remarkable afternoon, you were companion for my soul. I would like you to have this talisman of that time.

I'll be in touch later about the workshop planning. Those to whom I've mentioned it are delighted at the possibility. Thank you again.

Marion, may your remaining time at Esalen[8] be blessed by the muse, monarch butterflies, sun and quiet.

With love,

Jill

View from Esalen. ©Mellick

[7] JM visited Iona in 1971. She returned in the '80s to see Robin Hunter, whom she had met there, and to be in Iona's sphere again. Robin was dying of breast cancer and asked JM to go to her cottage to collect certain things precious to her, which she gave to JM.
[8] MW and Ross were staying on at Esalen for several weeks following the workshop.

∞

March 15, 1989

Dear Jill,

If I have written to you before, please understand I am working in three different realities.

There is Esalen, seductive, Great Loving Mother who would like me to do nothing but rest, eat and enjoy the beauty.

Then my writing, which is my inner dedication, very opposed to eternal rest. And another reality that has to do with my analysands in Toronto.

New possibilities here, my husband and I finding a renewed life.

I tell you it has been three explosive weeks.

Either I dreamed I wrote to you or I did write, but I'm not sure, so I will now. Thank you for your wonderful letter. I was so moved by what you wrote about our time together. I felt very open to immense joy that afternoon and felt the love and understanding that moved between us. I am so happy that our being together let your psyche move as it wanted to.

You must be in Australia now. Sorry about the change of pens. I hope you are having a meaningful and happy time with your family and friends.

And Jill, thank you for the exquisite little vase in terms of all it means…

With love,

Marion

∞

November 1, 1989

Dear Marion,

Greetings from earthquake country. At Esalen, you and I spoke briefly about your doing a workshop for the Institute of Transpersonal Psychology in 1991. I'd like to talk with you about that briefly some time over the upcoming Santa Barbara weekend. As a faculty member, I'm not directly involved with workshop planning, but I'd like to pass on to the relevant people your preferred dates, format, travel arrangements, and fee. We all hope you're still open to the possibility.

If you think it is a good idea, I would be happy to supplement your presentation at some point with a short creative arts session—only if you want a rest! I could take the group through some creative writing/art processes. I would design them specifically for and around your presentation or adapt *in situ* to whatever is happening.

While art focuses on product and art therapy focuses on pathology, I help people use the creative process purely for psychological and spiritual growth. In workshops, I usually choose a theme—for example, sacred spaces—and provide participants with art/writing processes designed to explore the presence of that theme in their lives. The response is so encouraging, sometimes overwhelming. I feel inadequate to the demand. You might already have someone or something in mind to supplement your presentation or prefer to present alone. Whatever you decide is fine. I'll just be delighted to have you at the school.

The time we spent at Esalen continues to nourish. Again I thank you for that gift of time, energy, and love. I wish time and distance permitted more. I'll check in with you at Santa Barbara to see whether you can talk about dates and so forth for the workshop during a break.

With love,

Jill

∞

JM Dream
November 10, 1989

Marion has filmed me swimming (something she had told me to do in the dream). The film shows me smiling, swimming in the four directions. I cast water into the air before swimming in each direction.

She has some art pieces of mine on the wall.

I say to her, "You really do care, don't you. You care without being responsible."

She tells me that her feelings about me come as somewhat of a surprise to her.

I ask her to help me to learn how to feel and not just think.

I awoke feeling as though we really *are* connected and even feeling as though, at some time, we might end up working together. Beyond the workshop offer, can't imagine how. Anyway, warmth and love in the dream.

∞

November 17, 1989

Dear Marion,

Welcome home. I hope your trip brought you as much inspiration and nurture as you brought all of us. It was a joy to be with you—as always. I'm so glad you and I had a chance to talk a little. I've felt very close to you in spirit over these months, since our Esalen time. I'm so happy that your little Iona pot has a home with your statue, "Echo."

Marion, your original offer to do a workshop this coming March is too much to resist. Let's not wait until 1991. I think it is possible to plan it—if we stay small. Would you enjoy leading a two-day retreat for around 20 participants from the institute and transpersonal community here? We could hold the retreat at ITP[9]; it occupies the larger part of a beautiful old mansion in the meditative and lovely grounds of a Catholic retreat center. If you'd like, it could be a women's retreat.

Santa Cruz tells me you'll be working with their group from Thursday, March 15, onwards. Could you come to ITP the weekend before March 10 and 11? This is the beginning of a one-week term break for students. It would also give you two or three days between workshops to rest and gather psychic energy again.

The intent of the retreat would be rest and renewal—we could even call it "Rites of Renewal: A Spring Retreat" if you like. A retreat format would allow you to share material in whatever way your intuition leads—a way of working and being that I value in you and practise myself. Participants also value intuitive presentations and would be open to experimentation. I think you'd find them exciting. Let me know your thoughts. And if you would like other suggestions. I'm open to whatever feels right to you.

After Santa Barbara, I'm even more excited about the possibility of helping groups deepen their experiential understanding of your material through creative artwork and writing. Let me know if you'd like me to offer a creative session. I did adapt some of the creative arts processes I've been developing and teaching in recent years specifically to themes you explore. I'd like to give the group some opportunity to work creatively with your material. With you present, each member's sharing of his/her creative process and work would carry healing insights for other members and often can generate a sacred, even numinous group energy.

However, this idea might not fit with how you work. If it doesn't, I understand. We shall develop a format that respects your wishes and

---

[9] Institute of Transpersonal Psychology, then in Menlo Park, California; it later became Sofia University, located in Palo Alto, California.

rhythms. After all, if the retreat cannot be designed to renew you as leader, then where is the feminine principle?!

Marion, I'll call you when you've had a chance to let the rhythms of your life settle in again and had time to consider this. I do hope I've seriously tempted you. My intuition says strongly that your connection with the transpersonal community here would be a synergistic one. It would be a joy for me—and the students—to have you here.

Meanwhile, I send you much love.

Jill

∞

JM Notes

Friday, November 30, 1989

I received a letter from Marion.[10] She surprised me by her openness about her positive feelings about me. She invited me to look within and see what, if anything, I hoped for *personally* from our time together, not just from her being a workshop presenter

January 20, 1990

I noted in my journal but did not include when I wrote to Marion:
Why, I'd just be content to walk along a beach exchanging nonconformist views on colonial culture; talking meaning; content to listen to her talking about aspects of her life; content for her to respect me and to express her belief in herself and belief in me. And—good grief! Where did this come from? I'm seeing us somehow, one day, *creating* a joint offering. In your dreams, Jill. Nice to imagine, though.

---

[10] This letter is missing.

∞

January 20, 1990

Dear Jill,

Thank you for the glorious pictures of yourself beside the blue Pacific.[11] Your Christmas pic is a joy to digest. What richness you have experienced and how well you express it. It brings up my own memories of some of the happiest days of my life in Greece and much later in Japan.[12] Our responses were very similar.

I'll look forward to seeing you and sharing at the SEN[13] conference. Perhaps we will also be together at the Dunes.[14] I must say I can hardly wait to get out of the Canadian cold. I await the miracle of warmth and color. The Ravaged Bridegroom[15] is finished, due to enter the world on February 5th. I'm not yet in balance after the long, long period of concentration and these days of vulnerability.

All the best for 1990.

Love,

Marion

---

[11] JM had been in Australia for Christmas, visiting family and friends.
[12] JM had traveled to Japan and Greece in 1989 with Jeanne Shutes and had referred to the visits in a Christmas letter.
[13] Spiritual Emergence Network.
[14] MW, together with colleagues, was offering week-long workshops at Pajaro Dunes in Northern California.
[15] Because MW always handwrote her letters, names, she underlined names of books.

∞

JM Notes

March 16–23, 1990, Pajaro Dunes Workshop
March 24–28, 1990, Spiritual Emergence Network Conference

Months later, neck still troublesome, I had been working rich, long days in my consulting room with frozen peas on my neck during sessions and a support collar when I taught. I decided to give myself a week of rest and renewal. I chose a BodySoul[16] workshop at Pajaro Dunes,[17] an hour and a half from home. Marion and one of her two co-leaders, Mary Hamilton, were offering it.

The workshop was scheduled to take place the week before Marion and I were each to present individually, together with other presenters, at the Spiritual Emergence Network Conference.

After a morning of patients, I drove south to Pajaro Dunes, arriving as dusk was turning an unfamiliar landscape more unfamiliar. I eventually found the house where participants were gathering for the first meal. Almost all participants were there. I was only thirty minutes late. Dinner was almost finished. All were socializing around the kitchen, dining, and sitting areas. My introversion was coursing through my veins, but I told it to be social anyway.

Marion moved away from a conversation and came to greet me alone. She was quiet, rather formal. "Hello, Jill," she said with a serious tone I couldn't read.

"Marion!" I spontaneously embraced her.

"You've a lot of courage to come when you have a patient *and* a student in the workshop." She paused.

---

[16] BodySoul Rhythms© was the name of the series of workshops offered by MW, Mary Hamilton, Ann Skinner and eventually others. It became a series of training workshops and was eventually placed under the auspices of the Marion Woodman Foundation.
[17] Pajaro Dunes is in Northern California, north of Moss Beach and south of Aptos, approximately two hours south of San Francisco.

"I've spoken with each, and we have found good ways to stay separate and contained in our own material," I said.

"I hope I have something new to offer you," she said almost shyly, hesitantly.

I smiled. "You do," I replied. "You."

Conversing longer was difficult: I was exhausted and hungry; Marion was jet-lagged. I also suspect too much needed to remain unspoken between us right then for idle conversation to carry real energy. So, I was relieved to get my bearings without too much talking.

I settled into the house and room assigned me. It was within walking distance of the workshop space. The first morning, as I walked along the sandy path between long, pale grasses to the main meeting house, two green snakes crossed my path just in front of me. I knew this workshop would not be without lasting repercussions. On a later day, I decided to take a beach walk along another path during one of our long early afternoon breaks. Again, two small green snakes crossed the sandy path in front of me. They exactly resembled snakes in a recent dream.

Pajaro Dunes: Late afternoon shadows, ice plant, beach and shallows. Pastel on paper, 30 x 20. Jill Mellick. Image is photographed through glass so shows reflections and mutes the colors. ©Mellick

The group was sizable, perhaps twenty-five to thirty. I was easily able to keep my own work contained and separate from my patient's. She did ask me once to sit with her during an active imagination. I was happy to do so. Marion and I sat together with her. My student and I were at ease, too, in the workshop; much of the doctoral work she and her cohorts were doing was rooted in experiential learning modalities.

Each day started with a round dance to Greek music. Marion would present in the mornings. Then followed a long break and an afternoon session of creative expression—movement, dance, mask work, shadow work. Marion would sometimes participate in the afternoon work herself while always giving priority to the work of the individuals within the group.

A group "altar" began assembling itself on the fireplace hearth with treasures from beach walks, drawings, candles.

At Marion's invitation one afternoon, she and I danced together. We faced each other, hand to hand. I matched her—a familiar role for me—and let her take the lead. She was unusually at ease being physically close to participants and letting participants feel at ease with more physical closeness. My body was a little startled; it was unaccustomed to such closeness other than in highly personal contexts. Marion and I ended up swinging slowly and gently from side to side, then back to back. Then we took each other's fingers and clasped hands strongly. She put her arm around my waist, holding strongly. I in turn put mine around hers. The music ended. Our dance was complete. It wasn't perfect unison, but it was generous and satisfying. And I kept feeling, somehow, that it completed something. I had no idea what but was content to let it be.

Partway through the workshop, I knew, with a twinge of wistfulness, that this would be the last workshop I would attend. My inner life had reached a place of transitioning out of workshops after this one. This surprised me, although I did not doubt it. I would go on to attend university classes in poetry, acting, improvisation, and art as well as many conferences; this was indeed the last workshop.

Each evening after dinner, one or two women would tell personal stories. I often found Marion seated, usually with others, but somewhere on my side of the circle without knowing how that had happened. One evening during dinner, I was sitting with Ross, who had decided to accompany Marion to the workshop. Mary Hamilton, Ross and I were roaring with laughter over some cultural difference between Canadians, Australians and Americans. Marion looked over with curiosity and pleasure to see Ross enjoying himself and who or what was making him laugh explosively.

Different participants took turns leading morning meditation. Marion asked me to lead one. Trained in raja yoga as well as having frequently adapted the practices for doctoral and non-yogic groups, I was accustomed to leading meditations. I led with my zither and chanting. After teaching the group to chant the *bij* mantras,[18] I led them through a meditation on waves and ocean with the open-tuned zither.[19] To conclude, I led them back into their bodies, asking them to open their eyes slowly, look at the floor and not at each other, and then to take their time reorienting to the physical space around them.

All except Marion slowly sat up. Finally, she pressed a hand to the carpet and half-rose to a sitting position. She looked into the distance a long time without speaking or moving. Then she appeared to pull herself out of some inner place and said, quietly and simply—for all the world sounding like a headmistress from my youth—"Thank you, Jill." She was disciplining herself to return to her leadership role. She had invited me to lead the group in mask-making later that morning, because her colleague in drama work, Ann Skinner, had been unable to join her and Mary in leading the retreat. I had to refuse, with regret; I was due in Palo Alto the rest of the day to teach. I returned that evening.

Each day we took a long break between morning and afternoon sessions and were free to join others or be alone. I usually walked along the beach, with its patches of sun and fog, waves and small white birds running in the shallows. Sometimes the wind grew strong. On a couple of days, I

---

[18] *Bij* or seed mantras are associated with each of the chakras, traditional energy centers in the body.
[19] Musician, composer, and friend La Raaji taught JM how to open-tune and play the zither.

To Pajaro Dunes. ©Mellick.

returned from my walk and sat facing the beach, trying to use my watercolors. Nothing worked. I'd been looking forward to this time each day to be able to paint, but every painting was turning out badly. I was frustrated.

A later painting of Pajaro Dunes. Acrylic, 40 x 30, Jill Mellick. ©Mellick

The sunlight was warmer and there was less breeze on the landing of the back steps away from the ocean. Mildly ill-tempered with my failed attempts and with my attitude toward them, which directly contradicted everything I was teaching my doctoral students about process being more important than product, I stomped out onto the top step. My housemates were off somewhere or asleep. I pulled out a long piece of heavy watercolor paper, soaked it in water, and then dropped color here and there. In about twenty minutes, I saw with surprise that the essence of my experiences walking along the beach had just moved down through my arms, hands, and brush onto the wet paper, spreading in different ways according to the pigment I was using. I had been trying too hard. The image had to express itself without effort. Why did I keep forgetting this simplest of lessons, a lesson I taught all the time? I could never do it again. Well, at least I had one decent image to bring home.

Afternoons at the retreat were focused on movement, often in triads, or on creative expression. For the last dance at the workshop, Mary chose a Chopin piano piece. I found myself dancing, eyes closed, to my mother's expert playing of the piece.[20] I found myself dancing in gratitude for and love of my mother. Then I knew I had to leave her metaphorically and make my own way. I didn't feel as though I had legs with which to dance. I dropped to the ground, found my center, rose slowly again. I moved away, turned back, found myself returning as an aspect of the archetypal mother, and my personal mother became my daughter. I rested my hands on my mother's invisible shoulders as she continued to play. I felt such love for her, tenderness, compassion.

Tears were flowing down my cheeks almost when the music began; I knew my two workshop companions for this last movement work were metaphorically holding the circumference of our field. Marion, moving amongst the triads, sat close to us, attention unbroken as usual. I didn't mind; I was there for me, and other than slightly opening my eyelids to stay physically oriented, I danced with my eyes closed. Faces of beloveds came in turn. I took each of their faces in my hands, farewelled each, let go of threads to earlier selves. The music stopped. My hands were lightly holding the opposite elbow. At first, I couldn't reenter into the physical

---

[20] JM's mother, Letty Katts, was a pianist and composer. Her deepest self was present in music, both when she played and when she composed. JM loved to listen; too, mother and daughter played together. Letty composed, practiced, and played until her death at 88.

room. I finally did. I noticed Marion was still watching. We reconvened. I didn't want to talk, and didn't.

The next morning Marion commented quietly, "Such sadness in your dance yesterday, Jill. *Such* sadness."

At the end of the week, Marion and I were each scheduled to present at a conference to be held nearby. We were shifting roles. She would no longer be a workshop leader but a speaker. I would no longer be a participant but a workshop leader.

As our Pajaro Dunes retreat was drawing to a close, Marion approached me and said calmly, firmly, "The one thing I want to do at this next conference is to spend time with you. I want to have dinner with you each evening. I want to walk on the beach with you."

Marion and Jill at Pajaro Dunes. ©Mellick

Being a reserved Australian and wary of my vulnerability to Northern Californian easy intimacy and generous hyperbole, I appreciated her expressed wish and knew better than to take her literally. I also knew that Australians were more concrete in their expressions of intention. "I'll lend you that book if you like" meant that two or three days later a call would come saying, "I'm dropping off that book on my way into town. I'll leave it in the letter box." By then, I had had many experiences of words expressed with kind intention at the time but not often—particularly in Palo Alto in those tumultuous years—acted upon. I learned to accept them for what they were: genuine expressions of good feeling in the moment.

So, I replied to Marion truthfully with that context for my response, "And I, you."

∞

The Spiritual Emergence Network and the Institute of Transpersonal Psychology present the first international conference on The Energies of Transformation: The Dynamics of Spiritual Emergence in the Body
March 25-28, 1990,
Asilomar Conference Center,
Monterey, California.[21]

Marion and I glimpsed each other during Jean Houston's keynote. Jean's fulsome, passionate presentation left my Australian reserve uneasy. Seated elsewhere, Marion looked overwhelmed and tired. We waved. We didn't talk.

Sometime the next day, we made contact. Marion meant what she said. Exactly what she said. I wondered if perhaps Canadians more closely resembled Australians in certain cultural aspects. We spent each dinner

---

[21] The long list of presenters included MW and JM.

together. After dinner the first night, we stayed for some of the "Hopi" ceremony. Marion said she enjoyed it; I said I didn't. I had spent too much time in the Pueblo culture to think that anything that professed to be derived from it, particularly from the Hopi culture, was the real thing. We walked each other to our separate housing both nights. The second night we wandered "home" arm in arm, content in each other's presence and discussing our different experiences of the ceremony.

Sometime the next day, Marion made contact. "Let's just spend the rest of the afternoon and evening together, Jill. We could go for a walk on the beach before dinner, have a quiet meal together, and then just see what happens."

"Won't you want to take a break?"

"No. Being with you I can be myself, so I can completely relax. At least *I* can. Can you?"

I adjusted my expectations yet again, recalibrating culturally. "Yes, I can."

We agreed on a time and place to meet. Marion was delayed by completing a radio interview and helping a woman who asked for help with her dreams. It was almost 5:30. We walked arm in arm down the wooden path to the beach and along the white sand. We talked about the Pajaro Dunes workshop and gradually made our way into other, more personal material.

"Ross enjoyed so much talking with you. He said, 'I met your friend, Jill.' I thought about that and took notice: he said, 'your friend.' I realized that this *was* how I felt; I look for Jill in a room the way I look for Mary. Then I thought, 'But I hardly know Jill. How can this be?' But we're soul mates." She said it with a paradoxical tone of surprise, acceptance, and lack of drama.

She kept walking, thick hair tossed by the wind, face toward the length of the beach. I was on her left, so she was between the ocean and me. She was considerably taller than I. Most people are.

Walking the beach near Asilomar, Northern California. ©Mellick

I leapt into my own unknown. "I feel that, too, Marion. It's … strange. As though I've known you for decades—have always known you. As though we don't need to talk about things or share history. It's just … there. Then I start to doubt myself. I say, 'Come on, Jill. You really think you should trust your intuition on this? Everyone wants something from Marion.' But when I look inside, Marion, I don't seem to want anything."

We drew apart and regarded each other for a moment. Marion said firmly and calmly as she looked down at me, "Well, I trust *my* intuition, Jill." She continued. "I totally let go in your meditation. It was an exquisite experience for me. You weren't nervous. I would have felt it. Your meditation went straight into my soul, Jill." (Marion used first names frequently. She was not aware of it, but it was heartwarming for most and seductive for many; she had no idea of her charisma, an obliviousness both endearing and challenging.) "That meditation took the group, the *week* into a whole new place." I was surprised. She continued. "I was sorry you couldn't lead the mask-making that day."

We walked on, our steps in rhythm in the sand despite the difference in height. Then Marion said, "When you were dancing at the retreat—you were never before or after your body. You're present in it every moment. I envy you that. I'd give anything to have your body awareness!"

"Well," I laughed, "I'd give my eyeteeth to have your soul. *You're* never before or after your *soul!*"

Marion had an unusual capacity for and confidence in nonsexual, nonmaternal, physical closeness. She put her arm around my waist. So, it felt natural for me to put mine around hers. We continued walking. I sensed we each were relaxing into a trusting, peaceful companionship, experienced as robust physical presence. We had always known each other. So much didn't need to be said.

The ocean breeze blew against us. We leaned into it, late sun on our faces. Neither wanted to speak much.

I eventually heard myself say, relaxed, laughing, matter-of-fact—as though I were checking whether she knew her car was back from the shop—"You do know I love you, don't you?"

She joined my laughter. "I think you've given me some idea. And you do know I love you Jill," she said, equally matter-of-fact.

For both of us, it was just a rather ordinary comment on what *was*—not a dramatic declaration or overwrought revelation. No overtones, no undertones. Comfortable. We walked on, speaking occasionally—inconsequentialities, which we continued throughout dinner.

After that afternoon and evening, I assumed Marion would spend her time with others for the balance of the conference. In her extroversion, she was always warm, generous, and consistently open to connecting with others. I stepped back. This was not the time for one-on-one anything.

Marion did, indeed, do that. However, she would eventually find me, and we would dine together while enjoying conversation with those at our table. I was surprised and warmed—if still being careful with my

The forest near Asilomar and along Seventeen Mile Drive is magical at all times of day.
©Mellick

anticipation. I knew Marion's capacity and reputation for unintentionally stirring projections (and attendant neediness) onto her as the Great Mother. I didn't want that for her or for me. I enjoyed our time when it appeared while also personally and culturally recalibrating. I didn't hold my affection and friendship back from her; neither did I seek it. This was like an unexpected, intense but lighthearted shipboard experience without the romance. I was happy to enjoy us for who we were in the moment.

The conference organizers had mentioned that they might ask me to conduct a yogic fire ceremony, so I had brought the accoutrements. At short notice, they asked me to conduct it one afternoon after workshops and before dinner. It wasn't formally on the schedule. It was late notice and an inconvenient time, so I was reassured; few if any would come (it was a glorious day at the beach). However, I dressed in my formal yogic robes, prepared the materials—dry cow dung, havan samagri, ghee, the copper homa[22] pot. When I learned that the organizers had put me in the great hall, I thought this unnecessary and slightly embarrassing; we would have a handful of people at best. I'd probably set off a fire alarm. Oh well. If anyone came, we could gather around the small fire. I arrived early to set up. Some of my doctoral students came; I was glad for their presence. At least someone would be there. I didn't know why, but I asked them to sit in a semicircle about eight feet from me.

When I next looked up, a man appeared at the back of the hall, standing in the bright, daylit entrance. He screamed obscenities at me from there. "Fucking spiritual stuff. You think you're so fucking spiritual. It's bullshit." He bellowed his litany again and again. His clothing made me wonder if he were a veteran with trauma. There was nothing to be gained either for him or for me from engaging. I stayed rooted to my cushion, meditating. I was glad I had surrounded myself with my students. His presence was a perfect complement to the conference and resulted in my focusing even more on my job at that moment.

Slowly people came. The hall filled. And filled. How did they hear? Soon it was two-thirds full. I internally adjusted what I was going to do according to the increasing numbers. People steadily filled the hall. I felt small and was small, sitting up front in orange robes with a small copper pot in front of me. I noticed Marion slipping in. The more people there are, the simpler a ceremony must be. I continued to revise it quickly in my imagination.

---

[22] *Homa* is a ritual fire ceremony performed at transitions. It originated thousands of years ago in Hindu tradition and symbolizes release of the old and embrace of the new. It is often performed at sunrise, sunset, births, holy days, blessings, and deaths.

After I had explained the ritual and started the fire, I invited those who were so moved to come up one at a time to the fire to pay homage to one of the three aspects of spirit: creation in the form of the inception of something new; sustenance for the maintenance of something; or destruction in the form of release of something no longer needed or dissolution of a perceived obstacle. [23]

A line of people formed in the center aisle. I kept chanting. Each came forward to offer a pinch of havan samagri herbs or a rice grain when the mantra reached the place where we all chanted *Svaha* (the Sanskrit equivalent of "amen" or "so be it").

The copper pot contains the fire consuming the dung, ghee, havan samagri, and rice grains in the homa ceremony. ©Mellick

---

[23] In Hindu ritual, these three aspects of energy are personified as Brahma, Vishnu, and Siva.

The ceremony requires the person conducting it to put personal self aside in order to allow the ritual and its antiquity to carry the strength. When I returned to my room, disrobed, and reinhabited my personal self, I felt how tired my back and neck were, how unprepared I had been for the size of the group and how my constant adjustment of the ceremony to the increasing numbers had taxed me. I was glad I was familiar with how to reenter my regular, flawed personhood. One must have a human home to which to return.

I showered and dressed in mufti before dinner. Over pasta, Marion said to me, "Did you see how many came up to the fire?"

"I was focused on the fire and the chanting."

I didn't know what Marion experienced until later in the week. It seemed she was deeply affected by the power of the ancient ceremony. As we walked to our rooms one evening, she declared with conviction and a kind of "Wake up!" tone, "It was because of how *you* were during the fire ceremony that so many came up. More than seventy-five." To my concealed discomfort, she added other extremely generous comments, then finished her demolition of my persona of the moment by saying, "I thought, 'The spirituality is in her face. She's a priestess.'"

I was silent, most embarrassed, touched. I couldn't and wouldn't take in the comment. My experience was that I was just there to tend the fire while each person did inner work. (A *kachina* in a Hopi ceremony is not a person who assumes the role of a kachina. Personhood is set aside, and a kachina dances during the ceremonial. Then, when the dance is complete, the kachina morphs and becomes a personal Hopi again. So it is with yogic ceremonies. Marion might have seen "a priestess." I didn't. Marion might have seen seventy-five people come up. I didn't. A ceremony was happening but Jill wasn't there.)

Marion was undeterred. "You *must've* dreamt of being one in a previous life—a dream when you were a child or adult, haven't you?" Why wouldn't she drop this? Finally, my sense of amusement, which has saved me in many an unpredicted situation, kicked in. I burst into laughter.

"Not one, Marion! I started recording my dreams when I was eleven for some reason—and I've never stopped. I've dreamt of rituals—as many do. But no! Not *one*!"

After dinner that night, my friend La Raaji[24] held his concert.

I glanced across at Marion. I felt as though she were one of my family sitting there. Marion seemed to treat me similarly. Jill was Jill. Marion was Marion. Yet, they were linked somehow, along some Möbius strip.

During La Raaji's concert and his laughter meditation, Marion sat on the floor, laughing belly laughs. She joined in fully; we all breathed deeply, grunted, relaxed, laughed, sang with gusto the song La Raaji led us in: "Got the spirit in my ankles."

After the concert, most people gravitated to another large room for free-form dancing solo, in pairs, in groups. Marion danced with abandon alone, with others, with a group. So did I. We each loved dancing. After a while, she came to where I was waiting for the music to begin again and said, "Perhaps we could dance more quietly over in the corner, Jill."

"Sounds good!" said the introvert.

We found a corner, raising our forearms when the music began, palms coming close as we began to move. Each of us had had many experiences of mirroring exercises where one partner moves and the other mirrors the movement. But this was not mirroring. From the moment our palms moved closer, *we* were not moving. We were *being moved*. Our hands must have moved closer because at some point our palms were pressed together—my small hand with its practical fingers and Marion's long, slim fingers. Her hands carried the grace she believed her body did not.

We found ourselves being swayed wider and wider, hands making waves. At some point my body must have turned, because we were facing the

---

[24] La Raaji is the name Edward Gordon found for himself. A brilliant, highly trained musician who devotes his music to spiritual purposes, he first met JM years earlier at a concert he gave at the Yoga Society of San Francisco. They have remained close since.

same direction and Marion was holding my form from behind as we continued to be moved. Our bodies became one organic form, moved by some unknown force. I had danced for years but never experienced this. Nor have I since. We were moved in unity, in rhythm. No effort, no *trying* to match, no thoughtful going back and forth, giving one the lead and then the other. Our separate selves just surrendered to being one form moved by some larger energy.

Unlike the morning dance at the beginning of each day of the Dunes retreat, the responsibility for choreographing did not fall on Marion. Nor was I moving solo as we'd each done in the afternoon sessions at the retreat, trusting my body to move as it needed. We became an energy form being moved independent of space and time. It was mindless, effortless, joyful. Even though my eyes were closed almost the whole time, I was aware in my inner eyelid that someone took a flash photograph of us dancing like women in the Eleusinian mysteries. For a second, my ego noted the intrusion, mainly on Marion, but then personal awareness faded; we were beyond self-consciousness. We were surrendered to something moving us, our eyes closed, hands locked. At one point, we were kneeling on the floor, one knee up, one on the floor. Marion was still behind me. The energy rocked our bodies back and forth, back and forth, my hand on her knee, hers on my thigh. The music stopped. We continued rocking and must have been moved to stand again.

At the end she just said, "Oh, Jill." We were still moving a little. She put my hands to her face and covered them with hers for a few moments. She kissed each of my palms. I realized that she, too, had experienced our being danced and that this might be new for her, too.

"You have exquisite hands," I said. She did. "They dance. Sometimes, last week, I'd lose track of what you were saying because I was mesmerized by your hands. Someone should video them so you can watch them dance."

The music started, and we found ourselves being danced again. Eventually she said, as surprised as I, that we were just one body.

"*And* I *think* the music has stopped," I said, amused at us. We both wanted to dance a little more. But the time had passed. Like schoolchildren at the end of lunch break, we reluctantly collected belongings and, dazed and thoughtful, wandered together back to our rooms.

We parted quietly. I lay awake for some time, trying to absorb the un-known without analyzing it to shreds. Then some impersonal peace washed over me, and I fell deeply asleep.

"Being Danced" Jill sculpted this to express Marion and Jill's experience at Asilomar. ©Mellick

∞

April 6, 1990

Dear, dear Marion,

I'm still dancing with you! I do miss our daily contact. Still, I delight in the unexpected yet effortless blessing of our old new friendship in whatever forms it will take. It seems so abiding, so familiar, so just there. Happily independent of space, time, and explanation. I've been having conversations with you in my heart often, but time to write quietly has been difficult to find. So much to attend to on my return. This afternoon, however, the chimes are chiming quietly in our now complete and flowering Japanese courtyard, and I am ALONE!

I did drive up to hear you in San Francisco that Friday evening. I can hear you saying, "But Jill, you've heard it all." Well, I haven't. Your point about post-patriarchal, conscious goddess consciousness was important. Colleagues with whom I went said, "Marion's talk reminded me of what my work's all about." Some of my students had a wonderful weekend with you in San Francisco and came to class inspired. Likewise the teacher, of course. I've been describing some of Mary's and your exercises and we're trying to adapt some for in-class use, I hope with your blessing. Let me know.

Apart from just wanting to be in contact, dear Marion, I also want to tell you something. It will probably be the only time we ever talk about this.

It began with the dancing that night. There was such a profound grace. We were exquisitely one with that river of energy, so completely, so joyfully in synchronous rhythm and loving movement with each other as though we were being danced by Her. I felt not only the delight of dancing with my friend, but a conscious, embodied surrender to the Tao.

But as if that weren't enough grace for the evening, after we parted and I was back in my room, I found myself suddenly and undramatically experiencing simple surrender of personal wishes and needs. . . . I felt body and soul transcend that ever-present, heartbreaking polarity between what one wants and what life presents. It just left, and the peace that washed over me, Marion, the experience of being held by a greater love enfolded me all night as I slept deeply. . . . As I emerged from the experience and the numinosity, I understood how our joyful surrender in the dancing had opened me to this. My gratitude runs deep, dear person.

Over this time, there's been more synchronicity in the air around here than cherry blossoms. My life and my energies are dancing together. Of course I know challenges will still come, but perhaps they won't come with a soul-blanching pain. Now I begin to see again integration of all into a not-always-numinous or synchronicity-filled life, but an integration rooted in something larger than me.

I can't switch gears to write about 1991 workshop plans here. They are on the move and the faculty is delighted to accommodate in any way. More when our academic calendar is made final.

I hope your weekend workshop at Esalen went as beautifully as the others have gone and that you and Ross are now enjoying quiet days of writing, companionship, and spring. Please give him my warmest greetings. I look forward to laughing and talking with him again.

Don't worry about replying—please. Keep the time for you. I know how much correspondence you must get and I also know how lovingly and promptly you reply. I would like to be one of your friends who doesn't expect replies, one to whom you write or not, as you feel like it.

I send love all the greater now there is more of me to send it.

Jill

PS The Pajaro Dunes watercolour I did is too big, I think, for you. I'll attempt a smaller one, and if it turns out I'll send it.

PPS My parents arrive tomorrow from Australia. Spare a thought for my need to make everything just right for them!

∞

Esalen
April 13, 1990

Dear Jill,

Strange to see the sun shining on Good Friday. At home, the day is always grey, cold, blustering, unsettled—sometimes the sun shines in the evening. I'm most always glad when it is over. But, I find myself even now unsettled with the indifferent sunshine. Ross and I are going to a monastery this afternoon for a service. (He sends you his warm regards.)

Your Japanese courtyard sounds perfect—something I always wanted, but our weather wouldn't make possible without constant work fighting the elements. Thank you so much for your wonderful letter. Yes. Of course, my blessing on using any of our exercises you wish with your students.

My experience of the dance was exactly like yours, Jill. I was totally surrendered. It was unforgettable. Being "danced by Her" and then the grace and release that came out of it for you. Well, I know that release and I see you showered with cherry blossoms. I thank Her with you.

I know I don't have to write, but I just want to acknowledge this magnificently shared moment in time.

Things are paradisal here. I wonder how I'm going to adjust on Thursday.

Don't worry about the painting, Jill. It was a moment and recreating it is not easy....

Love,

Marion

∞

June 21, 1990

Dear Marion,

Welcome home. I hope that your latest trip brought you a healing combination of rest and nourishing exchange. You must be headed off for your beloved island soon. How much you must look forward to that time of natural rhythms and hours of solitude.

Many thanks for passing on the materials to Mary. I received a lovely letter from her. How I wish I lived closer to you each. The closeness I feel with each of you is so patently and humorously in contrast with the physical distance.

Marion, I hope I finally have some idea of what the school is able to do and for what it is hoping around your intensive.[25] I've outlined it on the next page for you. I would very much appreciate it if you could give me some response before I go away for a month on July 18; then I can let the Dean know before I leave so he can begin further planning. This has been a full, full spring for me—many wonderful things, beginning with Pajaro and Asilomar. At times it has felt too full. Ego and physical strengths have felt pushed beyond their limits many days. I taught new courses: one, transpersonal and traditional therapeutic techniques; the other, the use of creativity and intuition in group process. Both were exciting challenges, but exceedingly demanding of all levels of me. Too, there was a lot of "negative mother" floating around last quarter. My extraordinary clients inspire me, challenge me, teach me—but I need to work less hours if I pretend to begin writing again.

My parents' five-week visit in the midst of all of this was joyful, mostly easy, fun, and exhausting. The experience that came that night at Asilomar has been hard in the living. The ego rages against the higher wisdom of the Self, which seems to offer few immediate external compensations. Analysis and sand tray work help. I pray for the kind of courage and trust in the inner work that you have. I watched how deeply I trust my clients' inner work and increasingly get out of the way so it can proceed. Ah, but trusting my own is the real and continuing act of faith.

I'm tossing it all in for one glorious month, mid-July through mid-August. We're off to Paris and Amsterdam, the van Gogh exhibit, and then to mainland Greece, Crete, and Santorini, to just be with the sky, the turquoise water, olive trees, paperbacks, quiet friends, my still healing body, and my soul.

I'm enclosing a photo of the sculpture that our dance engendered. It's the first sculpture I've been able to do since the accident. Would that my hand could truly express what I experienced.

---

[25] "Intensive" was a term often used instead of "retreat" or "workshop" at this time.

Your presence, loving wisdom and our connection continue to nourish me, dear Marion. How often you are in my heart and thoughts.

Much love to you as always, dearest friend.

Jill

∞

November 15, 1990

Dear Marion,

Writing to you is a selfish indulgence. You told me that you are overwhelmed with correspondence. You are also probably returning from the Common Boundary Conference to an even larger pile of mail than usual. However, as I have told you before, I never expect an answer. I delight in one, but never expect it. Knowing that you take time and energy to receive my message is connection. I've thought of you often in the times of light and the times of darkness. I hope you have found some ways to have that dream shell better protect your shining fish self now. I hope, too, that old accident symptoms are abating. I know that one only too well, including the tinnitus.

This fall, my respite from my patients, from my own physical challenges, and from words has been a figure-drawing class. What a joy it's been. Two of the models, one male, one female, just take my breath away. So at home are they in their exquisite and generous bodies. We often paint to classical music, and each painting gesture reflects not only one's response to the shapes of the bodies but also to the shape of the music. It's like dancing on paper. Often I arrive with much physical pain after a long afternoon in the therapy office, not knowing whether I'll make it through the evening. After half an hour, the pain goes and this full absorption takes its place. Quite a healing.

There are not enough of these parentheses in my week, however, and I find myself writing psychic checks on an illusory credit line of the soul, a risky game.

Not all of the imbalance is my own fault (she said defensively). The school scheduled me to teach three doctoral-level classes in one quarter, despite my protests, so I've been teaching two large classes in psycho-spiritual development through creative expression—painting, movement, poetry, clay, collage—and one on traditional and transpersonal skills and schools of psychotherapy. This, is in addition to about sixteen hours of psychotherapy.

We are an experientially-based curriculum, so each class brings forth deeper material in the students. I have to become a stronger and stronger and larger container. I also feel more and more challenged to do less and simply be there as fully present as I can be. This is a constant edge for me, for my animus, and sometimes a student thinks I should "perform." I've done that too well in the past. I wish I knew how to give less than 101% of me. That would be true wisdom.

My therapy load has not eased up this fall to accommodate the teaching. Usually, I can allow natural attrition to ease the full load. Not so this year, and the depth of my own work that seems to be coming forth these last two months has been profound, something I think my ego fights against daily. I am constantly finding myself at the bottom rung of the ladder and having to leap. Then I land, only to find that it wasn't the last leap at all, and that there was an even wider chasm, less courage, and more fear.

I know this must be a strengthening process, but many times I pray that this cup could pass. I thank God I have an analyst with length and breadth of life experience, a great sense of humour, and a conscious feeling function that stays fearless in the face of my highly wrought thinking defences.

When it's not amusing, it's stretching me to breaking point to make the constant transition from defenceless, childlike analytic states to teaching the very therapeutic techniques and creative exercises that are splitting my own soul asunder.

Students, as you know so well, project their best and worst selves onto teachers. It's so important and exhausting to stay real, conscious, and responsible about this while helping them work through the polarisation. Sometimes, after two days of teaching, I come home and just weep for a while. There's no more ego strength left.

How do you do it? I need to learn to wear it all a little more lightly. On these nights, I do something incredibly banal, such as watching TV or playing with the dog to keep me in balance. It's a strange life, this, that we lead—hours and hours during the week in archetypal realms. It's just as well that I have relationship, friends, creative pursuits and travel to keep me balanced.

The creative expression workbook I'm writing is getting short shrift, needless to say. I have wonderful assistance from two talented students, so when I do work on it, we get a lot done. I plan to take the manuscript to Australia over the three-week Christmas break and work on it a little.

I miss you, Marion. I miss the ease of our companionship, the words, the movement, the silences that speak of deep places, effortlessly understood. As you know, I'm blessed with love and friendships, yet there is a place in me where the tide only comes in when you and I are together. It doesn't really have much to do with what you give me, though your gifts to me are many, or what I'm able to enjoy occasionally offering you, like the guided meditation. It's some other grace like an iris out of season or flute music overheard unexpectedly and just present for delighting in. I look forward to our time together in February. I'm tempted to go to Santa Barbara, but think I shall not. I think I would feel greedy for some time alone with you, which the circumstances of the workshop would not provide. It's also close to when I leave for Australia. We'll see.

By the way, I hope you received the photos of the sculpture I made of our dance. I don't trust the Canadian mails too well.

Much, much love, dear Marion, and my thanks for giving this letter your loving attention. It has been nourishing to take time out to write to you.

With love,

Jill

∞

February 10,1991

Dearest Marion:

Thank you, thank you for your loving generosity. I really don't know how to tell you how much your blessing on and your part in this creative venture mean to me. My heart is full, dear friend.

Your letter[26] also arrived on the same day I had had a lovely dream about you. Both letter and dream brought respite from a dark time in my inner work. So I am grateful for this, too. (Our paths cross at these pivotal times for me—they have for years.)

Well, here is the manuscript. For heaven's sake don't take all of your two precious days of rest at Pajaro for this! Don't worry about keeping it. It's too heavy to carry around. If or when you're done with it, could you pass it onto Mary? I asked her last June if she would like to vet the movement exercises. Of course, if you want it for any reason, I'll give Mary another copy.

I think the organization's pretty self-explanatory: the main body of the text is in one volume; photography and lengthy captions are in another; original, unillustrated creative writing and commentaries are in a third. I did this to make it flexible for design and production needs.

I've transcribed (and taken the liberty of editing) the material from the tape so that you can get a feel for it.[27] I'm sure I can find additional material if you want on other tapes I have, but I think this says a lot.

You continue to be daily in my thoughts and meditations in this painful time for you. It must be so mixed for you right now—the

---

[26] This letter from MW is missing.
[27] Presumably JM transcribed something of MW's and sent it to her, but the transcription is missing.

delights of being in a warm place and teaching with Ross weaving with the pain of the distance and the not knowing....

Until we meet, my love as always,

Jill

∞

JM Notes

February 1991

I picked Marion up at the airport. My neck was in pain, and she was exhausted from holding a workshop. She decided to just stay in her hotel room that evening and not come over for dinner. I retired, exhausted from the effort of trying to appear out of pain and relaxed when I was feeling anything but.

We checked in with each other by telephone the next morning. I picked her up at 10:30, and we spent the day together. She came over to the house, and I showed her around. She took to Ashi (miniature schnauzer) immediately and Ashi, to her. She was genuinely interested in everything she saw. I was careful not to overwhelm her.

"You have a Japanese sensibility," she commented.

"Jeanne and I seem to.[28] And a Southwestern. Oddly enough, they go together."

Then she asked, surprisingly, to see photographs of me when I was younger—"in your twenties." She commented, "You're prettier now." We ended up on the sofa together while she looked through an album she'd

---

[28] JM shared daily life with Jeanne Shutes, Jungian therapist and literature seminar leader; their work and much of their personal lives were independent of each other.

asked to see with me. "Your father is a handsome man! My goodness! I know that type!"

One photograph she questioned led to my relating a truncated version of an old, long, serious romance—including a recent meeting for coffee and the peace it had brought him and me. Marion said she had gone through a similar experience last year. She had met him and done the same thing. "We agree," she told me she had said to him. "You're an anesthetist, and your job is to put people to sleep. My job is to wake people up!"

I gave her lunch and took her back to the hotel. However, when we had driven a street away from the house, I felt an old fear: had I left the stove on?! Granted, I had come by the fear honestly. I grew up in the subtropics; wooden houses predominated, fires were common, and my mother had the same fear. I felt foolish confessing I wanted to turn around just to check. To my surprise, Marion said, "I have exactly the same fear. I've had it all my life." So much for shame. Later that afternoon we began the workshop. Marion responded to someone's appreciation, saying simply to the group to my surprise, "Jill's my friend."

Marion leads the workshop for Institute of Transpersonal Psychology/Sofia University students at the Women's Club, Palo Alto, CA. ©Mellick

Jill, Marion, and Ashi the miniature schnauzer who reminded Marion of her dog Duffy. Marion also has a copy of Emily Dickinson's poetry on her lap. Jill has her zither on hers. The experiment eventually resulted in "Emily Dickinson and the Demon Lover." ©Mellick

I picked her up at the hotel again and brought her over for dinner. She said grace. After dinner, we went into the sitting room and talked. Our conversation moved to music. I went to the studio and brought back my zither, which I had played at the retreat. She asked me to play while she held Ashi. I offered the zither to her to play, but she said she wanted to learn from me. Nevertheless, I nudged her into playing it. I gave her suggestions: "Play it as though it is a lover … like waves in the ocean … be with the rhythm, not the sound." She loved it.

Then I brought in the keyboard and handed it to her. She asked for some music. I brought it but then had an inspiration. I took down a hymnal from the library. I knew we would both know the hymns. She played, and I sang. We continued until late in the evening, singing with Ashi plastered between us. That evening she told me stories about her parents and her childhood. My neck was hurting badly, but I delighted in listening. She was a consummate storyteller.

We shared inconsequential stories. My fiancé had always called me "Lady J." Marion looked shocked. "But that was *my* nickname! That—and Bubbles!" We dissolved into laughter.

The next day, I picked her up just before the workshop. She had been shopping downtown and said she had had a fun morning. She said she had bought things for both of us. I was surprised, touched. The afternoon session went well.

We came back for dinner. She spent time out in the inner courtyard garden while I fixed dinner. She was hungry, as she hadn't eaten much that day. I said grace. We each had a little rest, she on the floor in the sitting room and I in my office. Then I checked the Pachelbel tape she needed. I asked whether or not she still wanted me to do some creative expression work with her. I told her that while she'd said that she wanted me to do it, I was happy to do it or not do it. I meant it. I hoped she felt I was neither unhelpful nor pushy. She replied firmly that she wanted me to do creative expression in the workshop. She added, "Your presence is the psychological container for this workshop. You know that, don't you, Jill?"

I didn't.

When we went back to the workshop that evening, she included my work with creative expression. I simply suggested drawing the movements the participants had just made with their bodies, which seemed to consolidate and elucidate insights for the group. I took her straight back to the hotel after we finished.

Marion said as we were driving, "Really, the workshop is secondary to our having time to be together." Paradoxically, that gave the workshop even more import. It wrapped itself around our visit. It was our visit that I remember most. Monday evening touched something archetypal in me, something with which I'd lost touch, and I resolved not to lose touch again. It was also expensive. Raised in a household where the piano was the heart of the home, I had been without one too long. After Marion left, I bought a secondhand piano and, later, a grand.

Wednesday, I picked her up at the same time again. It was raining heavily. Before we got out of the car, I was still inwardly letting go of questioning the worth of my offering the previous night. As we were sitting there, Marion gave me little presents she had bought for me in the morning— note paper scattered with violets, pretty cards from Kew Gardens, and a journal in her colors: blues, purples, and aqua. She had written my name on the writer's line and hers below. She had also put a little note in it. I said I would like to read it later, when we weren't walking into the workshop. I, too, had something for her. I gave her my most beautiful stone from Iona. She said that she would put it next to the little vase from Iona that I had given her, which is next to her sculpture "Echo."

When we went into the afternoon session, I sat in the back and read the note:

> Dearest Jill,
> I have just returned from a glorious walk in the rain. I am full of our visit. Our evening together has touched depths in me that we had together last year—that deep, deep resonance in the body. We share so much history and so much present. Soul recognizing soul and so joyful to open into trust.

Contained, conscious, loving. My cross-examination of myself went out the window. I had a warm-hearted afternoon.

We drove home and followed the same ritual. As we were driving, Marion commented, "I didn't look at you while I was talking this afternoon because something personal would have happened—and, as you could see, it did at one point." (She had briefly mentioned me in the talk.) Instinct told me that having the same place to which to return might be renewing for Marion and that holding Ashi was nourishing for her. She felt as though Ashi were closely akin to her own dog, Duffy. (She and Ross also had shared two dogs, Byron and Samantha.)

We planned a mask exercise over dinner. Then I made the mistake of mentioning the possibility of a shadow party, about which she grew more enthusiastic than the suggestion warranted after I considered it for more than two seconds. I told her my intuition was saying no. We went back and together led them through connecting with a positive feminine energy. They made masks, danced with them, made sounds. I worked with J, who came to me, terrified of what she had made. We went to a corner and screamed together, atavistically. I urged her to bend down each time she screamed, as did I, so we both would stay grounded. I also held her hands. She appreciated my presence.

Thursday, the same thing: I picked up Marion at the last minute. This time I was out of breath. I had been running around all morning getting food from St. Michael's, a nearby restaurant, and picking up a watercolor I'd had matted for her.

In the evening we came back to the house. No sooner did I have dinner out and candles lit but Susan, my physical therapist, arrived unexpectedly to give me a treatment. I was nonplussed at her arrival—I didn't have it on my calendar. I recovered and gave in to Susan's treating my neck and the rest of me in the sitting room. Marion abandoned her dinner to watch what was happening. It ended with my body's having spontaneous kundalini shivers. I let them flow and didn't identify with them.

Somehow I managed to reheat dinner, and we finished. No planning about the evening session and whether they would do art—Marion just said we would do dancing.

The participants were doing trio work. Marion came over to me. "Jill, I don't think they understand what I mean by the mind giving metaphors. Would you be willing to demonstrate with me?"

"Of course," I said. I have always enjoyed improvisation.

She put on music intended to evoke what she had been describing about feminine energy. My body as always immediately responded to the music. I found myself dancing slowly in front of 65 participants. Marion quietly started to speak, giving me images: a moon with white clouds, picking peach blossoms, picking plum blossoms, gathering hyacinths, waves breaking on the shore, a starfish in the water. I kept my eyes closed and was in the dance. Closing my eyes was the only way my introverted self could stay focused. I was alone with myself and Marion's voice; my body was being moved by the music.

As we finished, people broke into spontaneous clapping. This was well-intended yet I felt mildly ill at ease; I had not been performing. It felt like clapping in church. Marion and I were simply helping them understand how imagery can give rise to movement. However, the atmosphere somehow had become charged. I turned to Marion, put my hands together, and bowed, smiling. Someone made a comment, and Marion simply responded, "Well, Jill and I have danced together before and know each other very well."

Someone said she didn't like all the suggestions, found them intrusive. I replied that it depended on how the suggestions were given and how they were received. If they were received as subtle criticism, then they would be intrusive; if they were received as a gift, then they were nourishing. I said I received Marion's images as a gift. The same woman then said that she wished we'd not spoken the night before during the drawing. I mentioned that both Marion and I had suggested they be free to ignore anything we said and added that perhaps she was more sensitive auditorily; this would make it hard for her to screen out sounds she didn't want.

At the end of the evening, B came to me and said she had told Marion she couldn't take her eyes off us: we were so attuned. Apparently, Marion would just shift the smallest amount, and I would be doing the same movement at the same moment; she would barely begin to move her body or suggest something, and it seemed my body was already doing it.

Afterward, Marion told me en route to the hotel, "I had trouble not laughing because the connection between us was so powerful that I no sooner thought of some image but you were doing it. It was a *long* piece of music. Seven minutes. I thought about cutting it off, but I could see most of the students were really learning something. Almost everyone in the group was seeing something and experiencing something very important, so I allowed it to go through to the end." She added, "And you are so beautiful. Your movements!"[29]

---

[29] MW experienced JM this way. JM ascribes her feeling for movement to genetics and osmosis, not training. Her mother, a composer, had been trained in classical ballet. JM grew up in an environment replete with resonance between music and movement.

I appreciated her generous comments and once again felt shy and squirmy. Music simply moves *me*. I remembered the callow young men in black tie with whom I had attended balls, and their shock when the music to which we were supposed to be shuffling together moved me otherwise and my conservative, colonial self turned into a wild woman. Music has always held unquestioned sway over my body—later to the detriment of my hypermobility.

So, Marion and I experienced last year's dance but this time in public and differentiated: she, the imagery; and I, the body. She was used by the muse to receive and offer images; I was apparently used by the same muse Marion heard in the music; that same muse was moving me.

H called. "I don't think I'll ever forget that dance. And to see Marion's face! The absolute hush that came over the room! It was a sense ... an expression of the feminine I've never experienced. You both embodied that evening *everything* that Marion had been talking about for three days. I wish we'd had a video and the men could get it, too! It was a feminine that wasn't threatening. Through Marion's and your connection, we could experience an archetypal energy."

I appreciated her call—and reflected internally that although teachers can't please all of the students all of the time, at least we can please some of them some of the time.

The next day I picked Marion up at 10:30 and brought her over to the house, but I left her with iron, keyboard, and zither for an hour and a half until I finished in my office[30] and picked up some soup for lunch. It was still raining when I returned.

We had lunch and talked and then decided to make a tape of her reading Emily Dickinson's poetry while I interpreted the poetry with the zither or a flute sound on the keyboard. We were quite pleased with ourselves at the end of the afternoon. She even said she would like to make a recording similar to what we'd improvised, for commercial distribution.

---

[30] JM's consulting rooms are at her home.

Marion holds Ashi. The sculpture, "Being Danced" sits on a Cochiti drum to the left. To her right, out of sight is a full, unedited version of Emily Dickinson's poetry. ©Mellick

One of the poems Marion read began:

> There is a pain—so utter—
> It swallows substance up[31]

"Have you ever felt that kind of pain, Jill?"

Marion saw my answer in my eyes.

"That's why we understand each other so well," she said.

I gave Marion a copy of *The Bone People*[32] with a little note:

---

[31] Fr#515 in: Franklin, R. W., ed. *The Poems of Emily Dickinson: Reading Edition* (The Belknap Press, 1999).

[32] *The Bone People,* a novel by Keri Hulme, is set in New Zealand and focuses on the cross-cultural redemption of three damaged, isolated individuals, two addicted adults and a child, who are thrown together.

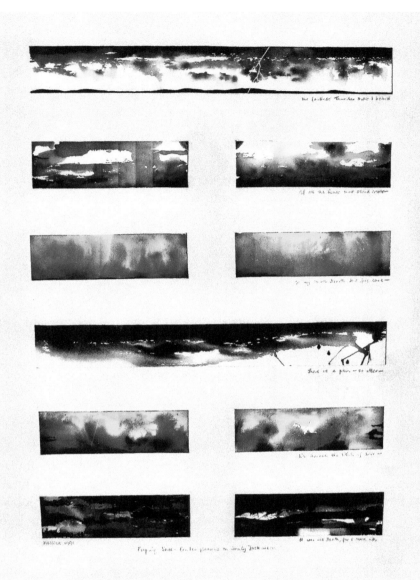

I Ching Reading. Keeping Still: Contemplations on Emily Dickinson. Watercolor 36 x 49, Jill Mellick. ©Mellick.
Quotations read from the bottom up.
"It was not Death for I stood up"
"We learned the Whole of Love—"
"There is a pain—so utter—"
"To my small Hearth His fire came"
"Of all the Souls that stand create—"
"The farthest Thunder that I heard"

Marion, dearest Marion,

Your note in my journal brought tears which christened its first page this morning. I also christened it with some images from our dance last night and my first Crone dream.

So, so much, yes, that almost has to go unspoken between us. Perhaps the dancing, the singing, and the music can better contain our souls for now. I am awed by the strength and breadth of our connection, from its easy, deep silences to its humour.

With love,

Jill

I wrote an inscription in the novel. (I didn't know it was a presentiment for us each.)

For Marion, who knows the music of the bones.
With love,
Jill

Later, just before she left, I mentioned that I had gone back to the old dream in which she had been giving me directions to do similar movements to those she had mentioned last night. Too, we had a brief, sad exchange about personal losses and our dread of Alzheimer's. I told her about M's early onset Pick's disease. We both said we would do ourselves in rather than become dependent.

I offered her the Pajaro painting of Ross and her walking through the shifting fog on the beach. I also gave her a way out of accepting it if she didn't want it. She loved it. She was struck by "those two tiny figures alone in that big world" and said immediately that she would put it in her bedroom. I managed to make it a light gift although it felt like a big gift to me.

She was gracious in her receiving. "I love the painting—and I love you."

Beach Ocean Fog. Pajaro Dunes. Watercolor completed during retreat, Jill Mellick. 24 x 8.
©Mellick

As she started to iron again, she asked me if I would like to join them on the island during June for the annual retreat. She said there would be a few of her analysands, another analyst, Mary Hamilton, and me. She said that if I couldn't do it this year, then any year it was open to me. I was delighted, told her that it sounded wonderful and that I would tell her soon. She was ironing a bright orange outfit. Soon someone arrived to take her to the Women's Alliance, and she was gone.

What we found and how we were together still baffled and delighted me.

∞

JM Dream
March 2, 1991

Marion is a sculptor.

∞

March 8, 1991

Dear Marion,

Welcome home! How good it must feel to be able to introvert for longer periods of time and to be with Ross again. This time last week, we were just beginning our tape. I feel your presence and your absence here. Your presence in the quiet, inner warmth I feel from our talks, silences, music, and laughter; your absence, in my wish for more.

The rain left early in the week, and today is piercingly blue. The sad hills are now emerald, and the trees are all pastel and burgundy buds. The deluge gave us some drought relief; I wish, however, it had stopped raining long enough for me to take you to the ocean. Next time ... (My critical self had a few things to say to me about not having taken you out—to dinner, for a drive ... I told my critic we needed to just let down between meetings and that it was raining, but she wanted me to tell you anyway!)

I can't begin to tell you what your presence meant to the students. There are inner—and outer— stirrings all over. Both men and women are saying it will take them weeks to absorb the insights, dreams, and potentials that emerged. (One woman, when asked by a male faculty member how the workshop had gone, told him she had only one regret: that the male members of the faculty had not been required to attend!) The students are prepared to do anything to get you to come back! What a wonderful catalyst you are. Thank you again for taking the time to be with them.

And thank you for the opportunity to assist you in the evening sessions. It was a privilege and a joy. I hope it was energising for you, too.

Marion, I accept with delight your invitation to join you all on the island this summer. Thank you. I would love to share in that experience. Please tell me what arrangements will work for you and the group; meanwhile, I'll make some temporary flight reservations so that I have something.

I would like to share fully in whatever physical and financial responsibilities and arrangements there are—food, gas etc. I'm a little concerned about pulling my weight physically (taking turns driving, carrying stuff ...). I don't easily acknowledge and respect my occasional physical limitations but they're real—as you saw. Sometimes my neck flares after flights. I can get it quieted down within a couple of days with ice, rest, and no lifting/pulling. I don't anticipate its happening but thought I should mention it in case this presents difficulties and you need to reconsider your invitation.

While you were being a transformative presence for the Alliance, I spent much of the weekend painting.[33] Then on Tuesday night I did the fire ceremony for my final kundalini class. For many, it was a continuation of

---

[33] The painting was the one of the I Ching readings thrown with the Emily Dickinson lines shown earlier.

your intensive. Each came to the fire (including those terrific nuns) and silently evoked/celebrated the presence of one of three energies in their present lives: creative, sustaining, or destroying (of obstacles). It also provided a way for some of the workshop people to sacrifice something if they were ready.

With classes finished, I am now free from regular teaching until at least September. Still have to attend faculty meetings. My rebellion got the better of me last week: no one was scheduled to do the opening, so I volunteered to take them through some improv[34] exercises. I had everyone "throwing" and "catching" sounds and words and images. That livened up our professional personae!

Jeanne[35] arrived back from Santa Fe on Saturday full of good stories about our Pueblo Indian and Anglo friends. The descriptions made me long for New Mexico, so we are going to go for Easter, when there are ceremonial dances in most Pueblo villages.

I hope your transition home has been smooth, nourishing, and not *too* overloaded. I also hope Ross had a marvelous time in San Francisco that weekend. My greetings to him and to dear Mary, whom I look forward to seeing.

Ashi sends licks and a persistent paw in your hand. I awoke this morning to find her standing on my stomach, eyeballing me through floppy grey eyebrows and shivering with calculated pathos. It worked.

Enough. What was it Saint Teresa said? "I apologise for the length of this letter; I did not have time to make it shorter."

Much love, dear friend,

Jill

---

[34] The improv exercises were originally taught by Patricia Ryan Madson, Drama Department, Stanford University; she worked with Canadian Keith Johnstone, author of *Impro: Improvisation and the Theatre.*
[35] Jeanne Shutes co-authored *The Worlds of P'otsunu* with JM (University of New Mexico Press, 1966).

∞

JM Notes
June 15, 1991

Left for Canada and ShaSha. Returned June 23.

∞

JM Notes

For several summers, I flew to Toronto and joined Marion and a group of nine women to drive to Parry Sound, from where we took a forty-minute water taxi to ShaSha, the island Marion and Ross owned in Georgian Bay.

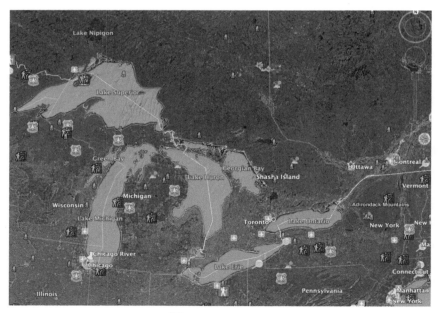

ShaSha Island, Georgian Bay. © Google Earth

Marion provided a sustained, physically and psychologically contained environment in which each woman could let down and experience her deepest core and feel it affecting others in a way they found inspiring, fun, moving, affirming. Each could not only be herself for herself, but also herself for others.

Five of the group were analysands of Marion's who, she felt, were at a good time in their analysis to devote a day to reflecting on their inner work and to being witnessed by nine others. Four or five of us were "facilitators" or "leaders," both of which words I dislike and which diminish the remarkable work these women presented over five days. We were actively involved in responding to various moments in each presenter's work when it felt timely and welcomed. The balance of our time was spent in active receiving. Receiving *is* action. Its quality affects others.

My times with Marion and the women on ShaSha taught me much about emerging parts of me I would not have otherwise learned. The last time we went, I found I could receive the women's verbal gifts to me and not just be one of the givers or one who just received what they shared about themselves.

ShaSha is small but heavily forested. Marion and Ross had two small cottages on rocky outcrops. Four of us slept in the main cottage,

The Woodman's cottage, "Miranda," on ShaSha. ©Mellick

The deck of "Miranda," the Woodman's cottage on ShaSha, shows their guest cottage. Three retreatants would stay there. ©Mellick

"Miranda," four in the Japanese "teahouse" cottage close by. Mary Hamilton and one analysand slept in the cottage on Colenso, a separate island owned by Mary and her husband, John.

How we joined up with the others driving to the Parry Sound departure point for Georgian Bay and ShaSha has slipped from memory. Somehow all ten of us convened where the water taxi was ready for us. It was at least a two-hour drive to Parry Sound and then forty minutes in the water taxi. Each of us was limited to one small suitcase. At Marion's request, I also brought my small guitar and zither. Marion mentioned that the First People of the area knew the channels best; one of them would weave the water taxi between mysterious islands, some with mansions and others with cottages. The journey in the boat was a vital part of the initiation into our week on ShaSha.

At the island's jetty we would clamber out to lug our pared-down belongings along the short jetty and up the rocks to the cottages. Marion carefully chose who stayed where. She liked to share a mattress on the floor in the sitting room of "Miranda," the main cottage where we gathered

The deep waters of Georgian Bay. ©Mellick

One of the jetties at Georgian Bay. ©Mellick

The Woodman's cottage, "Miranda," on the rocks beside the bay. ©Mellick

daily. She and close friend Eleanora Woloy, M.D., analyst from Virginia, would bunk there and awake to the view of the bay, which was either shrouded in mist or crystal clear.

Early that first week, she said as she was making morning coffee, "I was so excited that you were coming. I even said to Ross, 'Why, Jill's coming!'"

I told her that I was happy to be in the guest house if that worked better for the composition of the group, but she replied firmly, "I want you here— in the main house." So from the first year I went to ShaSha, Marion arranged for me to share the only bedroom and its mattress with a different analysand each year. I shared nights with either physically fragile or high-profile analysands. I sensed, too, that Marion was also quietly taking care of my permanently damaged neck by asking me to share the one comfortable bed. I would wake to the quiet murmuring of Marion and Eleanora in the sitting room, often broken by stifled laughter.

We were all gone for a week: two days of travel and five full days on the island. I captured some of the essence of those weeks in the watercolors I later painted for Marion's and my joint book, *Coming Home to Myself.*

View from ShaSha. Jill painted these indigo watercolors for their joint book, *Coming Home to Myself.* ©Mellick

Marion and Ross had given a name to every place on or near the island. The "grandmother tree" grew on an island opposite "Miranda." Marion loved that tree. Standing at the sink, she pointed out how its boughs, rather than evoking an image of a cross, lilted at the ends so the dark tree, almost monochromatic, looked like a strong figure, arms outstretched, hands open to hold all.

Marion named the great body of water that was Georgian Bay, a huge yet proportionately small part of Lake Huron, "The Beyond." She would lead us through damp, dark paths closed in on both sides by great rocks, each

The Beyond. ©Mellick

Two images of favorite rock formations on ShaSha. ©Mellick

From the southern tip of ShaSha, Marion contemplates what she called "The Beyond." ©Mellick

Marion contemplates Georgian Bay from one of many lookouts on ShaSha. ©Mellick

of which she and Ross had named. One hollowed-out tree that had fallen was a mother tree, and all lay in it yearly so each could feel its enclosing warmth. With Marion leading, we made our way through trees, grasses, wildflowers, and moss to the southernmost tip of the island to sit on rocks and look at the Beyond.

Gradually each year we always dropped our personae. None of us wore makeup. What need? We might have started out the week with a little persona, but it fast devolved into T-shirts, no makeup, environmentally friendly shampoo and bare feet or tennies.

In the mornings, we gathered for a group ritual, nature-based and usually led by quiet, grounded, wise, calm Eleanora and, at times, by Marion. Then we would repair to "Miranda." One of the five analysands would share her material with four fellow analysands, Marion, and the four facilitators. The analysands would share music, paintings, stories, insights, stuck places. They always sat in the corner of the main room, which afforded the receivers an uninterrupted view of both the presenter and the bay behind and on both sides of the presenter.

Loving to paint in addition to my full-time work as a Jungian psychologist, writer, and half-time professor, I quietly drew—with permission—while someone presented. Drawing let me focus deeply on the essence of the presenter's material. I have records of the sketches—mainly portraits. The original of each belongs with its subject. The atmosphere generated permitted my hand to draw in a way I doubt it could have otherwise.

Eleanora Woloy leads one of the morning rituals that opened each day's retreat on ShaSha. ©Mellick

Marion leads one of the daily morning rituals at ShaSha during a retreat week. ©Mellick

Mary Hamilton, Marion, and Jill work with a retreatant, ShaSha. ©Mellick

Marion works with a retreatant on ShaSha.
©Mellick

Often, during a presentation, a group response evolved organically and became part of the presentation. Too, when the presenters had finished, we would create a ritual for them, either at their direction or based on our imaginings. Each was as individual as the island's rocks. We immersed some in water. We cradled others. We sang for others.

After a late, relaxed lunch, we would explore the island with or without

Marion, swim, nap or take time alone until dinner. Those of us who wanted to brave the icy June waters would step carefully down the rocks into the bay. No one was around, so we could swim without suits. I love swimming, especially free of a suit, and swam daily, as did others. What delighted me about the water was its clarity and that patches of warm water were right next to patches of icy-cold water. I never knew which I was going to encounter next: water that would take my breath away or water that cradled me. One of my roommates used to go down early each morning when mist was still hanging low, slip off her robe, and enter the water soundlessly and gracefully. She seemed to step out of a painting—and she stepped into one of my watercolors later.

The first year, I dutifully brought a swim-suit. I stripped quickly, even leaving my straw hat on, and pulled up my suit. Marion, whose humor was always just below the surface, quipped in mid-conversation with Eleanora, "It looked better when you just had the hat on!" and continued to talk with Eleanora. Soon even the hat was gone, and we all were swimming unimpeded. Mary let me braid her hair as we sat free of suits on the warm rocks. We could have dis-appeared into an Impressionist painting.

Charcoal drawing by Jill of retreatant, ShaSha. ©Mellick

Jill braids Mary Hamilton's hair in the sun on the rocks at ShaSha. ©Marion Woodman

Marion arranges wildflowers and grasses in the main house, "Miranda," on ShaSha.
©Mellick

Meal preparations and serving used what finery the cottage afforded—a candle here or there, a small pot of wildflowers or grasses that Marion had arranged, un-matched plates and cutlery, two long pews, a long wooden table, and much laughter.

After dinner the singing would begin. Music infused each day. Usually, I was designated wandering minstrel. I don't enjoy being the center of attention, but, with my small guitar or zither, I delighted in accompanying a hesitant soloist, a rowdy group folk song or Broadway musical number or haunting folk melody. Marion commented toward the end of the first week,

Jill uses her smaller guitar to accompany ShaSha leaders and retreatants in the evenings. ©Marion Woodman

which came too soon, "Your music has added so much!" I appreciated her comment, but my experience was that it wasn't "my" music. It was the group's music; I loved playing along.

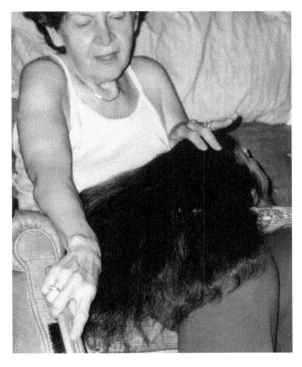

Marion loved to brush my hair. I love to have my hair brushed. So, it was a good, sybaritic fit. I would lie with my head in her lap, and she would brush and brush far longer than I had anticipated. As I have an endless capacity for having my hair brushed, it worked rather well. I was uneasy at times that others might feel less tended. My unease was misplaced. Marion gave each participant personal time, which she chose well—and I always happened to be the only one with long hair in the group.

It stormed severely one night. Rather than shelter inside, we gathered and huddled on the deck of "Miranda." Wind and rain lashed our faces and penetrated the all-weather jackets we'd been told to bring. Marion reveled in the thunderstorm and the lightning. For her, I'm sure, it was a

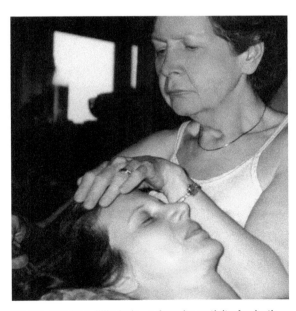

Marion brushes Jill's hair—a favorite activity for both. ShaSha. ©Mellick

Shakespearean play come to life: like the storm in *King Lear* when the king is wandering, I suspect the changes in weather were both synchronistic and classic pathetic fallacy[36] for her—although nature's empathy for whom was a mystery into which I did not pry.

One evening Marion asked if we would be willing to listen to something she had written. She wanted feedback. All assented with enthusiasm. Marion read. It was so quiet that I could hear, as well as Marion's deep voice with its well-timed hint of a Katherine Hepburn crackle, the slight sound of the water on the rocks. She finished.

Marion greets an approaching, fierce storm, ShaSha. ©Mellick

Silence. She was waiting for our feedback. Several spoke in glowing terms of how what she had written affected them and how important they found it. I was Australian enough to believe Marion. I had also worked as a freelance editor during the years I studied for my doctorate in psychology. Later as Director of Doctoral Research, I had to give constructive feedback to doctoral candidates. I'd also been fortunate enough to have published more books by then. She had a draft; she wanted feedback. Next? Happy to give it. I gave her polite, brief, constructive feedback, carefully modulated, given the environment.

The air became even more silent than when Marion was reading. Having been a psychotherapist for many years by now, I knew when quiet was just quiet and when it was full of portent; this was the latter. Too late, I became aware that I had committed a cardinal sin. I saw, with dismay, that I had slightly shocked all. Except Marion.

---

[36] Pathetic fallacy in literature or art is the attribution of human feelings and responses to inanimate things or animals.

The island worked its mysteries: quieting, slowing, expanding, warning of limitations, giving freely of its forested, rocky beauty.

When we would leave ShaSha, sometimes with Marion and sometimes without, we were parting with a new beloved. Once when we left, Marion and I sat in the bow of the water taxi. We were all singing Leonard Cohen's song "Suzanne." We were literally living part of the song's imagery. One does not leave garbage on the island but takes it back to the mainland. Marion and

Marion takes quiet time after a morning working with retreatants. ©Mellick

Readying to depart, Marion walks to the jetty on ShaSha. ©Mellick

Jill waits for the water taxi. ©Marion Woodman

I were sitting in the bow behind two huge, dark garbage bags—and a bunch of wildflowers and grasses someone had picked and tucked between them: the line from the song "… she shows you where to look among the garbage and the flowers …" came alive.

Marion sometimes stayed when retreatants left and sometimes returned with us. This time, she returned and she and Jill are seated in the bow. ©Mellick

Leaving ShaSha with "the garbage and the flowers" (Leonard Cohen). ©Mellick

Each of the years I flew up to Toronto and thence to ShaSha had its own character. The weather varied. The group of people, of course, determined much of the week's flavor. Marion trusted not only the individual presenters but the collective energy of the group in a way that taught me yet again how much positive animus and action I was accustomed to bringing to situations.

One morning the facilitators met early, as we often did, to reflect on how the week was evolving. This particular week was flowing well, yet we sensed presenters could partake of even more that they had available to them. Marion asked if any of us had had a dream the night before. I'd dreamt of a church. The front half of the church was devoted to religious matters. The back half was set with a large smorgasbord of excellent food. However, no one was eating. When we finished sharing our dreams and reflections, I, unsurprisingly, asked if there might be anything we could do to help the presenters draw more from what was available to them.

"Oh, I don't think we need to do anything else, Jill," Marion responded. "Your dream has already changed the energy." That tested me. Certainly, my dream might reflect the fact that participants were not dining off the available riches. But wasn't it also identifying a problem? How might we help them dine at the smorgasbord? At least I had the wits not to say this. Sure enough, when we convened as a group that morning, the sharing and reflections took an effortless dive. I received an invaluable lesson: when something is brought to consciousness in a group, whether it is expressed or not, the consciousness of the group changes. Another lesson for my problem-solving self.

We were assigned in pairs to cook one dinner. Being one of the few arriving long distance, I had to plan ahead. Rice and vegetable curry seemed an easy solution. I could bring rice and pick up vegetables at any grocery store at which we stopped. I am content to cook but—unlike my pursuit of writing, art, music and other creative activities—I am not a passionate cook. However, I did want to put my best effort into the rice and vegetable curry. My years of training in raja yoga and Sanskrit had been regularly punctuated with lessons in vegetarian cooking.

"*Oh look! Californian health food!*" the Canadians exclaimed when I placed the simple meal on the table together with small bowls of chutney, raisins and almonds. I had not known until then how acculturated I had become.

Marion, by being herself, provided a sustained, contained, and strong environment in which each woman could let herself feel her core self and, by being herself, let it flow out to others in a way others would find moving, inspiring, fun, affirming.

On our last morning that first year, Marion and I were alone in the kitchen cleaning up. "I hate to see you go, Jill."

"I hate to go."

We continued cleaning up. She turned away from me to

Marion relaxes in her rocking chair, ShaSha. ©Mellick

replace plates in cupboards. "The memories are here; I'll see you after you're gone."

When she turned around again, I hugged her. "They're in me, too, you know."

Cleanup continued. As Marion was drying plates, she looked out to the bay and said quietly, "I don't say much when the feelings run *really* deep, Jill. You've seen me at conferences and things, embracing people and talking." She looked across the water to the grandmother tree. "But when it is *really* deep, it doesn't get expressed. I hope you understand that."

I had not understood that. I had never assumed. Quite the opposite. Even though we had had our experience of the dance, I had not assumed Marion would sustain these feelings. She had. I inwardly determined to revisit this first of several weeks at ShaSha and my assumptions in general when I arrived home. Our years of experiences of ShaSha became part of the book that Marion and I later wrote, *Coming Home to Myself.*

Marion and Eleanora embrace during a farewell ritual, ShaSha. ©Jill Mellick

At the end of that first summer, after we had all returned home from our various travels, I spoke to Ross one evening. Marion was out. He said he remembered our delightful and humorous conversation at Pajaro and mentioned that Marion had spoken about "music, music and more music." He called me as "a great soul," an expression I quickly learned he liked to use with those for whom he had respect and affection. I delighted more in his authoritative, professorial voice than in the compliment.

∞

June 1991

After that first week at ShaSha, I wrote to Marion, sent her the photographs I had taken, and included a poem that had announced itself:

Jill and Marion sing on the jetty while waiting for the water taxi at the end of a retreat at ShaSha. ©Mellick

Marion relaxes as she contemplates Georgian Bay. ©Mellick

Marion's expressive hands in an iconic pose for her: her left hand around her walking stick; her right, "talking." ©Mellick

Marion at rest, absorbing the beauty and quiet of Georgian Bay from ShaSha. ©Mellick

On your hands

You are too close for dreaming yet;
your image casts graceful shadows
on the rice paper walls
of my heart. It seems
you have always been there.

Moving through air,
your hands:
their strong lines
reveal the fine brushwork of your soul.
They betray your silence,
draw tales from the heart.
As their brushwork lines unfold in space
I come to see
the untold you.

Long, fluid tapers, your fingers,
contemplative, purposeful,
tie your apron (one of your habits),
slowly brush hair,
delicate, knowing, firm.
They cup their elegant, languid bones
to light a match
against a twilight wind—
bold monk with fragile flame
in a cold corridor.

Your hands caress an unseen presence,
a figure on an ochre vase
touching a lover just out of sight;
your fingers hold your walking stick
like a lover's hand,
tracing each joint
as though the last you would ever hold,
lightly, lightly.

Stroking strings of harmonies,
they strike,
find keys to memories held
in cell and bone;
turning thin leaves of poetry
they pierce the already pierced heart
still deeper;
plucking an iris and summer grass,
they silently place
five blooms ascending
in pitched ecstasy.
Then their stillness
rocks and flows
like dawn across the lake.

Like the gulls we saw,
not knowing each other yet recognising still—
not, perhaps, needing knowing any more—
I see the delicate, dancing line
of your fierce calligraphy.

∞

July 24/91

Dearest Jill,

The pictures are fabulous! You caught the essence of so many moments and the soul quality of each person. I love the panorama.[37] Somehow I am going to put it together in a long frame. Ross hasn't seen the photos yet but I know he will be delighted. Many, many thanks. I will show them to the ladies in the fall and they can choose what they want. I loved the rhythm of the whole set. You can feel it settling in, the night of music, the farewell, the cottage alone, then the wake. You poet, you!!

---

[37] The panorama was of "the Beyond."

Marion farewells retreatants leaving by water taxi. ©Mellick

En route from ShaSha in the water taxi. ©Mellick

Yes, the transition was very difficult. How I missed you! But I had my autoharp[38] and I just keep quietly working with it. Loving it. I also have Emily and the possibility of our working together in the fall. I took Cynthia Wolff's biography [of Emily Dickinson] to ShaSha and had to deal with some harsh appraisals, some of which I agreed with, some of which I found very narrow-minded. Still, she is a magnificent critic and I am going to temper my own writing by my new perspective. Reading her will cause some changes. Will get it worked out, Jill, and increasingly, I do not believe in rushing.

Perhaps you are now in Santa Fe. I do hope your neck is better. It grieves me to see you in such pain. You seem to have everything—grace, elegance, easy rhythm in your life flow, music, poetry, wisdom—and then that forever pain. How I wish I could brush your hair often.

So happy you enjoyed meeting S. Isn't it remarkable to find a cousin whom you can relate to from 1748.[39] That is not part of my knowing but I can rejoice in that sense of *root* for you. I sense that depth in so much of what you do—who you are.

Ross is adjusting to his very disciplined diet.[40] Fraser[41] is steady. Bruce[42] and his son are driving August 2. The other nieces and nephews, next week or early August. Ross and I had a fabulous three weeks together and now it is family time. We are leaving for Victoria in August, mid-August. Ross's sister is not steady. Still, life is awesome.

The fresh air and rest on ShaSha have brought new energy and hope. I am happy to see you in so many places on that beloved island.

Marion

PS I'll keep your so-utterly-Jill hat for you here. Once in a while I wear it. Also I found your gel and luxuriated in a warm shower. Blessings, Dear One, M

---

[38] The autoharp is the same instrument as the zither, but musician and composer La Raaji taught JM to remove the dampers that created fixed chords and to open-tune the instrument. Marion bought one after hearing JM's.
[39] JM's cousin and family reside in Toronto.
[40] RW had developed Diabetes Type B.
[41] Fraser Boa, Marion's brother, Jungian analyst and maker of the documentary on Marie-Louise von Franz, was being treated for cancer.
[42] Bruce Boa, Marion's brother, an actor based in England.

∞

Somewhere in Denver

Sept 27, 91

Dearest Jill,

This is one of those lovely days when I hide out in my hotel room before
going on to speak tonight. Oddly enough my trips have become my rest
periods—no phone calls, no real pressures of decisions, no-one I have to
see. I had a fabulous rest in Lincoln, NE in a great four-poster with lace
and silk sheets and wonderful old coat hangers that would hang over the
shower rod on the huge old iron tub. All day the sun played on the leaves
outside my open window and the robins sang, and it felt like being in our
parsonage when I was a child. I was in a total bliss state all day —reading,
still sleeping, remembering. Now I'm in Denver, returning to Toronto on
Sunday.

Thank you for your phone call—always so good to hear your voice. The
ladies are delighted with their pictures. C especially can hardly believe
what she is seeing. They are wonderful, Jill.

Things never go quite as planned. Robert Bly[43] and I did the film
together—that's a saga in itself, but I now find I am part of the editing. We
had worked out our storyline through the film, but lost it in the third
episode. I am trying to find a new path through. It is taking a lot of time,
but most interesting and different and enjoyable. I love working with
images. I don't know how it will emerge. Two of the editors want to make
it into a documentary; one, into an art form . . .

Fraser has finished his chemo and radiation. His poor broken body brings
tears to my eyes every time I think about it. His eyes look out and seem to
say, "What are you going to do to me? What have I done? No more—

---

[43] Robert Bly, the poet, and MW did many live presentations and one film together.

please—no more torture." Still, his spirit is strong. He is still trying as hard as he can to live. We're all trying with him. In all of this, I am finishing Leaving My Father's House. That too is going through loops I never anticipated. Still I see that each is necessary and I'm just trying to be calm and patient and let each happen as it must.

I'm not at all ready for the Dickinson recording, Jill. I'm sorry about that. I think I told you that book I read last summer threw me through several loops which have to be rewritten before we do the tape. I'll just quietly do it some weekend …

The conference is only two weeks away in San Francisco. I can't believe it. I won't be able to have dinner, Jill. The way we work is chaos, controlled chaos. I may arrive there and Robert[44] will say "I found a new fairy tale. Let's do it." I'll read it and say "Terrific." Then we work minute by minute at night, in the morning, at noon. Each time I just pray the thing will hold together but it does make for excitement. We're also doing an interview together. It's all enough. We'll (you and I) meet at some point and look forward to real time together in January. I think you said you were going to be there. I do hope it is good. Sometimes it is fabulous and sometimes fearful. This is dangerous because it is on the shadow.

Dear one, I love you. I hope all goes well for you at work and with your dear ones. I do look forward to seeing your dear face.

Love,

Marion

Did I tell you how much I loved the poem on my hands?

---

[44] Robert Bly.

∞

JM Notes
Date unknown, Santa Barbara

Marion and Robert Johnson[45] were offering a weekend workshop. Jeanne and I drove down and stayed at a hotel, which also gave us opportunity to visit family and mutual friends. It must have been late summer because I swam in the pool. I also slipped in the bath—the only time I've done that. A tiny indentation in my shin memorializes it. My scream brought our visitors running to see who was murdering me in the shower à la Hitchcock.

Marion and Robert took turns presenting. More accurately, Marion didn't lecture or present; she spun words that made more—or less—sense depending on how deeply into herself she was diving. With or without logic, they spun a web; one found oneself spun into the web.

One afternoon, Marion and Robert were to present together. Marion waited on the stage for Robert. He never appeared. Someone was sent to track down the elusive Robert and ensure that he wasn't in trouble. Meanwhile, Marion found herself standing on the stage alone, minus Robert, with a large audience. She used her half of the time as she had planned and then—Robert not having appeared—she chose to read us a short story she had written. It was a draft, clearly only lightly disguised as fiction, at least to Jeanne's ear and mine.

Much later she told me that following the afternoon presentation, she went in search of Robert and eventually found him, reading, relaxed. "Where *were* you?" she asked, incredulous.

"I went for a walk on the beach," said the deeply introverted, unrepentant Robert. "I knew they wouldn't miss me and that you'd do fine."

---

[45] Robert Johnson, 1921–2018, was a Jungian analyst, author and lecturer.

At 10:00 P.M. on Sunday evening Marion called me. She had a playful intimacy in her tone at the beginning—especially when I didn't realize it was she. We talked for half an hour. It was a brief, warm love fest.

She said that after I had left ShaSha, she saw me so often on the sofa playing the guitar. I told her I was glad I'd left my hat there.

"Well, it'll be waiting for you there next year."

I spoke about how she had come across during the workshop; she exclaimed that this exactly mirrored her own experience. "Yes, yes. Access to all three energies: crone, mother, puella."

She later commented, "I'm sure you saw the moment when it became personal."

"You held for a second until you could put it together again," I replied.

Later in the conversation I mentioned, "You spark when you're with Robert. You're playful."

She said she was ready to do the Emily Dickinson recording, but not organizationally as yet. "Do you still want to, Jill?"

"Of course."

I told her about my book. I did not ask her if she would be willing to write a foreword. While I hoped it might be possible, I didn't want to distract or detract from our personal exchange.

She said, "The weekend didn't feel complete to me without calling you! At least we got that hug yesterday."

∞

Postcard
Dec 2/91

Dearest Jill,

These sombre ducks look out at the world as I feel this morning. Ross and I have just returned from a fabulous time in London, England, our beloved London. Its museums, art galleries, ballet, opera all as glorious as ever and while other things are sadly deteriorated, our world was still intact and we were so happy. Now it is back to work and picking up the load of responsibility. I'm looking at the whole thing through lids that shield the onslaught. Thanks for your lovely call. I love you dearly,

Marion

∞

December 14/91

Dearest Jill,

I hope you are having a splendid time in Australia—a very special occasion. I do understand your conflict about coming to Pajaro this year. And, dear Jill, it would be wonderful to be with you, but you know what we will be doing. To walk on the beach would be wonderful. You could get to know Ross better too. And dear Mary will be coming.

I may be in terrible conflict too. Fraser is not at all well and I feel I cannot leave if the situation is too bad. That would go against everything in me. We must trust the gods in this. Please no mention of this to anyone. It is very present to me and I need to tell you so you won't feel the pressure of a decision which may be unnecessary. Even now I am trying to "operate" with a broken heart.

But life is still beautiful. And I do love you dearly.

Marion

Thank you for your beautiful card.

∞

JM Notes
February 1992

I decided that I would not participate in the BodySoul Rhythm retreat at Pajaro Dunes but that I did want to stay open to seeing Marion and Ross if it fitted with their responsibilities and rhythms. I took myself on a painting and meditation retreat; I rented a separate apartment at Pajaro and stayed quiet, except for meeting Marion and Ross when they wanted.

Exploratory collage Jill made while on her personal retreat in an apartment overlooking a canal at Pajaro Dunes. 12 x 10. ©Melllick

As Marion had feared (in her previous letter), halfway through the workshop she received news that her brother Fraser was dying. She had to return to Canada as soon as possible. They needed to leave the workshop immediately. I was available, free of agenda; I was more than willing, if it felt right to them, to drive them from Pajaro Dunes two hours to the San Francisco airport.

Marion sat beside me, Ross behind. Marion was in shock but cloaking it with conversation. Finally, I thought what might give us relief from talking in the face of imminent death would be music. We sang. We sang every hymn, every calming song we could think of until we reached San Francisco International. Marion and Ross did gradually let down on the drive—as much as was possible under the circumstances.

Only in considerable retrospect, I saw that my unconscious understood the deeper implications of my choosing to be nearby that week; if things went smoothly, I would have a renewing personal retreat and some quick connections with Marion and Ross; if things didn't go as Marion hoped, I still would have quiet time for me and be there if they needed help from someone not involved with the BodySoul Rhythms work. I didn't know this when I made my plans, of course. Mary Hamilton and Patty Flowers, the administrator, handled the fallout with the group from Marion's sudden departure. In a later letter, Marion refers to the group's traveling to Canada to complete the workshop with her.

∞

JM Notes
March 15, 1992

Marion called me after Fraser died. I wanted to be present to all of her. Still, when we hung up, I wished I could have been even more present, more articulate. No matter that she found the flowers I had sent so beautiful, no matter that my presence at Pajaro and taking them to the airport had been "just right" she said, no matter she said she loved me. I wanted more *from me*. Who knows what? Perhaps it was a futile wish to be more, more *something* in the face of the absolute authority of death and grief. Marion said everything that needed to be done had been done.

∞

March 26/92

Dearest Jill,

I have your dear letter here with me in Atlanta. I am receiving your meditative purples and vibrant yellows.

Thank you for your congratulations on my honourary doctorate. Truly I am most honoured. I am sure you had much to do with it and I delight in our love of each other. I'll write to the Board very soon.[46]

I'm sending this with love,

Marion

∞

JM Notes
Week of May 4, 1992

Marion called about ShaSha, among other things. We shall be away for a week. She invited me to stay with her on the Saturday night before we left for the island if I wished.

The retreat started on June 14 and ended on June 19—much the same as last year. Marion asked if this year I would mind sleeping on the sitting room sofa in "Miranda." She assured me that it was comfortable. She said Eleanora and Mary would be at the retreat. She said she would be in touch with me after St. Simon (?).

Marion told me she had written a formal letter to ITP[47] saying how appreciative she was to be unanimously elected to receive an honorary doctorate.

---

[46] MW was to receive an honorary doctorate from ITP, the Institute of Transpersonal Psychology, now Sofia University, at commencement ceremonies in June.
[47] ITP, the Institute of Transpersonal Psychology, later to become Sofia University.

∞

May 15, 1992

Dearest Marion,

Congratulations on the release of *Leaving My Father's House!* It is a poignant, strong, clear, textured book with so much richness. Of course I read Mary's story first. How much it offers women in their own journeys. Jeanne has already stolen it from me, so I haven't finished it. I never cease to admire your vision and capacity to put it forth.

I hope your trip to Saint Simon (?) was successful and that you are having a chance to rest before the next journey. I wonder how it is for you being "out there" again during this time of mourning and healing.

I'm so delighted to be joining the pilgrimage to ShaSha again. I really had assumed that either you wouldn't do the retreat this year or that the group would probably have a different constitution—so Mary's letter telling me otherwise ... has been a lovely and unexpected gift.

Thank you for your kind invitation to stay over on Saturday night, Marion, which I accept with pleasure. How lovely to have a little time to connect before we join the group. Will Eleanora be staying with you that night, too? I have plane reservations up (no nonstop flights available so I go United through Chicago). I'll take a 7 A.M. out of San Francisco and arrive in Toronto at 1:50. By the time I get through baggage and take a bus to the city, I imagine it will probably be 3:00 to 3:30. Let me know what time suits you for me to arrive at your place. I'll be perfectly content exploring the city or meeting with friends until you're ready for company. Would you like to do some grocery shopping for a meal we could cook together at ShaSha?

Incidentally I'm assuming you'll bring your zither, so I'll just bring the guitar. As I'll be bunking on the sofa, do you want me to organise a sleeping bag and sheet and pillow?

ITP is happily announcing your acceptance of the honourary doctorate and your appearance next year at graduation, so that is all sorted out now.

Jeremy Tarcher[48] loves my book! He made my little writer's heart warm all over with compliments. I really didn't know whether it was worth a damn or not, Marion, so his comments were so encouraging. He even said it spoke directly to him as a person, which pleased me most of all. That's the good news—that, and that he wants to publish it. The bad news is that he is having difficulty convincing Putnam of its audience. He phoned me last Friday; he is in New York this week trying to educate Putnam about his market and said that if he is unsuccessful, he will personally try to place the book with another publisher. I am touched and grateful, not to mention happy.

Japan was superb. Demanding but superb. I filled myself with beauty and art and new ritual, both social and religious, for the two weeks. The learning and insights are without words; they just permeated my consciousness, and I find myself changed subtly on my return. We spent a week in Kyoto wondering through blossoms and gardens and temples. Then we went up into the North Country for three days. Most days, we saw no other Westerners—except for the day that we literally bumped into a close friend in a rock garden in Kyoto! He was on business in Tokyo but we had not expected to meet other than for a quick dinner on our one night in Tokyo. Talk about synchronicity! I also saw one of my physicians at the airport and two ex-students—all by happenstance!

One magical day, we hopped a train and went to a small village where we spent the morning inside a temple complex replete with sand garden, exquisite rocks, incense, temple bells, multitudes of cherry trees and long views of the ranges beyond; we followed with an afternoon in a small hot springs resort, bathing nude with Japanese women in the open air. I returned home laden with rolls of undeveloped film, memories, and Japanese art materials for use here.

I am coming to the close of the school year and feeling as though I shall just make it. The psychic demands of teaching are more challenging to combine with intense personal analysis than with my work as a therapist. This second analysis makes the first look like a romp in the sun! I am in such deep places right now that I often cannot even remember much of

---

[48] Jeremy Tarcher was a groundbreaking publisher who founded the imprint J.P. Tarcher. The imprint was purchased by Putnam and eventually purchased by Penguin.

what took place in a session until I enter the room again. Probably a good thing: my merciless animus can't claw it to death before it gets a chance to breathe. This work truly does require "not less than everything."[49]

Leave me a little message about arrangements when you can, and I look forward to seeing you soon.

Much much love, dearest person,

Jill

∞

JM Notes
June 13–21, 1992

Traveled to Toronto on Saturday. Spent the night with Marion.

Marion made me comfortable, offered me tea or coffee. Having oriented me to place and time, she asked if I would mind if she just finished some notes she was writing. She wrote all letters and books by hand. Later she would have her book drafts typed and would revise them by hand.

Having been raised in Australia where bread-and-butter letters[50] —all letters, in fact—were handwritten in cursive script, this

Marion's sitting room in her Toronto apartment.
©Mellick

---

[49] Reference MW and JM both knew from T.S. Eliot's *Four Quartets*.
[50] An expression used more often in Britain or Commonwealth countries but also in the U.S.

seemed normal to me. It was inconsiderate not to write in cursive script; we learned the order in which the pages should be written in primary school. Somehow one was supposed to know how many sheets of paper one would use for a letter. The first page wasn't numbered; the second page appeared on the second sheet, the third on the third sheet. Then one turned them all over and wrote from back to front so that the first page had the sixth page on its recto. These were arcane habits that Marion and I shared so never discussed; we'd been English Literature majors and teachers, and families had raised us with these habits. In those transitional years between my car accident and the appearance of home computers, I prefaced many letters with an apology and an explanation of why the letter was not handwritten.

After long hours of travel, I relaxed into stillness. Marion, head inclined, was writing swiftly by hand on heavyweight writing paper. The one concession she had made by then was to move from a fountain pen to a ballpoint. All of her letters and notes to me were handwritten in ball-point. I assured Marion that I was comfortable relaxing quietly in a big chair reading while she finished. I quietly took a couple of photographs of her.

The next day we traveled to Parry Sound by car, thence to ShaSha.

Marion and Jill, ShaSha. ©Mellick

Marion brushed my hair again. A silent, peaceful ritual. She was open in her physical closeness with all of us and, reserved Australian that I still was in "public," I learned yet again to receive kisses and hugs from Marion and others, and to sit close in group settings. Marion talked about the whole world having become eroticized for her at some point.

We facilitators learned deeply about ourselves, too, in these weeks. I learned more about being seen as a creative, quiet, intense listener. I noticed how, if I were not pushed, I could stay in my heart, be playful in a trusting, safe environment. I learned yet again that I could trust that my creativity could be a gift to others, even when imperfect. ShaSha taught me once again that nature is deeply healing for me. I felt alive in a storm; when the wind blew; by any kind of water. I noticed that I

Jill and Marion hiking on ShaSha. ©Mellick

Marion and Jill singing with others, ShaSha. ©Mellick

concern myself with small things that use up my energy unnecessarily; that music, making music, and singing are healing for me as well as others; that I can trust my musical ear; that I *can* sing again; that singing is an avenue for my feeling; that my feeling[51] side can be fully present if given enough introversion; that its rhythm is much slower than my thinking or intuition, but that it's *there* and it's true when I'm not fussing about other things. Each of us came away richer each year.

During the ShaSha week in 1992, I made a stream-of-consciousness note in my journal. It wasn't meant to be "good writing." It does remind me of what an impact I felt at that time in my life to consciously receive affection from the participants:

> A twig snaps in my silent forest. The ground groans. A trunk splinters. Full moon. Small feathers drying on a warm stone. Ripples are tidal waves across my dawn. Archeologist, I tie my shoelace, wipe sweat from my eyes, move with them. Qumran. Caves, vessels. They find and enter my cave, open a vessel. A scroll of me meets air, fragments.

∞

Sunday, June 28, 1992

Dearest Marion,

You are daily and sometimes hourly in my heart and consciousness. I wonder where you are and how you are. Such a liminal time for you and Ross.

I'd like to write more but I'm deeply tired and need to rest before the onslaught of the next week. We are in the midst of adding a Japanese-flavoured studio on the back and, despite a wonderful crew, it is an inherently disruptive process to both inner and outer life! It should be finished before we leave to spend August in Santa Fe. Thank you, thank you for the sacred opportunity to be part of this last week. Thank you, too,

---

[51] "Feeling" in this context refers to Jung's description of feeling as a valuing function of the psyche, not to emotions.

for your open-hearted generosity in having me as your guest both in Toronto and on ShaSha (my neck, too, greatly appreciated having a bed again at "Miranda").

Most of all, thank you for who you are and for all the quiet, loving ways—from shared moments of laughter and sadness and song to quiet moments alone together. Your being and your friendship bless me a thousand ways.

I also only fully realise when I get home the depth of the healing I, too, have experienced. My dreams have been full of ShaSha. I share a dream from this week: you, Ann and Mary are offering a women's workshop. Each woman will be given "the wedding she never had or wished she had had." She will dress in full bridal regalia. She will go through the ceremony alone—no physical groom. The participants will all celebrate with her. I couldn't have consciously made up a better description for the inner marriage I see you're helping women experience.

I'm happy with the photographs, although last year's set was a little better perhaps. Still, it's a loving record. Don't worry about showing these to the rest. I've come up with a new way of distributing, which gets you out of the loop. This set is just a small memento for you.

I feel as though our artesian connection runs so deep, beloved soul, that I wonder I use words with you at all. Each time I do, I remember the grace of who you are. Each time I brush my hair, you are with me.

With love, as always and growing,

Jill

PS I can't think why you would want my Santa Fe address for August but here it is. . . . We are staying in a writer's house replete with catwalk views of the mountains, a hot tub, three computers, a loft, a fountain—and a guest house called "Lady Chatterley's Lover"?![52]

---

[52] The guest house was named after D.H. Lawrence's novel, in which Lady Chatterley takes the gardener as her lover. Lawrence spent significant time in Taos, north of Santa Fe, at the invitation of Mabel Dodge Luhan, a New York socialite who had married a Taos Indian. When Lawrence died, his ashes were brought by train to "the end of the trail," where Luhan and Frieda Lawrence got drunk, fought over the ashes, then took them north to Taos together.

∞

ShaSha Island
July 31/92

Dearest Jill,

Thank you, thank you, thank you—for your beautiful letter and for your exquisite pictures. They are different from last year—yes—but I think they captured the essence of this group. I know A will be thrilled with hers, and your feeling for the island is so sensitive—the water, the moss, the flowers. For me, you caught the week moment by moment and I delight in your record. For instance, some lovely ones of you and Eleanora,[53] as well. (I showed Marion[54] the one of me combing your hair. She looked at it a long time, then I made some comment about my "fat arms." She said, "Oh, Auntie, I've always loved your fat arms. They are so soft. I remember going to sleep holding their softness." So much for self-deprecatory remarks!)

Our ladies' week was the only good week we have had here all summer. Right now is fairly typical—pouring rain, heavy mist, cold with no sign of clearing tomorrow. The foliage on the island is the most beautiful it has ever been—primulas, day lilies, gardens of wild iris and wild roses, vervain, exquisite grasses and now the wild asters. Anyway, it is excellent for reading and resting.

Ross is lying on the sofa reading The Chymical Wedding.[55] He said it is magnificent. He is relatively well but the three weeks we went through before we left London have left a deep scar. Great soul! He says he is ready for "the occasion" of his death and it will be okay.

W is not in an easy passage. Dear woman is really facing the depths. I'll let her tell you about it (but she probably already has). She needs many

---

[53] Eleanora Woloy, Jungian analyst and close friend of Marion's.
[54] Marion Boa, Marion's niece, one of analyst Fraser Boa's daughters.
[55] The Chymical Wedding by Lindsay Clarke.

prayers these days. I am encouraging her not to come to the intensive if it is wrong to leave her introversion.

I'm sure your "Japanese-flavoured studio" will be beautiful. I hope it is finished, for your sake.

Dear Jill, I hope you are having a splendid time in Santa Fe right now. The house must be exactly right. I think of you with deepest joy so many times a day, and I love seeing your hat hanging on the fuse box beside mine. Our connection is indeed artesian.

Dearest love,

Marion

PS Mary is fine. Her daughters are at camp so she and John have each other for two weeks.

∞

August 9, 1992

Dearest Marion,

Your letter arrived and, as always, it arrived at a synchronistic time for me, a time when the darkness had me temporarily in thrall. I have been talking with you in my inner world (descents are darker and deeper . . . but mercifully brief—these days).

I was so relieved and grateful to know that you and Ross had made it back to a wet and misty ShaSha again after those harrowing three weeks. You had been even more in my thoughts than usual (if possible) during that time. How glorious the wildflowers must be! What exquisite flower arrangements you must be creating.

Well, the offerings were made for you and for us at the shine on Tsikomo[56] yesterday. What a journey! And how its spirit reminded me of our times on ShaSha. Eight of us went, all dear friends with close connections to spiritual life, the inner life and a love of simple, organic ritual. Each of us made the pilgrimage for different reasons. We also took Ishta, a white, blue-eyed, wolf-husky mix, and Penny and David,[57] married minister friends committed to radical theology, community renewal, social justice, and the re-inclusion of the feminine in Christianity. It was David's fiftieth birthday.

We met at Gip and Patricia's[58] centuries-old rambling adobe compound in the small northern town of Nambé. They are turning their buildings into a retreat centre. Their sensitive children came, too.

Gip presented us each with *pajos*, string-wrapped feather carriers for our prayers. He and his son had made them the night before and had lain them on their home altar to "cure." They had also prayed that these feathers might be worthy bearers of our offerings.

We drove twenty precipitous miles on dirt, deep and high into the reservation of Santa Clara Pueblo. Tsikomo (Shining Mountain)[59] is held sacred as the emergence place of and center of the world for the Northern Pueblo peoples. Certain areas are open to non-Pueblo people. When we could drive no farther through the fir-covered mountains, we squeezed into Gip's four-wheeler and drove two more miles to the foot of Tsikomo. We had ascended from 7,000 to 10,000 feet.[60]

---

[56] Tsikomo, variously spelled and meaning "Shining Mountain," is the Tewa name for the highest point in the Jemez Mountains and sacred to Pueblo Peoples of New Mexico. Pueblo communities often refer to it as the "center of all."
[57] Penny and David Mann, Congregational ministers who have worked in settings predominantly directed toward social justice issues and actions.
[58] Dr. Patricia and Gip Brown and their two children lived in a compound in Nambé. Patricia headed the PHS Indian Hospital Mental Health Division. Gip became State Personnel Director for New Mexico.
[59] Tsikomo Mountain is on Santa Clara Pueblo land. It is open on the north side in specific areas to non-Pueblo people.
[60] The highest point on the mountain is 11,561 feet.

Another 1,500 feet to climb. The sun was shining, and we began our ascent through unmarked paths through the forest. The altitude had us all panting and conserving energy.

One hour later, we arrived at a meadow. Above the meadow somewhere is a pinnacle with an understated Pueblo shrine, the birthplace. We didn't approach it, of course. It's sacred ground for the Pueblo people and not ours to approach. At the very moment we looked up, thunder crackled across the sky and we all knew we were in the presence of the gods.

We moved quietly to a small, natural formation of stones that we deemed "our shrine." One by one we approached it, whispering prayers into the feathers, some laying down special objects—sacrifices, offerings, symbols of gratitude, blessings.

Small rock pool in which Jill left feathers for Marion, Ross, and ShaSha as part of her ritual offering on Tsikomo Mountain, New Mexico. ©Mellick

I was the last. I found, as part of the shrine, four tiny pools of water in a larger, encompassing rock. When I saw them, I knew what I wanted to do. For you, I took two of the small feathers and floated them in one of the rock pools. I thought: one for Marion, one for Ross. A third asked to join them there, too: for ShaSha. I sprinkled cornmeal—gift from Hartman, our dear Hopi friend[61]—onto the surface of the water. Then I completed what I needed to do for the rest of my own ritual. The second I finished, I felt rain falling on my face and beginning to splash into the tiny rock pools. It was gentle, loving rain.

We moved off to the left, where we sat in ponchos eating lunch in the rain, looking out from our 12,000-foot eagle's view of mesa after mesa and range after mauve range of the Sangre de Cristo Mountains and the Pedernal (focus of so much of Georgia O'Keefe's[62] creative energies). We were thousands of feet above Santa Fe, Los Alamos,[63] Black Mesa.[64] Rain fell in wide, bruised sheets from thunderclouds while sun gave fiery colour to other escarpments. We blessed each other with cornmeal and laughed and ate until Gip declared that the clouds were telling us to leave—now.

We started down the mountain quickly, following Gip. As we crossed the meadow, the lightning cut the sky and thunder encircled us. We quickly entered the thick forest and began our descent. Just as we entered the forest, the hail came. Endless, perfectly rounded pellets spitting on our raincoats, melting in our hair and eyes and soon covering the moss and pine-needle ground cover completely with white.

---

[61] Hartman Lomawaima, graduate of Harvard and Stanford, was Hopi Indian from Shipaulovi, Second Mesa. A tribal leader, he and Tsianina, Stanford graduate, author, university professor and half Creek Indian, were married in a traditional Hopi ceremony. Hartman was Assistant Director of the Arizona State Museum, active with the Smithsonian Museum in reappropriating sacred objects from museums. Without these, sacred rituals often could not take place. JM was his "Aussie sis;" he, her "Hopi bro;" and Jeanne, his "California Mom." He died of cancer before his 60th birthday. Hartman had ground the cornmeal and given it to JM.

[62] Artist Georgia O'Keefe created many of her oil paintings in New Mexico. She moved there permanently after the death of her husband, photographer and gallery owner Alfred Stieglitz, in 1946.

[63] Los Alamos was the secret residence of the scientists who developed the H-bomb, first tested in White Sands, New Mexico, then used to bomb Hiroshima.

[64] Black Mesa is sacred to the Tewa-speaking peoples of the Northern Pueblos. Once open to the public for ascent, it is now available solely to Pueblo people.

Hailstorm, Tsikomo, New Mexico. Acrylic 40 x 30, Jill Mellick. ©Mellick

An hour later Gip stopped. Without wasting energy on apologies he said to the group, "Does anyone have a gut feeling for where we are and which way we need to go?" We were lost. (Later he reviewed what had happened and realised that hurry and looking down because of the hail had disoriented him for the first time in his frequent ascents—but we knew there was more to our being lost than this outer explanation.)

Without missing a beat, we realised that we were each responsible for offering whatever strength, intuition, and capacities we had in what was potentially a serious situation. Our oldest member was 67; our youngest, 10. We had little food and water, no matches, and poor clothing for a possible overnight on the forest floor. One by one we internally set aside our usual ways of coping with stress and fear and drew other roles to play from the collective consciousness into which we seemed to move. Later we would give to each other names that honoured those natural roles we took on. Without discussing how we were to make decisions, we worked by consensus; and each person's capacities and physical limits became part of the "what is" of the event—again without discussion.

We climbed the mountain a second time. We lost the mountain. We sang. We were silent. We were chilled. We laughed; we trusted; we questioned; we let Ishta[65] pull a tired member up a steep slope. Once—prematurely breaking into "Amazing Grace"—we thought we were found but were not.

Two hours later, we came to a high enough point to orient ourselves from the surrounding peaks and began the descent again. Late in the afternoon Patricia and Ishta cried out that they could see the car. We were down, safe. The gods had quieted and the sun was shining again.

We are still absorbing the experience and telling each other, late into the night, our experiences of self and other. I wanted to tell you, too, about this experience because your spirits were part of that pilgrimage. Please feel free to share any of this with Ross if you wish.

On the day you wrote to me, I dreamt I was at ShaSha. You were sitting on a rock looking out to the Beyond.[66] Later, I cupped your face in my hands gently and held it with great love. Your eyes were closed but you knew it was I.

I cup your face in my hands, dearest one.

Jill

PS As always, there is no need to write unless you feel so moved. After all, this is your retreat time! It is enough to know that you have received this— and we have so many ways of being together in the spirit.

---

[65] Ishta means "blue eyes" in Apache and "Beloved One" in Sanskrit. An Apache man gave the dog to Dr. Shyam Kashyap, Patricia's yogic practitioner and Vedic physician, and she inherited him. He was her "beloved boy," her canine familiar.
[66] MW's "The Beyond" appears in the watercolors in *Coming Home to Myself.*

∞

September 4/92

Dearest Jill,

Thank you for your beautiful card. Thank God and Sophia you are safely back in this land of the living. Thanks for sharing that incredible initiation with us. I know well that lostness that comes from disorientation in nature. I'm rejoicing in your presence on this side of the veil and in your opening.

Tomorrow Mary, Ann and I set out to the country to meet the ladies and Paula[67] who want to finish the February Workshop[68]—twelve or more. What memories this relives, dear Jill.

Thank God you were there.

Love,

Marion

∞

JM Notes
October 22, 1992

Called Marion. I found I was able to tell her something highly personal with self-respect. She, of course, was receptive, loving, affirming.[69]

---

[67] Paula Reeves, Ph.D., psychotherapist and one of the later facilitators for many BodySoul Rhythms workshops and one ShaSha retreat.
[68] MW is referring to the Pajaro Dunes retreat when, halfway through the retreat, JM drove MW and Ross to the airport to fly to Canada when Fraser Boa was dying.
[69] JM noted few of MW's and her phone calls. The letter that follows refers to this call.

∞

October 25, 1992

Dearest Marion,

When it was finally time to break silence and reach out, you were there—right then and despite discomfort. Thank you for being available then, dear person. Our talking brought balm, blessing, hope.

I've learnt and endured much since January—all in the service of new beginnings, true. But at such a cost! These chosen, unchosen inner journeys bring one to one's knees—often castigating oneself for acting or for not acting, feeling unequal to either, breaking promises to oneself. What a shadow! I thank God for my generous, wise analyst's love and faith in me. One never knows on which side of the ravine one's tired body, soul and fate might put one. I do know I need respite right now.

It's hard to explain why it was so helpful to talk with you at that particular moment. It's not as though you haven't already given me insights from your experience with similar issues—and I certainly know your life has brought joy and fulfilment.

Somehow, being at a crossroad and no longer silent, I wanted to link hearts with my dear friend. Our talking braided another strand of a (still precarious) rope bridge across that ravine to the possibility for me of a full future utterly different from what I expected. It felt timely and good to tell you more about where I've been walking, to consciously remind myself that you are flourishing on the other side and there to greet me if I must cross this bridge. The self-accepting way you spoke, too, and mutual respect helped me to feel more self-accepting.

I wish I'd been able to turn my attention from myself to hear more about you. Ross told me briefly about your holiday—such a joy to see Marion Rose[70] so freshly budded! However, I have caught up a little. P said the

---

[70] Marion's great-niece.

UC Extension week went wonderfully; R told me you had decided not to do the film opening. She also said Ross was skipping his paper after all. I'm so pleased. I wonder how and where Bruce is, how your own heart is repairing from Fraser's death, how this less committed time is for you.

It almost does a disservice to the depth of our bond to constantly mention it. So I shan't. You know. Just touch the Iona pot and you'll feel it.

With love,

Jill

∞

December 12/92

Dearest Jill,

I was trying to send you a truly original piece of stationery. It is original all right, but not beautiful. But I'm going to send it anyway because I've spent such a frustrating half hour on it. In one of my forays into previous old boxes I've found these Victorian decals[71] I bought in England years ago. I did exactly what the instructions said to do, but now they are too dry to hold together. I kept them for someone I knew would appreciate them, and dear Jill, you would have but ... still, even in their brokenness, they speak. Thank you for your beautiful letter. I certainly heard your pain. I do hope you are gradually accepting what seems to be your destiny. Not easy, dear one, not easy. Trust that new doors will open easily.

---

[71] Popular in the Victorian era until the mid-twentieth century, decals are designs prepared on special paper with dry glue on the reverse side for wetting and transferring onto another surface, such as glass, paper, porcelain or metal. When JM was a child, friends would buy, collect and trade decals with one another.

Looking back over the year, I find your presence smiling at me or looking intensely into my stricken eyes so many times. What a precious friend you are.

The pictures you took of me at my desk electrified Ross. "That's you," he said. "I want those." So for our anniversary, I have put them in little connecting frames for him. I agree they are who I am.

Afternoon sunshine backlights Marion at her desk in the sitting room in Toronto. Ross felt that these two images caught the essence of Marion so she framed them and gave them to him for their anniversary. ©Mellick

Marion, seated at her desk, reflected in a mirror in the sitting room in her apartment in Toronto. The long watercolor below is the one Jill gave to Marion of Pajaro Dunes. ©Mellick

That introversion is battling to hold her space right now. My sabbatical year could quickly turn into time to begin organizing for a return to extraversion next year. Invitations to speak come in and I'm not sure yet that I'm going out again. At the same time I realized I cannot write from an abstract centre. I can, but it does not connect to people out there. So I have to find a balance. Ironically, in this time of withdrawal, the Bly/Woodman film is appearing for the next six weeks on TV in Canada.

Never before has any soul been so vulnerable. The camera picks up every innuendo in my eyes. People either love or hate the program. I feel quite detached from the praise and criticism. I was not performing. The woman there is doing her best and that's the way it is.

Ross celebrated his 70th birthday last week.[72] We had a soul party. His dearest friends of 70 years brought their own poems, songs, dances, sculptures. Amid 70 white candles and white roses we all participated. My gift was our waltz and, Jill, it was as if we were 20 or 2000. Dear soul!

I hope you are well. I do love you so much. ShaSha is going to be again the third week of June.

Dearest love,

Marion

∞

February 26, 1993

Dearest Marion,

Such a delight to talk with you![73] I had been planning to invite you after the Dean confirmed you're coming. I'm so happy you shall grace the new room. Jeanne asked me to tell you that she is delighted, too. The room is peaceful, private and filled with light. I think you'll be comfortable there. The Dean mentioned that speakers usually take 10 to 15 minutes. It's up to you, of course, but you are such an inspiring speaker that five minutes seems awfully short.[74]

---

[72] MW also printed a chapbook of Ross Woodman's poetry. It is to be hoped that it is with his archives in Canada.
[73] Date of phone call is unrecorded.
[74] MW had told JM on the phone that she was considering giving a five-minute address.

Such a year for you. A sabbatical spent on legal matters and politics ...
not exactly what you anticipated. I wonder how this week has been,
reading your notes from a year ago. I pray that it did, indeed, balance the
perspective on what was finished and what was not. I am holding you in
my heart as you gather in The Brother and release the brother. A daunting
and solitary task. I wonder how Bruce is, too.

... Odd how the psyche can be rent asunder in these journeys and yet the
outer life can continue and be continued uninterrupted. For me, I
experience heart and soul torn apart one moment in my own analysis.
(Boy, you aren't exaggerating when you talk about feeling as though one
is "on the cross." And it's as slow a death.) The next moment, I feel calm,
strong and present doing psychotherapy or teaching. I am grateful for the
ego strength I was given and for an analyst whose flexibility, astute heart
and wit walk fearless into the darkest burial grounds. I am well held and
moving through this despite myself.

...

Painting has been respite and meditation. The art show will still be up
when you are here and I want you to see it.[75] As I said, each landscape,
although not artistically daring, carries my experience of a pilgrimage
(there are some of Pajaro).

Let's stay in touch about plans. Let me know about airport pickups and
such; I'd be delighted to help in any way—you know that.

Much, much love,

J

PS The book is currently with Shambala.[76] A slow process, too.

---

[75] MW bought a painting of an Aboriginal women's sacred waterhole near Uluru in Central
Australia.
[76] Shambala Publications.

∞

JM Notes
Early March 1993

Phone call with Marion. She seemed subdued, almost formal although she talked willingly. No mention of ShaSha. They are not going to England; Mary[77] is going instead of her. Marion's affect was flat.

∞

March 23/93

Dearest Jill,

Thank you for your kind offer of a bed on my Santa Barbara venture. They are taking good care of me on that journey. Pacifica is also honouring me; hence the two journeys. I am steady at centre so I think all is well.

Your holidays sound wonderful. The Yosemite card is magnificent.

I appreciate the invitation to the luncheon, Jill, but I know I could give all my energy there and not have the focus for the graduation. (How do people wine and dine and then focus?) Will there be time to greet the grads after the ceremony? If so, I prefer afterwards.

Blessings and love as always,

Marion

---

[77] Mary Hamilton.

∞

JM Notes

When Marion stayed at our house, we always reveled in dressing down, not up. She had her own bedroom, bathroom, and studio in which to write (my art, writing and music studio). Sometimes she would sleep for hours to catch up with herself. She constantly said that she could completely let down when she came to us.

It helped that there was always a beloved dog. Marion was a dog devotee. She and Ross had had dogs most of their married life. She often publicly told the story of her being in England one summer working with E.A. Bennet—physician, analyst, and Jung's friend and colleague—when she received word that her loved dog had died. She went to the session, well organized and prepared for the hour. At the end, she mentioned that her dog had died. Dr. Bennet was shocked. My paraphrased memory of her description—it might well appear in a publication—is: "Mrs. Woodman! You have spent *all* this time speaking about other things when your *soul animal has died!*"

When Marion was staying with us, we would pad around as free of persona as we all were at ShaSha. Jeanne would often lend Marion her sweats. We enjoyed listening to Marion's stories. She was an inveterate storyteller with a knack for editing, good timing, and amplification. She was as in love with the stories as we were happy to have her relate them. One evening over dinner she spoke about being in Israel and wanting to see the Baha'i center there because Ross was senior in the Baha'i faith in Canada. Marion said she ended up wandering alone through the Israeli desert. No water. No map. Lost in the landscape for hours. Finally, she found her way out (dramatic details lost in the mists of time). She did, indeed, find the beautiful Baha'i center.[78]

---

[78] The Baha'i center in Israel is strongly associated with Haifa and Mount Carmel.

Having stayed with close friends ourselves in their gracious home on Mount Carmel overlooking Haifa, we refrained from asking Marion deflating questions such as "Why didn't you use a map?" or "Didn't you take water?" It would have denied the three of us the pleasure of her wonderful yarn—"a bit of good crack," my Anglo-Irish grandmother would have called it with delight.

Marion and Ross often came together to Palo Alto. When they did, they stayed at the Holiday Inn on El Camino Real. I would arrange for one of the best and quietest rooms overlooking the koi pond, a five-minute drive from our house.

Time with Marion and Ross together was invariably intense, fascinating, heartwarming, laughter-filled, deep, challenging, educational, and fun. Ross felt and said nothing by halves. Although he had been raised in a notably restrained, far-eastern part of Canada, his warm, intellectual, intense personality had survived his acculturation.

Ross and Marion in front of the bonsai deck at Mellick/Shutes residence. Marion is holding Ashi, the miniature schnauzer to whom she was greatly attached. ©Mellick

∞

JM Notes
June 1993

"Women's Sacred Watering Hole, Uluru," Pastel
24 x 30, Jill Mellick ©Mellick

Commencement weekend. Marion was to receive an honorary doctorate and be the commencement speaker at ITP.[79] She arrived on Thursday to stay with us. On Friday, she wanted to see my art show. She was drawn to one large painting in particular: a large pastel of an Aboriginal women's sacred watering hole near Uluru. I knew she and Ross had much fine art, so when she said she wanted it and was determined to pay for it, overriding my objections, I was surprised, pleased, and encouraged, given their collection.

On Saturday, Marion gave a workshop in the city. In the evening we relaxed in the sitting room. My head was bowed over the open-tuned zither. Ashi, our miniature schnauzer, was squashed contentedly between us. Later we repaired to my studio. It was hers when she stayed although some activities required our working together in it.

Tami Simon of Sounds True had told us she could find only one day she could book at a nearby recording studio, Music Annex, to finally record "Emily Dickinson and the Demon Lover"— Marion's words, my music: Sunday— Commencement Day. So, on Saturday, Marion was editing by

---

[79] Institute of Tranpersonal Psychology, now Sofia University.

hand the final copy for the recording we were to make the next day. When she would make and then read a change to me, I would respond spontaneously with something on the zither; it either felt right to us or it didn't. My music was a response to the words, tone, mood. Then, of course, we had to immerse ourselves in the tiresome details—neither of our fortés—of noting changes on two copies.

We arrived early at the studio with papers, zither, and drinks. After three intense hours of recording and rerecording, I gamely declared that I needed to *eat!* My body was protesting.

"Oh, yes, Jill," Marion replied. I waited for her to put her papers down so I could scoot us both home for a quick bite and then return. Quickly looking up at me, Marion said, "You go, Jill. I'm just going to make a few changes."

"Marion ..." I said.

"I'll be fine, Jill."

"Let me bring you back something. Sandwich? Cheese? Fruit? Tea? All of the above?"

"Some water—and a banana if you have one."

"A banana."

She was already lost in revisions again. I drove home and collapsed in the kitchen, refueling. Marion and I had less than three hours before we had to finish the recording, drive home, shower, robe, then drive to the venue for commencement.

I was back at the studio in twenty minutes with tea and banana. Only by being my bossy self—a side of me Marion knew and accepted with gentle, amused affection—did I get her to eat the banana.

We finished with five minutes to spare. By the time I drove us back to shower and change, my adrenalin would have fueled a plane. The windowless recording studio did not give me energy, but improvising music on the zither always did. Too, making creative changes as we went along gave me energy. Marion was in some state of suspended animation or adrenalin-fueled calm.

We showered, dressed, and donned academic robes. Ashi followed Marion and me around, curious. Jeanne took photographs of us with and without Ashi. All of us being dog devotees, we wanted Ashi in on the act almost as much as Marion did.

Jill and Marion preparing for Commencement Day. Marion gave the Commencement Speech and was awarded an Honorary Doctorate by the Institute of Transpersonal Psychology/Sofia University. ©Jeanne Shutes

Jill and Marion holding Ashi in Shutes/Mellick garden prior to leaving for Commencement, Institute of Transpersonal Psychology/Sofia University. ©Jeanne Shutes

Marion was awarded an Honorary Doctorate by and gave the Commencement Speech at the Institute of Transpersonal Psychology/Sofia University. ©Jeanne Shutes

The Institute of Transpersonal Psychology commencement began at 4:30. I introduced Marion and her accomplishments before she was awarded the honorary doctorate and she gave the commencement address.

Jill reads the tribute to Marion prior to the awarding of the Honorary Doctorate. ©Mellick

∞

Institute of Transpersonal Psychology
1993 Commencement
Portola Valley Presbyterian Church
Honorary Doctorate for Marion Woodman

Address by Jill Mellick on behalf of the Board and Faculty

It is a privilege and a personal delight to address Marion Woodman on behalf of our community. Marion, you never *planned* to become an international speaker or one of the most innovative Jungian analysts currently in practice. You didn't *plan* to write widely read and acclaimed books on Jungian psychology—books which broke new ground, books exploring the intimate connection between body and soul, books exploring the spiritual dimensions of addiction, books addressing the personal and global need for post-patriarchal masculinity and femininity.

No. You didn't start out to do these things. You started out rather quietly, graduating with honors in English from the University of Western Ontario and doing further graduate work at the Ontario College of Education. Then you taught English and Creative Drama in Canada and England for twenty-four years.

But something else was calling you. As you say in your book *The Pregnant Virgin*, "I was in midlife. ... I had almost everything middle-class life had to offer ... but I knew I had to find out who I was when all my support systems were taken away."

That decision took you to India—alone. In India, as you describe it, "I hoped I might find God ..." You found God "not in the protective walls of an ashram but in the streets seething with poverty, disease—and love."
India continued a transformation that was to affect not only your life but thousands of others. India led you into Jungian analysis, into analytic training in Zürich, into writing.

Marion, you have said that when you were writing your first book, it didn't really consciously register with you that people would *read* what you were writing! Well, read they have. Over 200,000 people have read your books—in fifteen editions and in seven languages. In 1980, you published *The Owl Was the Baker's Daughter*, a study of anorexia, obesity and the repressed feminine. Two years later you published *Addiction to Perfection* and, soon after, *The Pregnant Virgin*, both studies of psychological transformation. These were followed by *The Ravaged Bridegroom*. Your most recent books, *Leaving My Father's*

House and *Conscious Femininity*, were released last year. You have also been writer-in-residence at Esalen.

But if it never occurred to you that somebody would actually read your books, it was a further surprise that people would actually come to hear you *speak*! I know that the first time you came to speak at the Jung Institute in San Francisco, as a friend was driving you to the meeting hall, you passed long lines of people—all down one street and around the next corner. You casually asked your companion, "Who's in town?"

"Woodman," she replied calmly.

You were shocked. What could you have to say that might have real worth for all those people? You were sure that you should never have had the temerity to leave the church basement in Port Stanley. You have said that, as you waited go onstage, feeling odd and humbled by the challenge of the evening, you could do nothing except surrender yourself to any transpersonal energy that might carry soul and body through the evening. It did.
And that energy has carried you across thousands of miles and into thousands of hearts for twelve years: you have directed over two hundred workshops, given over two hundred fifty lectures, including an intensive for our students here. You have also made yourself accessible through audiotape and video, the most recent of which is a video series exploring the dimensions of a fairy tale with your friend Robert Bly.

Through these workshops—from the intimate to the large, sometimes involving over 2,000 participants—you have brought healing and insight to untold numbers. And you have stood patiently for hours afterwards answering questions as though each questioner were the only soul in the auditorium.

Through all of this, Marion, you have quietly continued your analytic practice and have responded to thousands of letters—by hand. Your integrity of heart and your capacity for deep, warm, and respectful personal connection are two of the great gifts you have brought to this, your second vocation. And these, together with your gifts for metaphor, spontaneity, down-to-earth humor, and translation of complex concepts into liveable visions, infuse others with real hope and real courage.

Unassumingly—and immeasurably—you have contributed to and advanced the fields of Jungian and transpersonal psychology. Those of us whose lives you have touched are the richer for your life, love, wisdom, and soul.

We thank you and we honor you.

The audience listened to this formal introduction and watched Marion bend her head of thick, curly grey hair to be hooded. They applauded noisily and then were spellbound by her four-point commencement address. (She had said two days before, "No, I haven't written my address, but I have some ideas, Jill." *When* did she write that?!) Marion's improvisational approach could sometimes leave me uneasy for her, but the timbre of her voice almost always became the warp and woof of even her most intuitive speeches. That commencement audience had no idea how we'd spent the day: recording, recording again, rewriting, changing the music to fit the rewrites, scarfing bananas, holding the dog in our robes.

From intuitive word and music exchange to formal hooding, our day had been lived in intensity. We began to come to earth when we returned home. The three of us ate a leisurely dinner exchanging stories, unashamedly and delightedly exaggerating travel tales and how we'd each got ourselves out of scrapes in strange countries.

∞

JM Notes
Friday, June 11, 1993

ShaSha retreat time again. I flew to Canada.

I stayed with Marion on Friday and Saturday nights in Toronto. I caught a taxi to her apartment. I assumed I would be staying in the downstairs ground-floor guest room that owners could reserve for visitors. Marion said I would not be sleeping downstairs but bunking with her as we all did at ShaSha, if that was fine with me.

After we embraced, she once more showed me down her hall into the light-flooded main room. Parquet flooring, Persian rugs. Afternoon light flooding in through the windows. Marion's desk was still on the window wall. Her bedroom was to the right of the sitting room. Marion showed me again where she had placed my long watercolor of Pajaro Dunes below a mirror in the sitting room. Then she took me in to the bedroom, where

Marion's sitting room and desk in her Toronto apartment. ©Mellick

In her Toronto apartment, Marion hung the painting she had bought from Jill of an aboriginal women's watering hole at Uluru. ©Mellick

she had hung my large pastel of the women's sacred watering hole at Uluru that she had bought. I was warmed to see how it just seemed to belong there. I have felt this experience often; someone purchases my art and later shows me where it lives. When I see it there, I feel a painless severing of some slim energy cord I still have with the piece, and at the same time my heart spontaneously warms. So, I was pleased to see that the painting of the watering hole really did belong with Marion. She had hung it above a bedside table. The colors of the room were the same palette as the painting: ochers, pale greens, mauves.

Bruce, Marion's actor brother, arrived unexpectedly. He was a large, handsome presence. Marion introduced us and mentioned again that he was an actor and visiting from England. He gave the impression of paying attention even when distracted. I wondered where these three siblings—Fraser Boa, Bruce Boa, and Marion—had inherited their gift for drama, for film, for acting. Bruce was an actor; Fraser had been an analyst and filmmaker of *The Way of the Dream*, the Marie-Louise von Franz six-hour marathon documentary, later a book; and Marion was a consummate storyteller, using this gift with an actor's timing in delivery and tonal changes to enhance workshops, addresses, and her books.

Marion's Toronto apartment sitting room. She kept her journals in the drawers.
©Mellick

Dinner was in her apartment; Marion did not dine out unless the situation necessitated it. After dinner, we settled down in the sitting room and conversed. Traveling from west to east, I still had good energy.

Marion must have decided ahead of time to share certain things. At the time, her doing so seemed spontaneous. In retrospect, I realized it was not. Marion had kept journals for years—as had I. She had a cabinet in her Toronto apartment in which they were lined up neatly and in date order. I had somehow imagined that

Marion would be more spontaneous and intuitive in her relationship to things. Not so. She was orderly. Very. Once, at ShaSha, she told me she could only be organized because she summoned up her obsessive-compulsive side from the soles of her feet to do it.

Marion went to the journals and pulled out two. She shared excerpts, quietly interspersing reading with comments. One of the things that struck me that evening was the utterly different style in which she had written these journals. If Marion professed to struggle with writing books, as Ross, too, said she did, the Marion of the journals did not struggle with writing. Her journal voice was one I hadn't heard before. It flowed without eddies or cascades. It was crystal clear. The narrative moved as smoothly as the River Cam. This was a voice Marion did not share in her books.

What she read took my breath away and eventually placed itself deep in my unconscious. At various points, she mentioned hyacinths; I've grown them ever since. We sat until late into the night reflecting quietly about the substance of what she had shared, the style, the fate of the journals. She was concerned about what to do with them. They were vital to her and held not only words but dried flowers and other mementos. It was equally vital to her that they remain private. She sensed something needed to happen to them and even mentioned *en passant* someone's possibly doing something with them long after she was gone.[80] At that time, she was still ambivalent and even spoke about the potential role her solicitor,[81] who later prepared agreements for Marion and me when we wrote together, might play.

I could not fall asleep after that evening. I was also jet-lagged, and my body knew that it was earlier than it was told by the clocks in Toronto. Marion gave me the window side of the bed. I lay awake a long time. Finally, exhaustion prevailed. In the morning I woke late. Marion was up. She was pleasantly vague when I asked her how she'd slept. I suspected that the dry air of the plane combined with exhaustion had turned me into a noisy sleeping companion; if so, she was too courteous to tell me. I can only hope that I was a quieter sleeper the second night.

---

[80] Joel Faflak, one of the executors of Marion and Ross's estate, confirmed Marion's request to privately dispose of the journals. (Personal communication, May 2021.)
[81] In the U.S., lawyers are lawyers; some go to the bar. In Australia, New Zealand, and Britain, lawyers are either solicitors who handle preparation of all legal paperwork or barristers who go to court.

Thence to ShaSha.

Marion fell once as she was walking us through the wilderness that managed to produce itself on such a small island. I saw her fall—she was ahead of me. She didn't cry out. She quickly assured us that she was fine, that she was pleased that she had remembered to tell herself to roll. However, something in my intuition felt as though there were a presage of something in that fall. I couldn't name it until much later.

At the end of that week, when the water taxi came to pick us up, I felt inexplicably heavy-hearted—not just the sadness of parting, but a formless foreboding. I asked two of the other retreat facilitators what they were feeling. They were feeling the same thing. It turned out to be the last time there would be such a gathering at ShaSha.

Before flying home, I didn't stay with my cousin as I usually did; her rambling Rosedale Heights house, near Marion's Toronto apartment, was being remodeled. Instead, my cousin arranged for me to stay in a nearby

Last view of ShaSha, "Miranda," and the teahouse. ©Mellick

Last view of Marion farewelling retreatants and leaders as they left ShaSha by water taxi.
©Mellick

B&B. What struck me about the elegant bed and breakfast was the difference between the deep courtesy of the heart that each woman had shown on ShaSha and the well-intended, rote courtesy that the owner of the B&B extended to me. She pleasantly asked me three times in one hour if I would like some fresh orange juice. It was as though my heart had developed perfect pitch for a while during and following ShaSha; my B&B hostess was, good-naturedly, singing out of tune. I flew home on Sunday, June 20.

∞

Summer Solstice, 1993

Dearest Marion,

It's not 4 A.M. but it might as well be; that's the kind of unrippled consciousness I am in. The only disturbance is that writing underscores that I am no longer with you physically. If I didn't so delight in watching you move, gesture, love, watch, wait, it might be easier. If I didn't so delight in how our songs, bodies, tales, and souls weave around each other, it might be easier. But I do so delight. And so your inner presence and outer absence vie with each other. Like the grandmother tree, I shall embrace the complements.

This morning I dreamt I was placing flowers in a fired blue vase. When I filled the vase with water it ballooned out to accommodate and then overflowed. Fascinated, I went to find a larger container. My soul is, indeed, finding ways to hold all the beauty and life it has received in these last days. I need to be quiet.

Jeanne knows how I am when I return from ShaSha. I make the transition slowly. She refreshes flowers in vases, doesn't expect details, doesn't force daily concerns too fast, lets me float in and out of paying attention—and makes sure the stove is turned off! That New England verbal parsimony and banter thinly disguise her acceptance, loving wisdom, and attunement. I also trust her to take care of herself while I take care of me. That helps. Ashi is less tolerant! R is away and that's fine for both of us; he loves the effect of ShaSha on me but perforce can only have a small understanding of the experience.

Marion stands in the writing, art, and music studio at Melllick/Shutes residence. She is holding Jeanne's copy of Emily Dickinson's poetry. The photograph was one of Marion's favorites and she asked to use it for public events. ©Mellick

I carry so many new images of you and about old-new roots in each other's souls from early June on: your bone-weary, gracious holding of your body upright while we went to my art show at your request that first evening; your academic grace of person and word at graduation; your multi-layered morning self, hugging my bespectacled equivalent! Your "Emily" self in all the week's fiery forms culminating in the Friday evening "Emily" photograph and in the strong-voiced one in the recording studio. You are in this house. Yesterday, when I went into your room to paint, I felt what had been possible there for you and gratitude for what you have left in its beams and bones.

New images not in this house only but in your apartment . . . midnight words and images still pierce me when I silently recall them (they did continually for the first twenty-four hours). The grandmother tree's wisdom held us firm in her loving embrace that night and continues to do so.

It was so strangely right to see that sacred waterhole painting in your apartment. As I said, that was the one image whose umbilical connection to me was still pulsing; seeing it there in your room, I felt how your conscious reception had midwifed it into independent life. Thank you, too, Marion, for the kind encouragement; your wanting a painting never occurred to me, so meant even more.

June 22

Daily life impinges ... gardeners, bills, patients, parents. ... Father tells me with quixotic, passionate intelligence that, on behalf of his church, he has challenged the entire state presbytery on six issues, including the refusal to ordain women. He is setting grounds for secession, if necessary, from an increasingly fundamentalist church body. I told him, in turn, that I was challenging a group to support a single-mother employee. I said I had learnt to do this kind of thing from him; he choked up. Mother couldn't be less publicly involved—but gave me fascinating information on Elgar's "Enigma Variations" (which I had promised D at ShaSha). What an oddly assorted, intense, tiny family we are!

Back to what I want to share with you before it is diffused into daily life.

Our time on ShaSha ... so many gifts, all healing and almost all joyful. Some challenges: amongst them, this year, was a deeper awareness of the autonomous forays of my animus. Compared with these experiences, academia was mere brushwork! When I'm tired, hurting, or forcing an inner transition from one feeling state to another, my animus still tries to handle things for me. Not being a feeling type, I'm slow on transitions. I see that I use animus (or social skills) as a container until I catch up. I know you've seen it. I do learn from seeing how you transit so fast and fully. Once, I used to be slightly disoriented; now, I learn. I also learn about more gracefully integrating yang energy from being with you and Eleanora. I appreciate your accepting all sides of me, dear person.

Marion works with a retreatant on ShaSha. ©Mellick

Our time on ShaSha … I also learnt about the sheer, strong, transparent beauty of soul. The women with whom you work are extraordinary women. And they are even more able to explore the depths they do because of who you are when you quietly move into that containing place. It can look or sound almost indistinguishable in you because there is less and less persona these days. But the difference is huge. Your eyes give me the sign: even when they are looking at a particular person, they are also seeing from and into the transpersonal—and you hold that all week! You let down a little at times … but that look is never completely gone.

June 23

I should bring this letter to a close. Writing to you daily could easily become a lovely addiction. I could go on about ShaSha but you and I know how I feel about it and about your being there. I pray you will have a lengthy and healthy summer there. Jeanne and I leave to join C and visit with Marianne[82] in Copenhagen on July 15. We'll drive through Denmark, Norway and Sweden, returning on August 7. C's husband, R, will join us in Norway. (C lived . . . in hiding for four years during the war.) I'm taking a copy of *Leaving My Father's House* to Marianne. She is a wonderful

---

[82] JM met Marianne Ammitzbøll as a masters student at ITP. She became a senior therapist and author in Copenhavn (Copenhagen)

therapist and ex-student of mine whose winter apartment/therapy office we're using in Copenhagen. She is a devotee of your work and is writing a book on menopause as spiritual initiation. Her husband, a literary critic,[83] has just finished editing a ten-volume literary history of the world.

As I hold you in my inner vision, I remember the poem I wrote, "On Your Hands." That new image also comes: glorious colours patterning your form from a stained-glass window.

Yet, really, how we are and who we are around each other now seems to run deeper than word or image. So I'll just delight in it!

For all the gifts you have given me in these last weeks, dearest one, thank you.

With love, widening and deepening,

Jill

PS I just burnt my quiche to smoking cinders in the microwave!
PPS I've just decided to send the photos under separate cover.

∞

June 28/93

Dearest Jill,

I started a note to you yesterday in a session—at the Noetics conference—a session that was going awry but then suddenly was fascinating. So here I am at noon determined to put this in the mail before leaving Washington. Ross and I have had a fabulous time at this conference. New boundaries broken in so many directions. All our intuitions reinforced. And people of such energy, such dedication, such wisdom in their knowledge. Ross is as

---

[83] Hans Hertel, Danish literary historian, critic, author.

on fire as I am and that is huge in our relationship. People in London, Ontario,[84] feel sorry for him because I have become "flaky" and here he sees I belong and he belongs with his Baha'i knowing.[85] It is great. I am so encouraged to go on with my work on dreams and the body.

This is to tell you how close you are to me. Having been so close for three weeks, I felt bereft when you were going back to California. But you are closer than ever in spirit. My love for you is very, very deep. I can't thank you enough for all you gave at the island. I'll never forget our hours of singing together. I love your paintings in my bedroom.[86] Ross looked at the large one and said quietly, "She's got it, Marion."[87]

Please tell Jeanne how often I think of her kindness to me. Her pink suit to keep me warm, good food and her surrounding love in all we did together. I do try to be civilised when I eat.[88] I really can't eat now without being conscious of my own comfort as I nourish myself. Please give her my thanks for all. Blessings for her trip.

I hope you have a wonderful summer ahead. I know you will. You make the most of everything. I hope your neck is increasingly without pain.

I love you, dear Jill.

Always,

Marion

---

[84] The Woodmans' city of residence in Canada.
[85] Ross Woodman was a senior leader of the Baha'i community in Canada for many years.
[86] Marion was referring to the pastel of the Aboriginal women's sacred watering hole near Uluru in Central Australia. The second to which she referred is the much smaller watercolor of two people in the fog on the beach at Pajaro Dunes, which JM had given her.
[87] Ross Woodman was a serious collector of modern art and a respected art critic.
[88] Jeanne had teased MW about standing while eating, quoting an old film: "Marion, only cannibals eat standing up!" Both had burst into laughter.

∞

Monday, July 5/93

Dearest Jill,

This incredible stationery was given me by [a dear friend.] The tragedy of her life is imaged in this paper. She treasures the tiny things of life and the extravagancies and nothing else makes any sense to her—nothing practical, nothing financial, nothing of this world. . . .

. . . I have devoted the last three days to <u>Father Melancholy's Daughter</u>.[89] WOW! I knew it would be potent and I certainly got the point. The important part of the reading was that I did not become complexed in spite of dire circumstances coming up . . . [in recent months]. I've just been solid, clear-thinking, making the necessary decisions. I loved the book, of course. Splendid writing. And quite something to capture innuendos of deeper insight. Uncanny similarities! My father, too, was a fatherless boy, beloved of his mother, much younger than his siblings, and to some extent an only child. Oh, Jill, how the web is woven before we arrive! Thank you for your presence all through the reading.

The wonderful pictures arrived. I think the "dark" one did take, didn't it? They are truly splendid and captured the week so well. Thank you for sending them. There has been some very powerful feedback from D; she is being moved to a different psychic space. Everyone who has phoned or written has been touched by the "soul" of ShaSha. The purple pictures come from that soul space.

Ross and I are still in London.[90] He has been through—is going through— has been put through—another huge psychic transition, accompanied by writing bouts of twelve to twenty hours per day. I'm containing. We don't dare move into the wilderness until this is completed. The Noetics conference blasted open all his defences and said "Yes" to all he fears to

---

[89] *Father Melancholy's Daughter* is a novel by Gail Godwin.
[90] London, Ontario.

say in conservative London, Ont. He is writing it with delight, but suffering horrible witch dreams as a result. We're fine, but taking no chances. NO and YES are very strong right now.

I have to comment on the adorable pictures of Ashi. She and I have such a soul connection. Still on pictures, I'm wondering if that excellent picture you took of me with "Emily" in my hands can be made into a black-and-white negative—I would love that for advertising. It captures my essence. Many of my analysands would like it. If you could send it to me, Jill, I would get some reprints and check out the black and white possibilities.

Yes, yes, the sacred water hole is so precious in my apartment. Dear Jill, how I experience you working with your animus, yes—challenging, encouraging, trusting the transitions. How blessed I am to have such a friend as you. So few people see me as a human being struggling to be more human, trying to hold the complements that are so ready to fly out at either end of the spectrum.

I too remembered your poem on my hands when I saw your pictures. I think I'll put the poem and one of the photos in our guest book.

Again, blessings on your trip to Scandinavia. Love to Jeanne. I hope everything opens with love to you both.

Dearest love—

Marion

Marion reads in the ShaSha guest-book during one of the retreats.
©Mellick

∞

July 11, 1993

Dearest Marion,

I have developed a habit of rising early and writing … hmm! Ashi is on my lap. (She turns thirteen this month; leaving her gets harder.) This is just a note to complete the enclosed. But beware! It might stretch!

When you first asked me about the "Emily picture," I tried to get a black and white negative for you. Instead, the best shop in turn printed the enclosed poor-quality black and white pic and provided no negative. Yesterday I located a smaller shop, which offers a black and white negative for $6 and 4 x 6 prints at 65 cents. However, I'm sending you the negative for now because you know better what you want. Keep it as long as you need. You should be able to get colour and black and white prints.

I am deeply interested in and excited about what transpired for you and for Ross at the Noetics conference. What a huge gate has opened. Small wonder you are staying still. (Do you know the "boat" problem as part of some larger picture now?) I am grieved (if not surprised) at the witches that have descended upon Ross through dream. Adrienne Rich says in "The Phenomenology of Anger" that "Every act of becoming conscious … is an unnatural act." The dark forces loathe acts of consciousness so, don't they? I wonder how Ross's health and yours are faring through this time out of time.

So you read *Father Melancholy's Daughter* … yes, WOW. I could hardly bear to read on at times, so exquisitely did it articulate that glorious, dangerous surrender to and taking on of the father's unconscious life. And then the separation—oh! It's like turning away from "God."

More difficulties with the [legal concerns]? What else was left to go awry? How necessary and how deeply tiring this all seems to be for you.

Am discouraged about the creative expression book. However, Jeanne and I have just finished the umpteenth draft of the American Indian woman artist's biography[91] and I shall send it to UNM Press soon. (They have asked to see it.)

As I mentioned, the publisher asked us to emphasise Jerry's "heroic approach to adversity." This has pushed me into taking an articulated position on feminine versus masculine structures and perspectives in narrative. I have just added a strong apologia for how we have constructed this biography. We *will* not turn it into a hero's journey in content or structure. It's not about protagonists, antagonists, beginnings, middles, ends or climaxes. It's not a narrative trajectory into success. It's cyclical, an indirect story of a woman, an American Indian woman; it just happens to have amazing external outcomes (like your life). You honour that feminine narrative form in the way you write, particularly in the woven quality of *Leaving My Father's House.* Poets, composers, African myth tellers exercise that choice. Few Western narrative writers do, really. I'm reading some feminist aesthetics on this—exciting.

Jeanne's lithe and beautiful fifteen-year-old granddaughter spent last weekend here. I delight in being with her; we're very close. We spend hours seriously discussing this T-shirt colour versus that T-shirt colour, and I am trusted to trim her long, thick hair!

A large, new pastel of mist over islands at ShaSha hangs already on my office wall where the Dickinson "I Ching" painting was hanging. That, our garden and the miniature watercolour of Iona[92] feed me in this overly busy time in the practice. Huge breakthroughs are happening with some people—occurring synchronistically with ShaSha. Yes, Marion it *is* all woven.

"Your" back garden is awash in "Marion-mauve" flowers!

---

[91] Jeanne Shutes and Jill Mellick, *The Worlds of P'otsunu: Geronima Cruz Montoya of San Juan Pueblo* (University of New Mexico Press,1996).
[92] JM was given an antique, miniature watercolor of Iona painted on bone and framed in silver by Robin Hunter, who lived on Iona and later, the Isle of Mull.

Here and Beyond. Pastel on paper, 40 x 30, Jill Mellick. ©Mellick

Stretch, it did! But it's a way to visit with you beyond what I do daily in my heart.

With love,

J

∞

JM Notes

Left for Scandinavia on July 15, and Marion returned to ShaSha on July 12. From the ensuing correspondence, it is clear that many phone calls occurred between our written communiqués.

∞

July 22[93]

Dear Jill,

I hardly dare put a date on anything. Time rolls through and I try to keep up.

My health has not been very well for some weeks. It started with surgery[94] and went down from there.

However, I think we're on the road to recovery now. Fierce heat here, but the house is well protected so we are in good form.

Ross is working very hard on a very good book. He is on fire and I am trying to hold a balance.

I really miss travelling. I need it to relax, rethink, restructure thinking and doing.

Everything piles up now, and I hate little piles. Anyway, time _flies_ and I say, "Marion, live it NOW."

Ross is holding steady. His Byronic nature does not like slowness. So we try to balance together.

I'm so happy you are there, Jill. I sometimes feel I cannot bring anything new into my aura (sp?). You hold a steadiness I need in this new passage—

Much love to you and yours,

Marion

---

[93] The year was not noted by MW although it would seem to be 1993.
[94] MW had surgery for early-stage uterine cancer and later was hospitalized for cellulitis.

∞

Excerpt from MW's book *Bone*:

November 15, 1993

Need to bring the events that led up to this diagnosis into sharper focus. Need to honor the intuitive flashes from my body that I did not sufficiently receive at the time.

The first one came on ShaSha ... where ten women were with me for an intensive in June. As we were waiting for the water taxi to take us back to the mainland we were singing together in "Miranda." ... I innocently asked Jill ... to play "The Red River Valley." As we began to sing "From this valley they say you are going," my throat blocked, the tears came. Everyone was shocked—none more than I. I tried again, but I couldn't sing. For the first time I knew I was leaving. I knew there would never be another group there. I began to feel myself moving towards a rendezvous with Destiny, the *Titanic* and the iceberg moving inevitably towards each other. Wrong analogy! Ego submits to Fate; ego cooperates with Destiny; consciousness makes the difference. ...

On July 12 Ross and I went to ShaSha together. We had two perfect days. July 14 I fell, or rather, my leg let go and I crashed on the rocks. Ross phoned the coast guard; within half an hour the police boat splashed in; three big, handsome guys secured my legs, stretched me out into a big sling, carrying me down the rocks, gently-so-gently drove the boat to Parry Sound, handed their bundle over to the waiting ambulance team who deposited it in Emergency. Ross and I returned to the island the next day, I with my crutches.

Marion walks through the woods on ShaSha. ©Mellick

So began the almost idyllic summer in the Lion Chair, in love with the loons, the sunrises and sunsets, and discussing with Ross his paper on the Baha'i faith.[95]

∞

JM Notes

On my return from Scandinavia, I broke out in chickenpox. I had caught it during our travels. I had had chickenpox as a child in Australia but not severely enough to become immune.

---

[95] Marion Woodman, *Bone* (Viking Penguin, 2000), page 12. Reprinted by permission of Random House/Penguin.

My notes from then through early in 1994 lack their usual specificity, but, reconstructing retrospectively, Marion was diagnosed with early-stage uterine cancer in early autumn of 1993. We were in constant touch during this time, when she was both in and out of the hospital. As Marion describes in the letter that follows, after the surgery, she went through external radiation for several weeks beginning mid-January 1994. Then her treatment ended with brachytherapy, a radium implant. I only find two notes about our many interactions, one from November in which I noted to myself my concern about her upcoming brachytherapy and another from Saturday, December 4, just noting that I had called her. Frequent other calls back and forth from late 1993 through early 1994 are not noted.

I do recall one scarifying phone call from Marion telling me what happened to her and for her when the radiation specialist started the four-day brachytherapy in early 1994. (I believe memory serves me correctly about the length of time she was to receive it.) Her reaction and description were stark and shocking. Brachytherapy should not be painful, or any pain should be managed immediately. It was painful in the extreme, and the pain was not managed.

∞

January 16/9:45 A.M.

Dearest Jill,

The candles on my creche for Christmas 1993 are burning out. The exquisite little figures from Switzerland, Austria, Germany, Israel, India have put forth their radiant message for yet another year. The angel choir has been singing for over a month. The coloured lights that surround my balcony will probably stay a bit longer. Certainly the meaning yet again will continue to goad me. I know there is something in my illness that has to do with a new understanding of Christ—Christ coming out of Mary— matter revealing spirit, but spirit differentiated from Father, from Son identified with Father.

Oh Jill, I think I have another very hard round to do on the demon lover.[96] I think I am not aware enough of the brutality of his perfection—that Nazi perfection—so intelligent, so handsome, so in love with music and the arts—so moving toward a super race that murders the feminine. Othello in spades—and Desdemona falling into the passivity that leads to murder—suicide. In this case—cancer.

I went into the beautiful hospital room on Wednesday—backlit, spacious, paintings on the wall—the grand machine in the middle, looked like an art deco sofa. It moved: the machine and the sofa around each other. It could measure the depth of radiation to 1/16th of an inch.[97] The handsome young doctor was enthralled with his magnificent toy. I was bewitched by the movement and by the intelligence behind all these laser beams and ceiling computers flashing different coloured lights. Suddenly, my soul jumped out of me and raised a fury, "These are the machines that will burn you. They are made to burn you," and my body, in equal rage, went into [severe abreaction].' . . .

You can see what I mean about a new dimension of this conflict. The radiation is supposed to begin next week. I am keeping in as close touch with the dialogue as I can. My Spirit is strong; my body strong; my sense of humour wild. My Crone takes absolutely nothing my "skipping" doctor says for granted. You must be very aware of what I am talking about. You were the centre of this technological world a year ago. Birth, death—and, the collision of planes. Please don't worry about me, Jill. Yes, it is a battle royal, but I love to talk to you. If you can take these missiles/missives without their upsetting the world you have to move in each day, I'll write to you instead of keeping it all in my journal—

Please tell Jeanne I loved her Christmas card. I loved the focus on her hands. She uses them in such an individual way. The photo caught that. Did you take it?

---

[96] MW drew an arrow between the words "Father" and "demon lover."
[97] MW had external radiation in addition to brachytherapy.

Also is there someone at ITP—president, principal—I should thank for my honourary degree? I would like to write if you send me a name and address. Pearly feathers of smoke in pearly mist. Dawn.

Dearest love—

Marion

∞

February 10/94

Dearest Jill,

Congratulations! I'm so happy that your and Jeanne's book—what a muddle! Start again. So happy for you and Jeanne, so happy that your book has been accepted by the New Mexico Press. It is such an important book, Jill, and will mean much to both of you if you do go to live in Santa Fe. I'm so glad.

Hope your time in Carmel was re-creating. I do know exactly what you mean about walking by the sea.[98] Ross and I are really missing our winter in California. The one glory about our hard winter is the frost on the panes. Literally, I sit talking on the telephone or just gazing and watch an invisible brush sketch the most intricate flower and leaf designs on the windows. They blossom into total panes covered with forests and every leaf is perfect. It is miraculous. Most of our windows were totally covered for over a week. I haven't seen anything like this winter (except in northern Ontario) since we were kids.

Yes, I'm halfway through the radiation. Two and a half weeks to go. The most obvious side effect is exhaustion. Ross asks me a question, I look him straight in the eye, try to muster my voice and go to sleep with my

---

[98] JM had spent a long weekend in Carmel and clearly MW and she had spoken on the phone several times, given the events to which MW refers.

eyes open. Dead out! Some nausea, Blake's bowllahula (sp?)[99] in my belly or some roaring God, everything in a primitive state, but my body is strong enough to deal with it and so is my spirit.

Thank you for the spring garden, Jill. It is truly the most glorious, wild pot of daffodils, tulips and hyacinths. They are expanding a foot outside the pot in every direction. Ross says it's the grandest "bouquet" we've ever had. And I laugh every time I experience its gypsy freedom. Mary[100] is fabulous. Brings us a "happy chicken" every once in a while and takes me to the clinic sometimes. We love to go together.

You are very present in my heart.

Dearest love,

Marion

∞

March 21/94

Dear Jill,

Happy springtime!!! It's come. It's raining and cold, but the light is spring light and I feel a quickening within me. I would not wish to go back to December 19 for anything. Please forgive this paper begun to "Polly" on Dec 19/93. It's the last piece of this I have and I can't find any other stationery.

B gave this paper to me a year ago Christmas. She has no money, no job and goes out with borrowed money and buys "the most beautiful" paper she can find. . . . I appreciate it partly because I feel her dreams and hopes,

---

[99] MW is referring to William Blake's concept of Bowlahoola, which he considered to be the stomach, heart and lungs, and was paired with Allamanda, the nervous system.
[100] Mary Hamilton.

and her determination to express them no matter what. She was . . . beloved. And beautiful . . . A femme fatale of the first order—even archetypal order. . . . she's doing her best to pull her life together. Dear Jill, I didn't mean to write to you about B. It's just I think about Wuthering Heights and how this archetype moved through that family from generation unto generation. I see it so tragically. . . .

I know I promised to phone and I probably will before you receive this. It has been the hardest two weeks. That time in the lead chamber left me with very little voice or strength. I'm trying hard but I cannot stay awake. Ross has succumbed to the flu and both of us have had to let life go by. Now we're beginning to raise our eyes above the covers. I do feel the quickening. Yesterday I even felt excitement over a new kind of bread. So you see, life is going on.

We had to cancel our England trip. That's what did us in. We both find our spiritual home in that country and I long for the downs and the ocean. The doctors all said, "Don't go." I'm not about to scuttle the ship if there is hope, so I'm taking the best possible care in the best possible ways. Dear Mary is going to England in my place. We spent several hours together yesterday. It is a huge challenge for her, but she's up to it. . . . I know they will treat her like a Queen. Another English friend, Peter Katham, is "taking Ross's place." Oh Jill, I love to watch the game of chess that life becomes.

Your beautiful roses—salmon pink Dresden china beauties—arrived at exactly the right moment. Oh Jill, I did enjoy your love beside me in those days. And I held the little buffalo[101] through the long hours in the hospital. Thank you for being so close during this long, dark winter. And now spring comes.

Dearest love, dear lady—

Marion

---

[101] The small white carved buffalo was the Zuni fetish JM sent to MW when she was first diagnosed with cancer. Only Zuni people may carve true fetishes. Particular families carve certain animals and entities. In the ensuing years, MW and JM exchanged the buffalo during health crises.

∞

May 1994

Dearest Marion:

I need to stand on the rock at ShaSha with a light rain making it difficult to light the candle—and share some deep breaths. Phone calls are good but I find it difficult these days to communicate the shades of feeling that emerge when we are physically together or when I write you.

You are consciously with me and I with you, almost continually these days—and nights. And images appear bountiful and unbidden at most unexpected times: in my last session today, I instantaneously relived the last time we planted flowers on ShaSha that misty morning (I had to stay quiet for a while; its poignant beauty grabbed my throat); at 2 A.M. the other night, your lovely voice echoed a comment from our last time on ShaSha. ... I cannot remember books, plays, concertos, politicians, cities, garbage days—never have. But I can call to awareness, in a nanosecond, complete *film reels* of our times together. My heart has a *fine* memory!

I sit in "your" room right now, typing on my new love, my laptop computer. Ashi is on your sofa, her small grey silky body tucked into a semi-curve; little black nose resting across a paw and buried in a corner; long eyebrows flopping into her eyes. I remember when you two first made friends as we dreamt up "Emily;" and how she became your night companion last June. What I wouldn't give to have you here for a week again—to spoil you, meditate together, sing quietly together!

Your voice sounds stronger; your soul's flame is burning taller and less fitfully in dark winds. I rejoice about that. I did not rejoice to hear from P that your digestion is still uncertain. Jeanne arrived home from our superb acupuncturist just now. She says that [her acupuncturist] helps post-radiation . . . membranes with a special medicine. She mentioned it in case it might help.

Your new exploration into yoga excites me. Jeanne and I went out for dinner Saturday evening, then went bookstore hopping, picking up three yoga books. I've mailed them in separate envelopes. I also bought Wolf's latest book—on dreams and physics—for myself. This is what I was speaking about in Perth[102]—how the very structure of dreams reflects and behaves within the laws of relativity. I'm deeply interested in Wolf's connection to your own healing.

Please accept the books as a way for me to be materially and lovingly active in your healing. If the books don't match with your inner direction, just hand them on to someone interested or send them back at your convenience. You know I won't be upset in the least.

You know, from your own teaching, how bothered Jung was about Westerners' doing yoga. However, my experience is that yoga also can be used to *heighten* body awareness and align body and spirit.

You might skim Mishra's book[103] first. (He was my teacher.) What still excites me about his work is his treatment of matter and spirit as inseparable. For him, they're all forms of the same energy manifesting at different octaves. Hewitt's book[104] is the most comprehensive (and accurate) Western summary of theory and practice; it's particularly helpful on diet, mantra, and breath. Rama's book[105] on yoga psychology is more general but is excellent on theory and is easy reading.

When you've had a chance to skim, I'd be happy to talk with you. Begin where you are intuitively inclined to begin—say, a brief daily program integrating body, breath, sound, image, and meditation. I wish I were physically close. We could do some practices together. Yoga is really an orally transmitted tradition. I'm sending, too, two recordings I made for teaching: meditations on the body and the breath. (I apologise for the sound; they're soft.) Again, hand them on if they don't fit with your inner work.

I wrote W a small letter today. My connection to that family goes deep. . . . We have treated each other with respect, tact, affection, and trust

---

[102] JM gave the keynote presentation at a transpersonal conference in Perth, Western Australia.
[103] Rammurti Mishra, *The Fundamentals of Yoga*.
[104] James Hewitt, *The Complete Yoga Book: Yoga of Breathing, Yoga of Posture, Yoga of Meditation*.
[105] Swami Rama, *Yoga and Psychotherapy*.

for . . . years. And I am fond of each of the lovely daughters. I wanted to acknowledge my ongoing affection for and connection to each of them as women finding ways to express themselves with creativity and integrity in the world. . . . My sadness . . . is carefully encapsulated—not in my head this time but in my heart. However, sometimes it is so private that it is private even to me. Not so good; it emerges at unpredictable times about unrelated, small events. I'll be disproportionately upset about, say, Ashi's going deaf so quickly. Then I realize that my heart has been fairly full . . . over the last months and it doesn't take much to spill over in secure circumstances. . . .

I keep NOT really saying how heartsick I am that circumstances prevent your going again to ShaSha and our all getting together there this June. So I'm saying it. I feel as though a beloved friend is disappearing into the mists of Avalon. My *body* keeps anticipating ShaSha. It's the oddest thing. It's as though there is a black hole in the summer that has as much inverse reality as ShaSha has had reality. It is in my blood and bones in a way deeper than I ever imagined, even at the peak of joyful awareness when I *was* there. I need to paint a second painting, write a poem or song, plant a tree or do something to ritually mark the profound gratitude and loss I

Dancing Driftwood, ShaSha. Pen, pencil, and watercolor, 20 x 16, Jill Mellick. ©Mellick

feel. How incredibly blessed I have been to have participated not one but three times! I hung my hat there physically and metaphorically. Thank you, dear, generous soul, for giving me feasts of the heart at ShaSha that will feed me all my days.

Somehow this letter still isn't at all a true reflection of the depth of the feelings I am having right now but as you know, my articulateness still only extends to the outer sac of my heart and becomes gun shy inside it. Being you, even in your exhaustion, I know you will read between the lines, join me on the rock, your hand cupping mine to protect a flame against the light rain, feel my loving embrace, and my voice ready to join you in quiet song over a candle and a guitar.

With such old and ever-renewing love,

Jill

∞

July 1994

Dear Marion:

I tried to reach you the weekend before last. (Did you receive my message?) I'll try you again today.

First, I want to send you birthday wishes that come with great love and rejoicing that you have not merely survived this searing year but prevailed. I shall be thinking of you and Mary celebrating together, I hope, as you have done so many times. I shall be attending a Pueblo Indian ceremonial dance on your birthday.[106] All dances are done for long life. I shall watch the dance with you in my heart.

---

[106] August 15 is celebrated in many Christian traditions as Assumption Day. The Pueblo Indian tribes, when forced to become Catholic, astutely made summer ceremonials coincide with saints' days so they could "dance for the saint" rather than be accused of practicing summer ceremonials danced for rain and long life.

I feel out of touch with you. Not surprising given what has been going on in our lives. At fundament, we are never out of touch. We meet in that field of total, quiet, loving acceptance of each other, of inseparable contact with each other's spirit. On the human level, I miss you. I want to massage your hands and hear that marvellous voice of yours; I want you to brush my hair while we listen to music. . . . If you still ritually step out to breathe deeply and contemplate at times, I want to light a match and candle some time with you again out on a verandah or rock somewhere.

This is a challenging time for me. The confluence of events in my life has been strong. However, I am still sufficiently *in* the dark not to be able to feel the numinosity of the dark yet, merely a lessening of meaning.

I plucked up courage to go to another [specialist.][107] I realized that the previous one evoked Great Father so strongly that I couldn't hold to my own self-knowledge but became caught in his expectations. He was dear—but so authoritarian. I fell hook, line, and sinker. If others are nice to me and tell me they have my good in mind, then I should feel fine about everything, right? It took me too long to figure out the fallacy in that to repeat it.

And then the interminable time waiting for tests. Two days after the last test, I sliced my left forefinger to the bone in the garden. It's still numb. A week after, I skidded in the kitchen on the newly cleaned kitchen floor with two boiling cups of black tea in my hand. I sustained extensive second-degree burns all over my face, neck, shoulder, hand and leg. The pain was breathtakingly intense for hours but the recovery process is blessedly quick. I am walking around looking like a discoloured lizard as the old layers shed and shed. We didn't know for days whether I would have scars or not. It seems I shall not.

And today, more information. Bad odds, Marion. Bad odds.

Too, it's also exactly a year since . . . . Once in, people don't leave my heart. Life might lead us apart but they always roam around in my inner chambers. . . .

---

[107] JM had a life-changing health challenge that required research and second opinions.

Jeanne, my soul mate, companion of the heart, is beside me unconditionally throughout. Yet she tires, physically and emotionally. She . . . harnesses her spiritual and physical energies carefully and instinctively. Her fidelity to our life companionship, mutual support, and utter (if at times exasperated!) acceptance of me are unquestioned. Without that daily succour, I doubt my heart and soul would be as they are. Even so, at times, I feel vulnerable in the world, Marion.

We leave for Santa Fe next Friday. We shall return earlier than usual, the day before my birthday at the end of the month, in time to host my parents for five days. I so look forward to seeing them. (My father has a literary research grant, which is taking them around the world in forty days.)

Forgive this being such a black letter. I'm not asking for comfort or reassurance or a response. Thank God you will never pity me. I dislike that more than anything. All I want is to create a moment's companionship with you in dark nights of the soul when they come upon me. I simply want to stay in touch even from within this place.

With great love,

Jill

∞

Marion Woodman
Will be closing her practice at
223 St. Clair Avenue West
Toronto
Canada
June 1994
"the readiness is all"

(Over)

Did I send you one of these? Lovely irony! They were printed in August before I knew I was sick. I had my timing. God has His, and I am learning more about "the readiness is all."

∞

July 6/94

Dear Jill,

Someone sent me this beautiful card and I love the little figures so much, I want to share them with you. This card is coming from the chaos of moving. Tomorrow the van arrives and we leave our cosy nest here on Windermere to fly into a wide, bright, sunny, exposed, shy world on Sydenham. I closed my office in Toronto a week ago, moved everything into my room at Sydenham. I was more deeply disturbed by that move than I had imagined I would be—but leaving fifteen years of solid concentration in Toronto to move into gentle, pastoral London[108] made me realize how intently I will have to experience self-discipline in order to think another thought.

Ross is ravaged by the move. Physical and psychic chaos together leave him in paralysis. However, he wanted this more than anything in the world and, if we can hold steady until tomorrow night, he will realize all the inner world down there is already in place. All the cupboards and inner workings had been put in order over the past five months. We may go to the quiet apartment in Toronto for a few days. He has faced reality— been forced by Destiny to stand on the solid ground of his own past and the last few weeks in horrendous encounters that seem almost miraculous. It's like God is saying, "This move is your birthing into the next world and you will finish your work here before you go." Anyway we're in it together.

---

[108] London, Ontario.

Your wonderful books all arrived, Jill. I haven't worked on them yet, but I am now moving towards my own inner regime. Many thanks for sending them.

Dear, dear friend, if I seem stunned, please accept that I am a bit. Last night, I talked to several people by phone who saw my "MW" nameplate had been removed from my office door and although they knew I was "closing my office," they felt I had died when I did it. They were crying as if I were dead. This 4:00 A.M. I think I'm wondering where I'll be waking up when the sun rises.

Dearest love—

Marion

∞

Abraxis, Ontario
September 4/94

Dearest Jill,

Every time I stand and watch the stars, I think of you and wish we had time and place for our few ritual moments. We are doing a workshop here forty miles north of Toronto. Glorious rolling countryside and grand clear open skies at night. So far, all is well though I expect some negative mother reactions today.

Mary is Professor Hamilton this week—managing, engineering, doing a superb job with body work. She is very funny as Professor Hamilton, compulsive about detail and then undercutting herself. Marvellous! And Paula[109] pushes her on. Paula has become a mediator par excellence. Southern Belle charm worth anyone's clear vision as a study in firmness and humour and intelligent holding of the opposites.

---

[109] Psychotherapist Paula Reeves, Ph.D., from Atlanta, Georgia.

Ann Skinner is here too, of course. Brilliant and funny. We miss you, think of how it would be if you were here with your music. This is our first workshop without any overseer or large group sponsor. We've learned a lot especially about pettiness.

Mary found two stones exactly the same and wrapped them in red string as you told her to.[110] They were so sweet and so meaningful. Private space. Thank you, dear Jill, for such a beautiful remembrance. I know your birthday is right in here somewhere. Mary, Aug. 13; Marion, Aug. 15; Paula, September 12; Eleanora and Jill, Aug. but not sure of dates.[111] Amazing constellation of women! I send you my special love every day hoping to hit the right one.

I am holding up well, not trying to do what I used to do in workshops, but making my crone indulgences clear without apology. A new place for me, full of conflicts but no alternatives because my body can do so much and no more. I am learning much about receiving—the graciousness of receiving. But sometimes I want to roar out against being the beloved old lady. I would smoke cigarettes and drink Scotch down at the pool if I had them.

I think of you, dear, dear Jill. I think you are passing through rough waters. I hope your book is off to the press and that you and Jeanne are utterly enjoying the red earth you love. As I begin to organize my inner life for the Fall I have your books close by.

Many, many thanks. They bring me close to you.

Dearest love—

Marion

---

[110] In Japanese Shinto shrines and Buddhist temples, private areas are quietly demarcated "Do not enter please" by a stone wrapped like a parcel with thick black rope. The stone is chosen for its smoothness. String is wrapped vertically and horizontally so that the knot is at the center of the crossing of the string.
[111] Eleanora Woloy and JM share the same birthdate: August 29.

∞

October 25/94

Dearest Jill,

I just received very bad news. I am alone here, silent, shocked. I am not going to broadcast this to the world because I am going to have to pull in all my energy now for my own healing, whichever way that goes. My oncologist just phoned to say that the cancer is in my spine on the inner surface and the prognosis is bad. So on this rainy autumn afternoon I write to you with my heart beating very, very fast. This is much worse than where I thought I was last year at the end of Oct.

Strangely I feel in excellent health. My skin is radiant, my eyes clear, I am gaining strength. Now all the doctors here have to offer is more radiation. And this is without hope. I doubt that I'll take it.

Dear Jill, how I hate to put this on you. But as I carry your nigredo with love, and therefore with no sense of burden, I ask you simply to offer me to God each day.

I send you this picture because I couldn't bear to put it on a Christmas card and yet I knew it was the one for this year. Do you see the Marion triangle a third of the way up, and the altar of the Virgin? The big tree went down and left its huge roots dangling in mid-air. They make a horrendous, bird-like, Kali face. If you put the picture in light you'll see it.

Dear Jill, how much I love you words cannot say.

Always,

Marion

∞

JM Notes

Excerpts from Marion's journal, which she later published as *Bone*, follow. They present her experience with disarming honesty. At that time, my perspective on what she was being told both differed from and was complementary to hers. Now as I write—having had brain surgery for a large aneurysm; bilateral breast cancer; metastatic cancer requiring neck fusion, radiation, and chemotherapy for over four years—my perspective has evolved, inevitably, yet again. However, I recorded and can recall my perspective on and responses to Marion at the time. These are what I include here.

Some people seem born with strong proprioceptive awareness. I've always been aware of what I was experiencing in my body even when I often overrode whatever was happening. Marion recognized this proprioceptive awareness during that first retreat at Pajaro Dunes and our later time together at the Spiritual Emergence Network Conference. She thought it rare; I didn't. Wasn't it something everyone felt? I rarely gave it precedence. (Now medical conditions require that I do.) Once, when we were en route to Parry Sound to take the water taxi to ShaSha, we stopped to buy groceries. I said I needed potato chips because I was low on sodium; I was feeling weak and tired. Knowing my blood pressure often caused physicians to ask politely whether I was alive, I had learned to eat a small amount of salt straight. The symptoms would leave as blood pressure climbed.

"*How* do you know, Jill?" I remember Marion saying, amazed, from the front seat. I had no answer because—rather narcissistically—it had never occurred to me that others experienced their bodies differently. I'd never stopped to think about it. Nor do I know how I have sensed in advance several life-threatening events. Had I not, I would not be writing this.

Marion grew up with the perfect complement to proprioceptive awareness: she was exquisitely aware of and attuned to the archetypal world. As she used to say personally and in lectures that because her father was a minister, she grew up with archetypal events—birth, death, and marriage—being the world she most naturally and easily inhabited. She recalled entering her father's church when she was about four. She saw what looked like a beautiful doll in a box. When she returned to the parsonage and told her parents, they realized with shock that she had entered the church when it had been readied with an open casket for a small child's funeral.

Marion was always more at home in the archetypal world. It was a constant discipline and lifelong path for her to learn to live in the human and physiological realm. I, too, loved the archetypal world. However, when I realized this inconveniently around puberty, I kept quiet—especially at my all-girls school with its focus on civic responsibility, academic achievement, and sports. So, my spiritual concerns were confined to time under the mosquito net after I'd finished homework. I would consistently do my version of meditation (not having read anything about it) and secretly write bad poetry, lights out. Only then would I take time for soul.

Marion's body was, as she declared in all of her books and lectures, her path to individuation, her path away from her eating disorder, her path to entering fully into her humanity. My path was to lend weight to what I knew in my body and inner world and do what I needed to do rather than always giving someone or something else priority. I knew my inner world intimately, but it was low down on the priority list for successful maturation. Marion and I were each ineluctably fated to connect body and soul; we just followed complementary paths to the same place. Our first conversation on the beach at Asilomar—when she commented that I was never ahead of or behind my body and I commented that she was never ahead of or behind her soul—prefigured this awareness of our complementarity in these realms.

∞

Excerpt from MW's *Bone*:

November 7–8, 1994

> Exhaustion. Couldn't wake out of the depths. Stayed in
> Toronto to rest before driving home. Jill phoned from
> Palo Alto, sensed there was something wrong. I told her,
> heard my own flat voice, I could feel myself vacating this
> body. With strangers, I can act. With her, I cannot. She
> was silent. We hung up.[112]

∞

JM Notes

Given what Marion had told me about her own experiences and given my
own, I heard in her voice a tone I associated with trust perhaps too readily
handed over to medical "authorities." Being less naturally at home in her
body, Marion was more susceptible to trusting declarations by the medical
establishment. It did not occur to her to question their declarations. She
told me on the phone that her physician in London had given her six
months and said that if she did not agree to have palliative radiation, she
would be "in agony" for the few months before she died.

My vigilance went on high alert. I have always been fiercely protective of
the physical well-being of those I love. I did quiet battle with myself about
speaking up with Marion: was I putting in an oar where it was not wanted,
even harmful, or might I be offering a branch to a loved one in quicksand?

---

[112] Marion Woodman, *Bone*, page 12. Reprinted by permission of Random House/Penguin.

Could I live with myself if Marion found the content of my next phone call intrusive? Yes—with regret for having intruded. Could I live with myself if I did not act and my failure to act colluded with a diagnosis and treatment that would kill her? No.

I called her back.

∞

Excerpt from MW's *Bone*:

> Later she [Jill] phoned again. "Marion, why don't you get a second opinion? You don't need to accept this diagnosis as absolute. I have a friend in the radiology department at Stanford. Let me talk to him."
>
> Some light went on in our conversation. Some spark was ignited. Something screamed, "yes," and fell silent—one crack of lightning bolting through a jet-black night.
>
> "OK, Jill," I said, but I didn't dare hope. I was thankful for a voice outside the darkness strong enough, kind enough, to reach my soul. Talking with the consciousness outside made me realize the depth of my despair. I feel my medical doctors have almost given up hope. That note from Doctor Cohen I happened to see on my cancellation insurance felt like a death blow. I told her [Dr. Cohen] I did not believe I am dying. She thinks I am in denial—a natural response after a death sentence.[113]

---

[113] *Ibid*, page 12. Reprinted by permission of Random House/Penguin

∞

JM Notes

When Marion received the first diagnosis of cancer with the need for surgery followed by radiation, I had sent her—for inner strength and companionship during her treatment—a small fetish carved by an artisan in the Zuni nation. It was a white buffalo made of alabaster with a turquoise "gift" bound on its back with gut string. When a Zuni carver makes a fetish, a gift is often included as an offering to the animal's spirit in return for our borrowing some of its spirit.

Buffalo fetish made by a carver in the Zuni Nation. ©Mellick

∞

Excerpt from MW's *Bone*:

> November 21, 1993, Sunday
> Jill sent me a little white buffalo with turquoise eyes. I hold it in my hand to feel the Navajo energy pouring through me from the earth into the sky and back into my heart.[114]

---

[114] Ibid, page 21. Reprinted by permission of Random House/Penguin

∞

JM Notes

Robert Mindelzun, M.D., husband of a close friend, was Professor of Radiology and a specialist at Stanford University Medical Center. Although I had been raised with the same hierarchical, colonial tradition of medicine as Marion, I had lived in Northern California long enough to learn (the hard way) a little about negotiating the medical world. Surely, I could use that for someone I loved. I called Bob and asked if he might be open to looking at Marion's scans. He was generous and willing.

∞

Excerpt from MW's *Bone*:

> November 9, 1994
>
> Jill phoned. She had received the letter I wrote after the red phone call of October 26.[115] Had talked to her friend Dr. Mindelzun. He said he would be happy to talk to me. Meantime I galvanized myself to phone Dr. Alistair Cunningham at Princess Margaret, made appointment for Friday, 25th. Feel tiny gusts of hope, but not daring to pray for wind.[116]

---

[115] MW is referring to a phone call she and a physician had had.
[116] Ibid, page 189

∞

JM Notes

Although almost a generation younger, I, too, had grown up hearing the word "cancer" whispered; everyone knew it meant death—probably sooner rather than later. However, by the time Marion and I were talking about her getting a second opinion, I had been exposed to other approaches and outcomes. Finding myself living with the luxury of choosing from some of the finest physicians in the country—Palo Alto being one of the most concentrated and best medical areas in the United States—I did not need to accord one specialist absolute authority.

The more I could step back and let Marion and Bob Mindelzun work together, the better. I preferred to be a connector, not a go-between. I knew that Bob, a caring, sensitive, straightforward, brilliant specialist, would treat Marion with respect. He did.

∞

Excerpt from MW's *Bone*:

> November 9, 1994
>
> Tonight phoned Doctor Bob Mindelzun. He was kind, assertive, treated me as if I were alive and worth talking to. He asked me questions that I should have had asked too, but I never thought to ask them.
> 1. Exactly what am I being treated for?
> 2. Is the problem located in one place?
> 3. Where am I being treated—in what part of my body exactly?
> 4. How do I know this is a tumor?
> 5. Who is the captain of the ship? Which doctor knows everything that is going on?
> 6. How advanced is this tumor? Is it a primary tumor?

He suggested I find an internist or gynecologist who is captain of the ship—one person who knows me and all about my treatments. That doctor may send me to a specialist, but he/she has to have all the facts and know all the treatments. Rarely is radiation done without a biopsy. Need to know one hundred percent before going into radiation again. The radiation specialist has to know for sure what he is radiating and where.

He echoed my fear of accepting radiation again. I think it would destroy any bones I have left. I told him about my 12-year problem with my back and how this pain is exactly in the same place, acting the same way, and how I finally was able to walk last year before the cancer. Told him of the family problem in that area.

Dr. Mindelzun asked me to send copy of CAT scan.

Hung up the phone. I felt genuinely respected in my personhood and breath came into my lower rib cage for the first time in weeks. Doctor Mindelzun said he would take primary responsibility for looking into my case, consult with a group of experts from the tumor board at Stanford, review all the findings, and make a joint recommendation.[117]

∞

All Hallows' Eve, 1994

Beloved Marion,

Your letter and photograph arrived. Of course, we've spoken since you wrote but the letter was crucial to our effort to absorb this. Do you feel

---

[117] Ibid, pages 188–190. Reprinted by permission of Random House/Penguin

my presence these days? Alone or with others, a chamber of my heart holds you constantly. I *physically feel* you there.

I can only begin to imagine how you are feeling. The effect of the chilling diagnosis and prognosis and the heartlessness of its delivery on you; dealing with Ross's devastation and courageous determination to be strong; your crucial internal shifts after Cunningham and your homeopaths; your anticipation of the award ceremony. I am holding all these emotions—for you and for me. I am enraged at the emotional treatment you received; my heart is knocked windless and weeping at odd hours by the news; yet I am also open, encouraged, focused, and hopeful— about your visit to your homeopath and your own healing plans. I am also overjoyed at this award![118] How fitting and timely. I hope someone takes a superb photograph of you both!

Marion, I had hoped to see you in San Diego. As that is not happening I want to visit you soon. I would like to fly up for a weekend in mid-November or early December—*and* make regular brief visits next year. (I insist on a hotel so let's not even talk about those logistics.)

However even more than doing what *I* want, I want to do what is helpful for you. If you don't *want* me to come at a particular time, I shan't— without question or hurt feelings. I know you need time alone—to move through this passage, to write, to be with loved ones—but please distinguish between those needs and misplaced concerns about burdening me or accepting support. (Remember, I fly all over; Canada is next door!)

We have to be very, very honest during this passage. I want to trust you to ask for support (hard as that might be) and trust you to respond honestly to possibilities I raise; and *you* in turn have to trust I shan't feel hurt if my suggestion doesn't feel right to you. We are both dedicated to the same transpersonal outcome here—a soul-full, love-permeated, dignified passage from one phase of your life to another whose form is not yet clear.

You told me it is no burden for you to carry my nigredo. Neither is it a burden to accompany you *as much as you would like—physically, and/or*

---

[118] MW had been told she was to receive an honorary doctorate from her alma mater.

psychically—during this second bout. No matter how personally stunned, grief-filled and outraged I am, I also feel strong, Marion. You won't have to worry about the effect of all this on me. The joyous love I have for you is stronger than my fears. I feel its sinewy, tensile strength; its roots descend so deep and its trunk and branches are so supple that this storm cannot fell it (like the tree in your photo). Selfishly, I don't want to lose your physical and emotional bodies—they are sources of endless beauty and love and delight to me—but I shall *never* lose my unbreakable, corded connection to your soul. My love grows in the marrow of your soul and yours in mine. *That* is what makes me strong. We'll face whatever we face here separately and together, beloved one; and I shall physically or psychically accompany you whenever and wherever you wish to be accompanied.

Always with love,

Jill

PS Let's talk on the phone soon about my coming up.

∞

JM Notes

Bob Mindelzun told me he would take Marion's scans, which he didn't think were well done, to the tumor board at Stanford to get multiple input. Time passed. Perhaps a week? Then Bob phoned me.

"Jill, I don't quite know how to begin," he began. "I showed your friend Marion's scans to the tumor board. *Everyone* agreed that, even though the scans were poor, not *one* of us could see *any* tumor on them. Arthritic issues but not cancer. I thought I'd better call you as soon as possible so you can tell her."

I remember where I was sitting when he told me. "Bob," I said, "I couldn't be more stunned—or relieved—or grateful. This is the best *possible* news. *Thank* you for telling me.

"I don't think I should be the one to tell Marion. I feel odd knowing before she does. I don't want to ask you to take more of your time, but could you please tell her? She trusts and likes you. She knows you're a top specialist. She'll take it *in* if you say it. And if possible don't say we spoke unless she asks. I'd never lie to her. You're so kind to tell me. I just think she should know directly from you."

Bob said he would do it immediately.

∞

Excerpt from MW's *Bone*:

> Talked to Dr. Bob tonight about my scans. Was shaking so much I could barely hold the phone. He sensed my terror.
>
> "I think I may be bringing some hope," he began. Then I could hear him. "There are a lot of arthritic changes in your spine," he said. I write everything down because in my nervousness. I can't remember, but I can hear and write without my brain taking it in, then I can study it afterward.
>
> "Osteoporosis and osteoarthritis certainly. There is a fluid collection, but I do not believe it is a malignant process. Difficult making a definite right diagnosis with this scan," he said. "Go to a major center if necessary—Toronto, Mayo Clinic, Massachusetts General—find out what it is before you have more radiation. More radiation may exacerbate the condition. Get a gynecologist and an oncologist. Review findings. Find out what needs to be treated."

Felt his energy opening mine. Toronto feels right.

"If the prognosis is bad," he said, "will irradiation improve it? Is the treatment palliative or curative? In that area, will it hurt your other organs? Is there a problem in other areas of the body? Any vital organs? Be demanding."

He distinguished between an oncologist and a radiation therapist. An oncologist is an internist who has taken specialized training in tumors. He will make decisions and independent evaluations, but may send a patient to a radiation therapist. He himself usually uses chemo-therapy. Radiation therapist is trained in tumors, usually only malignant tumors.

So energized after this conversation and telling it to Ross. Glimmerings of a New Day.[119]

∞

JM Notes

Bob's calling Marion directly was not only respectful of her right to know first, but it was vital that he be the one to tell her. I realized from older Australian friends and family members that her capacity to metabolize medical information was influenced by her generation's experience and acculturation. For Marion's generation, the word "cancer" meant death. More than that, cancer had killed in Marion's own family.

Marion was indeed free of cancer. She lived for many more years. As Bob Mindelzun and the tumor board at Stanford told her, the pain and numbness were caused by degeneration from osteoporosis and arthritis.

---

[119] Ibid, page 196. Reprinted by permission of Random House/Penguin

Now, having lived with cancer myself for seventeen years, four of those with Stage IV and "mets" (as metastases are affectionately known in the medical world), my experience of treating and living with cancer differs from Marion's—and even from mine at the time she was getting her second opinion. While I spend much time on treatment, stamina is circumscribed, and I depend on others' help, I am able to *live* with cancer rather than feeling my life defined by it. This is a luxury, this state of "living with." I have the finest, most dedicated, honest specialists who listen to me, and I have the finest diagnostic equipment on my doorstep. Marion had none of this in London, Ontario, until I could secure her a second opinion at Stanford; it was the tumor board's second opinion followed up by tests in Toronto that determined that she had neither a metastasis nor another primary tumor.

Irony also played a role. Ross had forthrightly told Marion she wasn't a born *writer* because she lived in images, not words. He was not being negative; he held her writing with high respect. Marion comfortably accepted his perspective. Whether Ross was right or not, it was true that Marion could not filter images scattered at her across a specialist's table. They clung to her, worked their way into her like a foxtail into a dog's ear. She once told me on the phone, shocked, "Jill, they're giving Ross *snake venom* for his eye!" (Ross had eyelid ptosis. The snake venom was indeed snake venom: Botox.)

I was only able to offer help at the time of her wrong diagnosis because, though similarly susceptible to images, I had by then been educated in other ways of working with the medical world in the U.S. (Once, when a researcher told me flatly that at most I had ten years to live because of a rare disorder—and that if I lived longer, I'd wish I hadn't—I fled his office and called my specialist urgently. I told him what the researcher had said and said, "Peter, give me a different image! Fast! I can't let his image take hold!" Peter[120] calmly gave me a different image of the condition's progression; that image has held true thus far for thirteen years.)

---

[120] Peter Cassini, M.D., neurologist, neurophysiologist and a clinical professor at Stanford University Medical Center.

Not only had Marion grown up when cancer was the pitiless kiss of death in rural Ontario and she had lost family and friends to it; she was wide open to the archetypal realm. The word haunted her with good reason. It took not only Stanford's second opinion but the recommended third opinion, using better scans, to let her concerns fade.

∞

December 4/94

Dearest Jill,

I tried to reach you yesterday, but there was no answer. I remembered Jeanne's card and thought perhaps you might be in Santa Fe. For your sake, I do hope so.

Nothing new has happened here. My body is in good strength; I am taking the best possible care of it. I go for my MRI in Toronto on Friday and receive the reading on Monday, December 12. I'm very nervous about that one. I've learned (because of your dear friend, Bob) what it is to live in life again and I don't want to go back under the veil of death. Of course, I know it will happen one day, but I'm starting to feel life in a totally new way.

"All is as God o'er-rules"—ultimately.

I struck out that line of etcs because I could hear my Doctor Radwyn telling me I am in denial "as always happens."

How are you, dear Jill? I do indeed hold you in my heart every hour of every day. I know exactly what you mean about the nigredo that "steals one's past, denies one's future and blanches the moment."[121] I wish we could sit together and you could play and I'll hold that dear wee dog and we'll sing our harmonies.

---

[121] This letter from JM to MW is missing.

Your response to my brokenness was magnificent. I felt your love surging towards me and mine surging as a result toward you. I felt that as I wrote to you. There was no-one else I wished to write to in that moment. What you have given me in Dr. Bob is priceless—whatever the outcome.

The reprieve has also brought new strength to Ross. He is writing again—a fabulous paper on Keats's final poems. He seems full of health and well-being. We both feel quite at home in our new condo. He is truly manifesting a radiant soul.

About your coming to London, Jill. I think it is magnificent of you to offer to come. We have a complication here over Christmas because both Paul and his family and David and his girlfriend are coming from great distances. They are coming to Toronto. We are all going to Marion's,[122] then the boys (and men) will come here with families. It is also possible that Luke will come from overseas. The four (Fraser's four) are desperately upset at the thought of Auntie not being here. I was their surrogate mother for ten years while Sonya[123] was sick, and even after she died. I really had no idea how deep their love is. David even offered to come back to London from Vancouver "to take care of uncle" and me. But there is a New Year, dear Jill, and we can make plans then. I don't want you to stay in a hotel, but we'll argue about that later. I enclose a check which I hope will cover flowers you sent to Dr. Bob. Naomi[124] said they were gorgeous. And his FedEx return.[125] And for you, either for flowers for Christmas or a long talk on the phone. The calls are a lifeline.

Darling Jill, take care of yourself.

Marion

---

[122] Paul, David and Luke are nephews; Marion, a niece.
[123] Sonya was married to Fraser Boa; they had four children.
[124] JM's friend Naomi Mindelzun, Dr. Robert Mindelzun's wife.
[125] MW is referring to the return of her scans.

∞

Christmas photograph titled "Seamless"
Christmas blessings, dearest Jill.
Love –
Ross & Marion

On the other side of the photograph:

Jill,

When Ross and I chose this photograph in October, we were awed by the invisible mysterious line between land and water. Now we hear "Seamless" with new resonances that have to do with the mystery between temporal and eternal worlds. Intuition is awesome!

Dear, dear friend, how can I
ever thank you for all you have been to me this year.

Dearest Jill, how I value our love for each other.

Marion

∞

JM Dream

Reunited

We are all reunited. We are all there, driving to the new cottage together. We are each talking with one another and aware that the others are there. The mood is light, excited. It is an hour and a half's drive. When we arrive, I realize that I have no idea how that time passed, that I drop into another reality when we are all together.

We arrive at the cottage, walk in. It is all newly painted white—a small place but a jewel of careful restoration with every wooden surface planed and painted high-gloss white in a traditional fashion. Not much furniture. Only two rooms. I recognize the sleeping verandah about which Mary[126] had told me.

I then walk into the main room. I walk to the door and see that we are right over the water. The lake is up to but not over the foundations. A hot tub is submerged in the lake; it is a secure wire cage into which water is steadily flowing from the lake. I turn and someone says, "We are the only people on this lake, you know." I realize that although we might have been the only people on ShaSha and have had to forego that, now we are the only people on this lake. This fills me with joy.

One of the group is nearby and we begin to dance together, moving effortlessly and delightedly in inward-moving and descending spirals, aware of little gravity. Others can see us. We all end up in one blissful, playful, loving, effortless sinking together onto the floor. This is our dance of joy at the return.

Marion and I have still not officially connected. Marion is talking with others. Our eyes meet quickly twice, a glance so fleeting that I wonder, for a moment, if Marion herself really caught it, yet I know she did.

---

[126] Mary Hamilton.

I finally excuse myself from a conversation, saying I want to greet Marion. I find her in the other room. A smorgasbord has been laid out. This has become a large reception now where there are many associated people.

Marion is alone and reaching for some small, white round food on the table. I stand quietly to her right. She turns, sees me, and swiftly comes toward me. The love between us is so powerful. I embrace her, holding her strongly. We embrace for a long time. I feel her distinct fragility and residual, permanent wounding. Marion is clear and persona-free after so much living with death at her doorstep.

So much passes between us in the embrace: the memory of those days when we connected through her darkness, the memory of the fateful call when she agreed to seek the second opinion. We let it all be there passing energetically between us. I have not yet seen her face.

Our embrace is an absolute affirmation of all that has passed between us these last two years. Marion almost cries out with the energy surging through her. Her etheric body lies down on a floor bed beside us. Her other body continues to embrace me. Then the sheer magnitude of the energy takes us both over. At the same moment, we feel it flood us and rush through our central energy channels. We are ignited by and united in the fierce and loving connection between our hearts and history. It reminds me of the dance we danced at Asilomar so many years ago now.

∞

Feb, 95

Dearest Marion,

That the possibility of a ShaSha reunion somewhere grows stronger delights me.[127] I cannot tell you what silent hunger I felt for what we

---

[127] Phone calls had come before this letter, as they usually did between letters.

all generate. I understood more deeply how our time feeds me for a whole year.

While I am greatly distressed at your ongoing spinal challenges, I am reassured that you have this new doctor who seems to be both intelligent and sensitive. I await news with impatience, to say the least. I hope you or Mary will call and tell me what he recommends. On and on and on this goes. Daily you are with me, beloved one.

It is barely dawn. The dove is mourning outside; crocuses and a single daffodil, visible in the lightening darkness. I am sitting at "your" desk, beside a half-finished pastel—the first in ten months. I have only been doing small mandalas.

Ashi roams, waiting for the house to arise soon.

We sent K to relax for a couple of hours while we cared for tiny J.[128] She has painful colic and cries all the time she is awake. But she stopped crying soon after her father left and was quiet while she was here. It was the same last time. It's probably wishful thinking that we give her tired little body some peace. My feelings for her are still more universal than personal. This little distressed being is in too much pain to be either winsome or attractive yet. If she looks like her parents, she will be both later. I hold her, and my maternal instincts just hum with satisfaction and content-ment. Not personally bonded delight—self-protection, perhaps. Her darling mother—who should not have died two weeks after giving birth— was working on a book when she was pregnant. So I rustle papers as I cradle her and she seems to calm. These visits are probably the only realistic way of being in her life. . . . What we can do for them at present is care for her sometimes and develop a bond, independent of others.

Doors I am not knocking on seem to be opening. My agent sent my creativity manuscript to a small Berkeley publisher, Conari—who liked my curriculum vita[129] better than my book! Mary Jane Ryan, the publisher,

---

[128] A friend died after giving birth; K, the bereft father, was caring for the infant, J, who had severe colic.
[129] "Curriculum vita" is less commonly used than "resumé" in the U.S.

and I had a marvelous meeting. We were alike—wildly intuitive; barely-tempered positive animuses (!); quick, impatient, gestalt thought processes; valuing the feminine and the primacy of emotional connection; and valuing spiritual integrity in work.

Hers is a rare and exciting publishing company—smart young people with inclusive values and practicality, and not New Age-y. They have a team of mainly women and minorities who base their business on good relationship, not good finance. Moreover, they only work with authors where there is mutual enjoyment and respect. In other words, they choose authors, not books. A wonderful concept. Their books sell well because they like and work hard for their authors and themselves. With this philosophy, the company has been highly successful in seven years—three million dollar turnover now and no failures.

Mary Jane asked me "dream" questions such as "What books would you most *like* to write? How *many* books would you be willing to do? What interests you *most* because that is what we want you to write about first!" She has asked me to write not one, not two, but a whole *series* of books! She wants me to take archetypal themes (some from my current manuscript) and explore creative approaches to each theme through a wide variety of the creative arts, beginning with three books: 1) on dreams; 2) on personal and family secrets; and 3) on losses/incompletions. Because of how she and her company are, I am opening to this. I am also stunned, curious, optimistic, excited—and cautious.

Cautious about time. Family . . . is my first priority. I don't want to jeopardize it by the unavoidable isolation of my work. Psychotherapy and writing are by definition solitary professions . . . . They must take second place to relationship.

Also want to protect time to paint. This New Mexico University Press book has absorbed much of our time in 1994. My soul feeds nonfiction but poetry, painting, playing the piano, and dance feed me.

With cautions in place, I have committed to the dream book. It is a natural. What better combination of things I love?! I'll get a head start on it in Australia. Marion, would you still be willing to write the foreword, if you can?[130] It could be as brief or as long as you wish. Your companionship and blessing would be so heartening. I almost left this out of this letter because I don't want you to feel pressured. However, I must trust you to listen to yourself and to be honest. If you don't have the energy or inclination—and I understand well that you might not—just tell me. I'd be sad but I'd support your decision, God knows, after all you've faced and are still handling.

I leave for Australia at the same time you go to Seattle. I return March 10. Three weeks feels long. . . . I'll give a creativity workshop while I'm there, be with friends (including G, perhaps, if he is free), work on the new book, and swim at home. My father is working on his own book for the University of Canberra and my mother needs piano time and has limited capacity for schedule interruption, so we'll have separate lives and happily come together for meals. It was always thus except when we tried otherwise.

Some inner darkness continues with intermittent flashes of light. I grow accustomed to it as my closest companion, especially in the night hours and early morning. I am stronger but still can sometimes fall hapless prey to my own dark gods' visions. Laying down hope, projections, and illusions is not for the weak, is it? I am grateful for my inborn persistence and resilience in the face of the impossible and for the abiding and healing love I receive from you and my other dear soul companions.

I shall be in contact before I leave to hear about your doctor's latest findings.

Until then, feel my love warming the marrow of your tired bones,

Jill

---

[130] MW had offered to write the foreword to JM's first manuscript accepted by Jeremy Tarcher but not yet published when Putnam bought his publishing house.

∞

JM Notes

For years, I had been mentioning Marion's books to patients when appropriate. Many had the same experience; they would start to read a paragraph and their imagination would fly out the window; they would find themselves pondering one sentence, one image. So they would confess to me that, no, despite their genuine wish to do so, they'd not finished "it." They wanted to. They meant to. They didn't. They were clearly moved by what they'd read. They just had to put the book down because short passages had had too much of an impact on them to keep on reading in a linear fashion. I found myself wishing some of Marion's most striking statements or descriptions could stand alone. Surely *someone* could pull those out of her writing and recordings. The thought occurred occasionally and flew away quickly.

Marion must have come to stay with us before, between, or after certain events that brought her to our area in September or October of 1995.

I had to make a supermarket run. Marion said she would enjoy accompanying me to a "Californian supermarket." She explained, "You have so many *fresh* items we can't get in Canada, Jill. It's a pleasure just to look." So we headed off on the most banal of tasks: grocery shopping. We enjoyed pushing the cart together and popping in treats as well as necessities.

I don't remember what made me think of it but I said to Marion as we were pushing the cart, "You know, Marion, several people I see have had a little difficulty finishing some of your books because they are like rich food. Readers take in a little at a time. It occurred to me that someone, some time, could pull out some of your more quotable quotes and publish them separately. You or Ross must know someone in London or Toronto who can do it with you if the idea appeals." I took care in my choice of words. Otherwise Marion would have instantly said, "You see, Jill. Ross *is* right. I'm not a *real* writer." The case was the opposite.

We continued to push the cart. I was pleased I'd caught the thought to mention it while Marion was staying with us. She could run with the idea or not.

We popped more necessities and treats into the cart.

"You."

"I what?"

"Could."

"I'm sorry, Marion. I was distracted by the woman in the purple tights. Could what?"

"You could do it. You understand my work. You understand me. You're a writer. But I'm getting ahead of myself, Jill. You're busy with your own writing."

"Marion, I just had the idea and thought *somebody* should do it."

"Yes of course. How thoughtless. You have a full schedule—teaching, therapy, writing."

"I didn't mean that, Marion. I'd be delighted. But qualified people—who know your work intimately—live close by and could work with you far more easily. I'm glad you like the idea—and thank you for the compliment. I'm sure you'll think of someone close by." We passed a woman with red curly hair flowing down to her waist, a silver bodysuit for yoga and a yoga mat rolled in her shopping cart.

"Goodness, things really *are* different down here, aren't they?" Marion said, bemused.

"I'm so used to 'here' that I don't see here, if you know what I mean."

"Jill, I really like the idea— but only if you'd like to do it with me—*and* have time. It would give us more opportunities to be together and…"

"Become old high school English teachers together?!"

"Oh, wouldn't that be fun! If you promise not to work too hard, I'd love to do it. You should choose the pieces."

We went through the checkout line, picked up several bags, and walked to the car.

As I turned on the engine, Marion said with mixed excitement and reluctant practicality, "Let's ask Jeanne. She can be our voice of reason."

I thought this an excellent idea.

We arrived home with more brown bags than the list indicated.

"Are you planning on feeding a small nation this evening?" Jeanne queried calmly. She had politely looked up from preparing for a literature seminar in her study/library. She was dressed for an afternoon of psychotherapy.[131]

"Marion and I have a question. Please be our voice of reason, ok? What do you think about a book that's just some of Marion's most quotable quotes?"

"Overdue," Jeanne replied and went back to reading.

"Jeanne, I haven't finished— I think so too. But Marion thinks I should do it with her."

"So?"

"*Well?*"

"I agree. Next?" She smiled benignly up at us and returned to her reading.

By the time Marion left, my creative daimon was dancing. Marion and I would be able to give every woman a chance to go to ShaSha, not just a privileged few. Perhaps I could even try out some watercolors of ShaSha?

---

[131] Both Jeanne Shutes and JM had therapy offices, each with separate entrances, at opposite ends of the house.

Marion loved that idea. I called my publisher. She replied, "How soon can you finish it?"

Marion left. Soon my studio floor was scattered with pages. Each contained a separate, typed quote. The wings of my intuition were coasting on currents. However, as my publisher had gently mentioned when I was writing the first edition of the dream book,[132] "We probably should start to think about *some* organizing principle…." I looked at the snow on the floor and wondered how these could possibly organize themselves. My body began to move to pick up pages and put them somewhere, without any conscious reason. Then I would pick up another piece and move that one. Piles began slowly appearing. I began asking the piles what they would like to be named. Mary Jane, the editor and publisher, asked me to write an introduction to each grouping.

∞

Undated

Dear Marion:

Just a quick follow-up to my phone call to make sure it is clear what Mary Jane[133] and I have come up with. Together, we are going to draft out a brief intro for each theme. I shall write a draft and send it to Mary Jane. It will appear under the title for that section, which will be opposite the painting. Mary Jane thought this was a simpler and cleaner way of doing them because then we don't have to repeat the word of the theme but can move straight into the brief commentary. We are picturing these comments as indications/invitations into the section rather than definitions. This *should* get around the difficulties of formal definitions.

---

[132] Jill Mellick, *The Natural Artistry of Dreams* (Conari Press, 1996).
[133] Mary Jane Ryan was founder, owner and senior editor at Conari Press. Conari had published JM's book *The Natural Artistry of Dreams* with a foreword by MW, and Conari was publishing MW's and JM's co-authored book.

I'll assume this meets with your approval unless you tell me otherwise by September 1. I think it's a good solution, and I feel much better about sitting down and doing this with a "someone else there." As Mary Jane said, "If *I* understand what you're saying, we'll be sure the average reader will understand!" So that is resolved, if not completed. I believe I'll be able to drop it from my concerns while I'm away now—I'm sure my mind will play with ideas, but that's different from worrying about it!

A piece of good news. As you know, I've been most reluctant to go "on the road" doing workshops with the dream book over this last year. I've just had no heart for it—being away from home, promotion, etc. I might have come up with a solution. I can agree to three, at most four, conferences or workshops a year only. That satisfies Conari and my wish for introversion.

All fine here. We are readying ourselves for vacation and can hardly wait. Jeanne and I are both tired and in need of R and R although repairing nicely. I shall come back to a full schedule of teaching and clients before Common Boundary[134] (again, thanks to you) and then Australia at Christmas. I do seem to clock up those miles during the year.

I'll be in touch, I hope, before you go off to London, but if not, I'll be thinking of you all and hoping that some of the concerns we shared . . . resolve themselves over the summer. Meanwhile, take care of that body we all love, dear friend. You are in my thoughts at least daily.

With love,

J

∞

After one of the times when Marion came to stay and work with me on the book, I sent her the slight, occasional poems that follow. Intentionally keeping them apart from the work we were doing, I hand-made a small book of them, accompanying each poem with a simple mandala.

---

[134] Conference at which both MW and JM were presenting.

Snapshots of a Brief Visit

For Marion
and for our friendship
November, 1995

Wrong Gate[135]

Racing downstairs
from the wrongly posted gate
I see from the back
your lion's mane.

In the space between heart beats
I see
you are in your life again:
stronger, less protected,
wiser, less weary yet weary still,
lighter, fragile.
I see
my tentative, tired,
habitually cautious heart
leap out to encompass you again.

I run and slow,
lightly raise an arm
curve it
around your tall shoulder.
Not a reuniting, this,
but confirmation:
you are never absent
from my heart.

---

[135]Referring to airport pickup of MW by JM.

Your Other Voice[136]

"Write from your passion!
You need—we need—I need—
this now!"
she says with force.
Impassioned, protective,
perhaps too strong, I too urge you.
"Write in that—other voice."

She senses, yet does not know—
in the way a passing perfume
on a spring night
betrays the presence
of unseen flowers—
what I heard that late summer night:
your other voice,
simple, strong, etched,
elegant as lilacs,
as your long fingers.

You quietly receive our fierceness
and tell us you hear another call.

For whom we do we really plea?

Fire Ceremony[137]

Across the autumnal table
you say—lightly—
"I'd like you to do a fire ceremony
for me—after I'm gone—
that is, if you would be willing."

---

[136] During dinner at home with JM and Jeanne, MW asked for input on her writing. Jeanne and JM responded similarly; JM also urged MW to use the voice in MW"s journals.
[137] JM refers to the fire ceremony, *homa,* that JM led and MW attended at Asilomar. MW asked JM to perform it at her funeral.

Across the candles,
I smile and nod.
We move on to laughter.

I do not say what we already know:
the steady fire
we share
across three thousand miles
already dances strong.

Later, glimpsing my small pencil sketch
you will cry, "That's it!"

In our separate lives
we each must form
from our heart's clay
the burnished pot
and light the dancing flame.

Chapel Visit[138]

We know this place in our bones.
A generation
and ten thousand miles apart,
we are together now
in our childhood home.

In the stained stillness,
a wrong note on the organ
crosses parallel panes of light.

We sit in silent harmony.
Our hands lie folded
as delight flows over
to lay warm fingers on yours.

[138] MW and JM went to Stanford University Memorial Chapel and sat silently, listening
to an organist practicing. The Chapel is nonsectarian.

An ancient, known thing,
this offering of gratitude
to the long, light-filled panes,
for your resurrected life,
for your irrepressible heart.
Joy sings in my ears,
accompanies Bach.
You are back.

Your Dance

What do you think
of my work with him?[139]

I hesitate.

You dance together well.
Yet, because I promise you
no less in friendship and in love,
than this,
my fierce, myopic, measured truth,
I shall tell you:

When he dances
I see
the beauty of the waves;
When you dance,
I see
the light on the floor of the sea.

---

[139] Over a dinner at home, MW had asked JM and Jeanne Shutes what each thought of her work with poet Robert Bly.

Price of Entry

The dream you tell
of sun and moon,
of velvet and stone,
echoes in my heart's cave
long after
you have fallen asleep
to enter again that chamber of dreams.
Who can really know
the price you paid
to enter into your life.

Brushing My Hair

My head in your lap,
you brush my hair
as only you can do.

Two women talking
of women's things,
we are each as old and young
as the moon.

Beneath the waves you see
what is hidden:
the slow shedding of old visions.
Even my hair grows weary.

We talk of destiny, fate;
of gratitude, anger;
of surrender, of standing alone.
At what precise moment
did we turn
to follow this lonelier path?
You speak of acceptance;
I, of proud, blind, slingshot attempts

to stone down the planet of my fate
in full trajectory.

Seeing my snakeskin sloughing off,
you do not flinch.
You brush firm and gentle,
patient and rhythmic,
until the last of my loss
lies silent as snow
in your green lap.
    The oils are releasing,
you calmly observe.
    I'd better wash it then,
I reply.

Like a cloudless sky,
I stand, washing my hair
as Pueblo women do
in the acequia madre
for ceremonial days.[140]
After, they dress in mantas, hold green boughs;
they dance for a long and fertile life.

I emerge
and, hair still wet,
farewell you.

Tonight, I pass the tall mirror
we each used in these last days.
Waves glow and dance
in a way I had forgotten
since last you brushed away my pain.

---

[140] On ceremonial days in the Pueblo Indian communities of New Mexico, women traditionally wash their hair in the acequia madre, the mother ditch. During many ceremonial dances open to the public, particularly the Corn Dance held in each village in summer, dancers wear special dresses, mantas and head dresses, and they carry fir branches or bind them around their upper arms.

I feel your hand still,
your hand brushing away
old sorrows, joys, and hopes,
your hand resting quietly on my life,
my new and unctuous life,
still, for these few moments,
in your hands.

Pansies

Returning from our farewell
to your room[141] I see,
still firm and bold,
the pansies:
lush violet
of sweet secrets
and senses overflowing,
dark lavender
of bruised twilight
and promises;
succulent yellow
of soul
and summer island light,
of losses
and laughter—
just as you arranged them,
fierce, fragile, and triumphant,
in this vase of lapis blue.[142]

---

[141] MW used JM's writing, art and music studio when she stayed. MW and JM wrote
Coming Home to Myself in this room.
[142] Lapis lazuli is often referred to in alchemical texts as a symbol of the Self.

∞

January 2, 1996

Dear Marion—and Ross:

Well, I certainly didn't expect to have this much to show you as a first attempt! However, as I said, your words carried me along without effort and also nourished my awareness when I was in Australia. Some quick notes about what I am sending:

• These are *first drafts* only. I am not attached to any one of them as a final. Change at will! I do not offend easily in the writing area! After so many years of professional editing, I have a happy level of commitment to and yet detachment from my writing.

• To date, I have used all books except *Leaving My Father's House*. I am rereading that now for quotes.

• Most of the quotes list an abbreviated title and page reference at the end. Some do not. These will be added later.

• The pieces (we'll be careful not to refer to them as poems for your sake![143]) seemed to divide themselves into sections. Once again, I'm not attached to the sections; change at will.

• The title of the book is a working title only. I welcome all ideas you have for a title that would do homage to and reflect the richness of its contents. As you both know, titles are my weakest point!

• There are numerous punctuation errors. I shall correct them later, but do change anything you think needs changing.

---

[143] MW did not consider her writing "poetic." JM plucked pieces of MW's work, made line breaks where they naturally fell, then worked with poetic devices such as alliteration, parallelism, and repetition. MW and JM then worked on them together. MW and JM agreed to regard them as prose poems.

• I've included a quote or two (not in real line form) at the beginning of each section. These were quotes that seemed to need to keep a different form from the rest. Delete or change if you wish.

• The line breaks are moveable feasts at this point. Once again, I welcome any improvements as I am not convinced of the correctness of all of them.

• How would these do, later, as a tape with Sounds True?! I would LOVE to hear you reading these with the same bone fierceness that you read Emily!

• I have tried to change as little as possible, using almost exclusively the simple rhetorical devices of repetition and parallel construction to occasionally increase emphasis. I have at times changed the order of the presentation of a section to enhance the cumulative tension in the section. Other than that, your words stand 95% unchanged.

• Any chance you would allow the Katherine dreams to be directly associated with you? They would make powerful pieces, but I can't include them as long as they are under another's name.

• Please skim the original to see what I have done and feel free to request anything you wish. I really would like to be a linguistic midwife here only—your words are both mother and child. This is all written in water at this time.

I shan't elaborate on the process again after regaling you on the phone—other than to reiterate that it has been a joy to do this much. Even if you change your mind about publication, I have been happy to just send these to you as a way of thanking you for the role your wisdom has played in my own life.

I'm so pleased we talked yesterday. We really needed to clear up the whole annual get-together!

With love to you both from

Jill

∞

JM Notes
Around 1995–1997

Only when Jeanne and I went to Kauaʻi again did I have time to experiment with the watercolors for the book. Sitting on the floor of the condominium there with a full, close view of the Pacific waves rolling in, I dwelt in my imagination at ShaSha. It did occur to me that this dual experience was odd, but my connection to water gave it coherence. I chose pure indigo watercolor pigment in tubes to make the paintings. I love the way indigo flows in water.

Marion came to stay several times over this period between conception and birth of the book. We worked on the manuscript and laughed as our old English university training and high school teaching did indeed take over. We could bat punctuation, gerunds, infinitives back and forth without rancor; we were united in the service of something larger: the

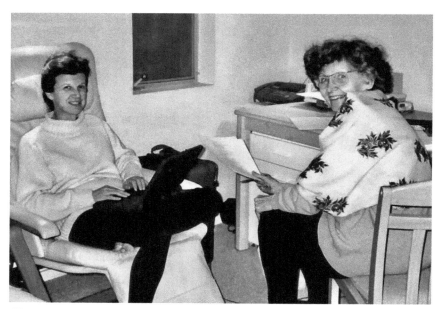

Jill and Marion work on the draft of *Coming Home to Myself* in the studio at the Shutes/Mellick residence. ©Jeanne Shutes

manuscript itself. The word reigned, not either's ego. We took breaks—usually at Jeanne's urging.

We did tussle over royalties. Marion wanted me to have more. I wanted her to have more. The book would not exist without her original words. She argued it would not exist without my reviewing all her work and creating the prose poems. I'm stubborn but Marion finally won.

Mary Jane Ryan drove down from the publishing house in Berkeley during one of Marion's stays to meet with us. We spent intense time in the sitting room generating possible names for the book. Without saying it, we took it for granted that it needed to evolve by consensus. Marion was always good at giving titles to her books. Jeanne always gave her literature seminars succinct, intriguing titles. I didn't consider myself gifted in this area. However, on this particular day, the atmosphere amongst us must have woken the muse, and she hopped onto my shoulder; I heard me saying as we were brainstorming, "Coming home to myself?" The energy in the room settled down like a dog for a nap. I don't consider it *my* title. It couldn't have happened without the three of us working synergistically in the service of those who would read it.

However, poor Mary Jane later received Marion's and my righteous indignation. She had sent each of us a mockup of a cover for the book, and we were decidedly unhappy.

"Jill, what do you think of this ... this *mockup*," Marion asked me almost as soon as she arrived on one visit.

"I hate it," I said flatly. Neither Marion nor I held back with each other, especially when it came to aesthetics.

"So do I," Marion said and uttered the exact words I was readying to say. "It's *wooden!* It's the *opposite* of what we're trying to communicate in terms of a woman's *occupying* her body!"

When Mary Jane arrived that day, Marion and I, united, broke the news in no uncertain terms. Mary Jane listened calmly and simply responded, "You're thinking like authors, not like a reader. Trust me, this will work."

Marion and I retreated into a verbal corner, each righteously gnawing at our aesthetic bones. We said no more other than to reiterate at dinner after Mary Jane had left that the proposed cover was exactly what we *didn't* want. This repeated itself when the book was also issued as a paperback with a new cover.

"*Wooden,* Jill! The woman is *wooden!*"

"She looks like a stick figure. She has no feminine *shape*," I exclaimed. "I grew up at the beach. *No one* stands looking at the ocean like that! At least no one with blood in their veins. And certainly no one in my figure drawing classes!" However, by then we knew better than to argue with Mary Jane. Mary Jane, of course, was right; the book sold out and has been reprinted many times.

∞

JM Notes

In early September 1996, Marion sent me a draft of *Bone,* her excerpts from her journals about her experience with cancer. She wanted my responses both to the sections that included me and to the manuscript as a whole. It was a difficult, difficult task. My introversion was shocked at what she was willing to share with a wide audience. The manuscript also brought back many of the moments we shared during that time, brought back my fear of and temerity in suggesting a second opinion, the agony we each felt from our very different places. I also feared that her undressing certain experiences in public would leave her vulnerable to misinterpretation, to entitlement by others regarding what they "knew" about Marion, and to a flood of needy women seeking her guidance on their own physical conditions.

∞

Tuesday, September 30, 1996[144]

Dearest Marion,

I'm so pleased we could carve time out from our separately crazy weekends to be together and to work on the poetry. I'm delighted to my toes that you are so pleased with what is emerging. That gratifying feeling of having one's literary efforts seen and appreciated goes both ways, you know.

And thank you again for your kindness about the royalties, dear Marion. You are, as always, truly generous, especially given that this book would not exist without your original work. Your generosity also makes me feel that the depth and extent of the energy I'm putting into it does not go unnoticed either—and as a writer, you know how much one appreciates someone else's really recognizing what it takes to put a simple sentence together at times. So thank you on that level, too.

Now to your very, very special and precious journals. First, dearest friend, I consider it a gift to have been given them to read, just for the sake of sharing them with you. I felt as though I were walking with a very, very quiet, deep place inside you. Thank you for your trust in letting me be with or revisit your healing crisis in a new way.

Clearly you seem to feel ready now to share with the public at large these very private moments you experienced with yourself, your family and your friends.

---

[144] These two letters refer to MW's draft of *Bone*. Her experience of cancer is included earlier, excerpted from the published book because it made sense to include MW's experience where it fitted in the timeline. However, MW wrote the draft later. She sent it to JM who responded. MW returned JM's letter with words underlined. JM wrote at the top the date she received the letter back; this is one of the few letters she did not date when she wrote it. MW wrote "Jill re Journals" on the letter.

I wonder, however, if your family and friends are as ready to have these moments—which include them and which were private moments from their point of view, too—shared with the public. Are you getting permission from each of these people to include these moments and their real names? I, for one, was startled to encounter things I had thought private between us appearing on those pages. And I am deeply considering, from my side, how I feel about having these times we shared—moments that I have considered until now part of my private life—now shared with thousands.

My feeling is that, in its current form, this material is too private for public consumption. Would you consider finishing this version for distribution to family and close friends with the understanding that they share it with no-one else? It could then provide the essential ground for a second version which could evolve in its own form better suited to public scrutiny, perhaps less historically particular, less specific, more focused on inner reflections.

You see, when I heard your talk on Sunday, I realized that there is a huge difference between hearing you talk about this material and reading it. When you speak, you are there to act as a physical, visual, and emotional filter and container—dropping in humour as you do so beautifully with your sensitivity to the pulse of an audience, pausing for emphasis, balancing intensity with banality, giving the hearer a breather every so often, gauging what is happening every second: what is too much, what is losing them, what moves them, what needs a shift in container. You are a master at this. You are also speaking in the past tense, which places a second level of mediation on the material. We can bear to hear the unbearable because you are embodying emotion recollected in tranquility.[145] When you *talk* about your despair in a lecture, you, the whole person, are there to act as compassionate witness to your own suffering.

In the journals as they currently stand, there is no possibility of mediation of content and no container possible other than the words themselves. And, because of the style of journal writing, every moment is happening

---

[145] JM is referring to William Wordsworth's term "emotion recollected in tranquility," which MW and Ross would know well.

<u>NOW</u>. When you write about spiraling down into doubt or fear, your readers are there until you come up. There is no Marion to contain them. In the writing, the container is the word, not <u>you</u>. The difference is huge and quite dangerous.

When you stand up, you speak your truth; you contain your truth. When you write, each word carries that function, not you yourself. No matter how transparently we write, we are not what we write. However, others will make us that. And their wounds will use your self-revelations in the service of grafting skin onto the raw places in their own psyches. If you leave these journals as they are, I fear that, rather than nourishing others, your material will be eaten alive. I wonder whether you would really welcome having each detail consumed by other eyes. Written words are frozen, picked over, subject to psychoanalysis. You and Ross and everyone you mention and every detailed description you provide will be subject to endless projection—used and fantasized about in others' psyches in ways we can't even dream of.

I have always believed that this writing project is a valuable one. I still do. I am not suggesting you do not continue. So there's no cause for that despair you mentioned. The journal's current, very private form will have its own priceless value for the chosen few; and I believe that completion of this private form will also open up the way for you then to give birth to its more public form, which will have its own unique value.

Well, dear one, this is the best I can offer. I must to bed. I have spent many hours reflecting and clarifying my responses to all of this for both our sakes and hope that these suggestions are received with all the love with which they are being sent. I love you too much to tell you what I imagine you would like to hear; I love you enough to offer you what you have entrusted me to offer you: my honest if probably flawed responses.

I hope England suffuses you with its autumnal elegance and that Stockholm seduces you with its charm!

As always, with love deepening,

J

∞

JM Notes

After battling yet again about who deserved more of the royalties, we sent this fax. (I knew Marion should get the larger part, but there comes a time when one has to bow gracefully.)

To:
———, Attorney at Law for Marion
———, Attorney at Law for Jill
Cc: Conari Press Legal Department:

We, Marion Woodman and Jill Mellick, are moving towards some formalization of our wishes for the continued life of our joint book should it survive one or both of us.

We agree that, should one author survive the other, all copyright and royalties revert to the surviving author until death. After the death of both authors, the copyright to *Coming Home to Myself* will be held equally by the executor or a person legally appointed by the executor of each author's estate. Royalties will revert to being distributed to the two estates on the percentage basis established at the time of the authors' original joint royalty agreement, that is, 40% Woodman and 60% Mellick.

∞

London, England
October 9, 1996

Dearest Jill,

Life is pushing right along for me these past three days. Ross decided he needed to rest for his eyes' sake so couldn't come to our beloved London.

Yesterday Ross phoned to say a buyer had arrived for ShaSha, so we are negotiating that sad farewell by phone. (I am insisting we go there once more to say good-bye. I shall pick up your straw hat.) And last night Bruce had an emergency for kidney stones. So, you see, I'm more than focused on where I am at in this moment. (Amazing, Ross was home for the buyer!)

I do, however, need to get a note off to you. Thank you for your wonderfully thoughtful letter. I know exactly what you mean and I am musing constantly on the whole endeavour. I certainly had intended to show it to everyone (including my doctor R) before publishing. It's a bind because this is already a gentle version of what my journal is and I don't think I can distance it any more and still call it my journal. Not that I need to, but I can't work in the old mode either.

I thank you for telling me you were ~~shocked~~ startled at finding things you had thought private between us appearing on those pages. I haven't had time to reread yet, but I will find what you are referring to. I would not for anything violate my friends' privacy. I have not put in anything which seems to come from my holy of holies. Facts are presented, in part, but the depths that they represent between me and my friends I have not disclosed. Nor do I intend to. You need have no fear, Jill. I am well-veiled and very much in control of what is edited out. If my friends don't like what I put in or feel that I put in something too precious, I would certainly take it out. My family have all read it and encouraged me to stay with what I have written. Some things about Ross I am not sure of.

Your point about the container, I understand. I'll think about that. I don't know how to make that container for this book. Of course, I will write an introduction, but this needs more consideration.

As I go out to London, I just need to say again how precious the "poems" are. I am thinking about them as well, dear friend. How well you know me!

Much much love, Marion

And again so many thanks for our time at your home.

Love to Jeanne

Love from us both to you both

Jill, I'm happy to work this at the next level or even two or three

∞

Christmas photograph titled "Our everlasting farewell take":[146]
Stewards of ShaSha 1983–1996
Love and Christmas Blessings

Reverse side:
Jan 23/97

Dear Jill,

We'll try once again! This image was a glorious mistake that I want you to
have. It captures us on ShaSha so accurately—that world between two
worlds—temporal and eternal. Our Avalon—our mists of Avalon. It will
live forever in our hearts. I think part of my ceaseless flu is the realization
that it is no longer ours. I try to be practical and know that we could no
longer care for it, but we still profoundly miss it.

I am so happy that you shared it with us. Forever you and I will have our
evening time alone under the Big Dipper, forever your zither will play and
I will gently comb your hair. Magic! Have been working on our book with
delight today. Will phone. Blessings in 97.

Love,

Marion

---

[146] William Shakespeare, *Julius Caesar*, Act V, Scene 1.

∞

Friday noon[147]

Dearest Jill,

I'm trying to put this in the mail today. I'm sorry I couldn't return it sooner. But I am working for both Pacifica and the Foundation and wasting no moment. I've been over it carefully. Hadn't realized in the beginning that you had what was at the beginning, at the back. Not quite sure of the integration now.

It is too long, I think. I found myself quite energized at the beginning, but then the tempo lags. You tell me what you think of what I've done and I'll think. I'm still very uncertain about my own health stuff towards the end. I'll phone next week, or next weekend might be better, and find out when we can discuss.

Thank you for your patience with it. Wonderful to be out of this ice and snow. The Tribute[148] does put me under great strain. I don't know why. I wish somebody else was/were in the spotlight.

Dearest love—

Marion

---

[147] Undated.
[148] MW didn't identify what "The Tribute" was; it seems some homage was being paid to her at Pacifica Graduate Institute.

∞

JM Notes

Marion was informed in 1996 that she was to be awarded an honorary doctorate by her alma mater, the University of Western Ontario, the following year, 1997. She invited guests to the ceremony. There were doubtless others who accepted and attended whom I did not know; I attended together with those I knew—Eleanora Woloy,[149] Paula Reeves,[150] Mary Hamilton,[151] and Ann Skinner.[152]

We stayed near Marion and Ross's townhouse and walked to and from their place on Sydenham Street opposite the park. The townhouse was spacious, elegant, mostly white except for Marion's study and its attached bathroom. As one went up the stairs, Ross's study and desk were on the left facing the park. In the corner

Ross Woodman's study in the Woodman's townhouse. ©Mellick

formed where the hall turned right, a Gerrit Reitveld chair sat, quietly stunning and placed below Guido Molinari's "Mutation Bleu Pale."[153]

A few semicircular steps on the right of the white-carpeted hall led up to a spacious sitting room, Persian carpet, huge Inuit carvings. Farther along the hall, a breathtaking Perspex bicycle by a Canadian artist leaned against the wall. My eyes were suffused by aesthetics that were, to me, flawless. I wanted to be quiet, to look at each piece, one a day, for a long time.

---

[149] Jungian analyst and author from Virginia Beach, Virginia.
[150] Psychotherapist and author from Atlanta, Georgia.
[151] Graduate of the National School of Ballet in Canada, professor (ret.) at the University of Western Ontario, cofounder of BodySoul Rhythms.
[152] Head of Voice Emerita at Stratford Shakespeare Festival in Ontario, cofounder of BodySoul Rhythms.
[153] Guido Molinari's "Mutation Bleu Pale,"acrylic on canvas, 1966, 50" x 68. Details courtesy of Joel Faflak, Ph.D.

The blue door on the left led to Ross's study; the chair is a Gerrit Rietveld and the painting, a Guido Molinari. Ross was a serious collector of modern art. ©Mellick

Curved stairs led to the Woodman's sitting room in their London townhouse. ©Mellick

Sitting room of the Woodman's townhouse on Sydenham Street, London, Ontario. ©Mellick

At the end of the hall, Marion took us down to her study. Warm colors: adobe, mauves, blues, dusty unsentimental rose, ochers. The furniture expressed the complementarity of Marion's passionate journey toward empowered feminine spirit, informed and energized by Ross, and Ross's

Marion's study in the townhouse on Sydenham Street, London, Ontario. ©Mellick

L to R: Eleanora Woloy, Jill, Ross, and Marion in Marion's study where several of us gathered to witness her receiving an Honorary Doctorate from her Alma Mater, University of Western Ontario. ©Mellick

passionate journey toward the masculine spirit, informed and energized by Marion. Now I understood at a physical level what Marion meant when she once said to me, "I must have my place in Toronto, Jill. When Ross is writing—he has no intention of doing this but— his creativity and writing take all *my* energy through the *walls*." We happily piled like a litter of puppies onto a daybed, with Ross delightedly joining "Marion's ladies."

Ross and Marion delighted in sitting and talking with those of us who flew to be present at the awarding of Marion's Honorary Doctorate. ©Mellick

Marion and Ross converse with those who traveled to be there before, during, and after the awarding of Marion's Honorary Doctorate. She loved having her world with Ross and world with us together under the same roof. ©Mellick

Marion and Ross in Marion's study standing in front of a piece from their art collection. ©Mellick

The ceremony itself took place in the great hall of the university. The audience was in darkness, and the dignitaries in formal academia robes were on the stage, including Marion. I was determined to get memorable photographs for her, so I followed sage advice received years earlier: take too many, and one of them might—if you are lucky—turn out. I was not lucky but at least I managed a few that were passable.

On the grounds of the University of Western Ontario, some of her close friends meet and speak before the ceremony awarding Marion her Honorary Doctorate. ©Mellick

Marion in cap and gown during the awarding of her Honorary Doctorate by the University of Western Ontario. ©Mellick

Mary Hamilton and Marion during the award of her Honorary Doctorate. ©Mellick

Marion addresses the audience after her Honorary Doctorate is awarded. ©Mellick

Marion signs her name during her Honorary Doctorate ceremony at the University of Western Ontario. Mary Hamilton looks on. ©Mellick

We went on to a celebratory dinner at Mary and John Hamilton's house that evening. Next day we would leave for our own "ShaSha" at Ann Skinner's family cottage by Lake Huron. This time we would focus on ourselves instead of other participants. We were amused when we admitted the idea scared us—*we* the center of attention, not others? We all had a deep desire to gather—and we each admitted comical trepidation at personally doing what we had witnessed Marion's analysands doing with dignity and grace. We spent a week together in the cottage. I had a small, comfortable, simply furnished single bedroom upstairs with a view of trees close by.

The leaders' retreat at the Skinner cottage, Lake Huron, 1997. L to R: Jill, Marion, Paula Reeves, Eleanora Woloy. ©Mellick

Within two days of being at the cottage, which had been sealed all winter, I was deaf in one ear, so I went to a local physician. I had prepared for just about anything this week—except for mold and being deaf. Whatever the physician prescribed restored my hearing.

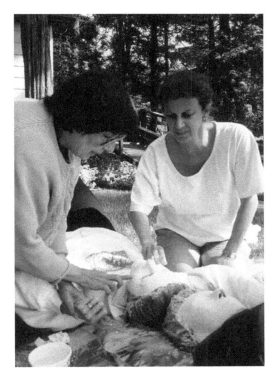

Each of us was more accustomed to leading creative work than being led, but we found we loved being led. For this week, we each led once and were led the rest of the time. We made masks. We painted. We moved. We spontaneously created rituals. We sat around the kitchen table, summer light filtering strongly through yellow curtains, and laughed. A lot. *Coming*

Mask making during the leaders' retreat at the Skinner cottage, Lake Huron. L to R: Paula Reeves. Jill, and two participants letting masks dry. ©Mellick

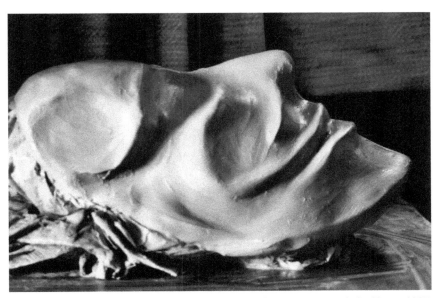

Jill's mask drying during the leaders' retreat at the Skinner cottage, Lake Huron,1997. ©Mellick

Leaders' retreat at Ann Skinner's family's cottage, Lake Huron. L to R: Ann Skinner, Jill, Paula Reeves, Eleanora Woloy, Mary Hamilton, Marion. ©Mellick

Home to Myself, Marion's and my book, had been printed relatively recently.[154] Marion wanted to ask Sophia, as she called the spirit that enlivened her soul, to bless it on its way, so she led us in a small ritual. The sun setting over the lake painted our faces warm shades of ocher.

During the leaders' retreat at the Skinner Cottage, Lake Huron, 1997, Marion held a brief ritual for the book she and Jill had just published, *Coming Home to Myself.* Marion asked for Sophia's blessing on its journey into the world. ©Mellick

---

[154] Marion Woodman and Jill Mellick, *Coming Home to Myself* (Conari Press, 1998).

The group watches the sun set over Lake Huron, June 1997. L to R: Marion, Mary Hamilton, Jill, Eleanora Woloy. ©Mellick

Nightly, we did what we always did on ShaSha. We sang lustily and self-admiringly. I accompanied on my travel guitar, falling again into a comfortable role as wandering minstrel. Blessed with a good memory for melody and a poor one for lyrics, I always brought fat lyric books. I was surrounded by singers as insatiable and unembarrassed as I. We'd sing late into the night.

L to R: Marion, Jill, Ann Skinner, and Paula Reeves "on Broadway" at the Skinner cottage. ©Mellick

Evenings were spent singing during the 1997 June leaders' retreat. L to R: Marion, Eleanora Woloy, Ann Skinner, Mary Hamilton, Jill with guitar. ©Mellick

Private conversations evolved spontaneously between pairs of us on beach walks, forested walks, over a cup of tea or coffee on the back lawn facing the lake. We spent an uproarious evening reading aloud from an enneagram[155] book someone had brought. The book, an approach to

Marion and Jill talk at the June 1997 leaders' retreat at the Skinner's cottage. ©Mellick

---

[155] The enneagram is a model of the psyche constructed as a typology of nine interconnected personality types.

L to R: Jill, Paula Reeves, and Eleanora Woloy enjoy the sun and view of Lake Huron.©Mellick

Beach, waves, and lighthouse, Lake Huron. ©Mellick

personality types with which none of us was intimately familiar, was a childlike delight. With uncontrolled amusement we recognized ourselves, each other, loved ones.

We walked on the beach. (A coastal dweller all my days, I didn't even know that lakes had beaches and tides.) We walked out on a long jetty at night; I sang a version of "Full Fathom Five," which Ariel sang to Ferdinand in *The Tempest,* in honor of a special moment that had arisen.

∞

June 17/97

Dear Jill,

I need to write to you before you are out of my bloodstream. After you left I felt, with a blow, how we had not gone for a walk together, I had not brushed your hair—in short, no private time together. However, we did have our work together. Again, thank you for your incredible gift in seeing my writing so clearly and taking the time to put your clarifying focus on it. I hope everything runs smoothly now to the publication. (Michael did his work and sent off the originals to you last week.)

I'm glad we didn't try out in front of people. If we are going to read them for Tami (Sounds True) I will have to do some trial runs of my own. I was almost speechlessly nervous that Sunday night. Thank you for the time you stayed at our home. You have no idea what it meant to Ross to know my friends. And he loves my haircut and so do I. "Cheeky" he calls it. "It took courage to cut it that way," he said.[156] He hadn't realized you cut it (I love it!!). You may wonder about the B on this paper. I bought the paper a year ago thinking I would try out Boa-Woodman. Just buying the paper ended the idea!

I know how much energy it takes for you to come all this way, Jill. I know, too, there is much left unsaid in the full group situation. I think it is remarkable that we can all share at the depth we do, and I think that will go deeper or change totally. For now, many thanks for coming again, for reflecting me to myself.

Always—

Marion

---

[156] JM had cut MW's hair at her request.

∞

June 1997

Dearest Jill,

You have been very close to me as Ross and I have crossed to the East side of the continent this past week. I have <u>loved</u> the journeying. There is a big, happy-go-lucky gypsy in me and she's on a long leash these days. So far our trip has gone as planned. Two days retracing the steps of my maternal grandfather (a UEL, United Empire Loyalist) who crossed Lake Ontario with nothing rather than leave England's rule. Three days with P and C and their glorious Marion Rose and new E. That child at 2 ½ can sing every song in <u>Sound of Music</u> with a verve that is alarming. Wow! Passion! E is a little Buddha.

The retreat was pure joy. Now Ross and I are in Bar Harbor waiting to take the ferry to Nova Scotia at seven tomorrow morning.

In all of this movement, I've been thinking constantly on our time together last week at Ann's, and our time together around the University ceremonies. I go back to the pictures repeatedly just to be sure it really happened. As I showed them to P and K in the wilderness of New Hampshire, I wondered again at the sheer magic of having you and Eleanora and Paula, Mary and Ann with us to share it. What an act of friendship your caring coming was, Jill! I shall never forget it. It was so wonderful to be in your physical presence again. I really felt I left the last veils of illness behind, and moved totally into the present.

Last week was extraordinary. I feel I pulled off some heavy outworn conservative veils—something about living in London[157]— without falling into ancient patterns of attitude and action.

Ross is roaring at me to stop writing letters, but I am determined to get this off to you before we cross into Canada. He sends you his love. I send

---

[157] London, Ontario.

you my dearest love, Jill. Such a friend! I look forward to your manuscript when I return. I'll write the foreword as soon as possible. Dear One, I hope all is flowing smoothly for you and your writing.

A big hug and kiss,

Marion

∞

Aug 18/97

Dearest Jill,

I'm feeling a bit like this old lady this morning.[158] Not dark, but holding on tight with a slightly pursed lip. I haven't been ordering myself at all this summer. My commitment has been to getting my blood count up and the radiation out—NOW. I think we may have succeeded. Now I look ahead to a fairly rigorous and structured two months and pull in the breath to hold it all together. One step at a time!

Am putting the materials in the mail for Conari today. Here is your cheque.[159] I hope you are having a splendid time in Hawaii. Many thanks for your beautiful birthday card and note. Truly I had a glorious day.

Much love always,

Marion

---

[158] Written on a card showing an image of an old woman.
[159] MW and JM split the advance for *Coming Home to Myself*.

∞

July 20/98   HAPPY BIRTHDAY

Dearest Jill,

We'll probably speak on the phone before Ross and I leave for England and Switzerland, but I know how time and space in one world cut me off from time and space in another, so I want to send you your birthday card now. This has been a precious year of sharing for us: I felt so close to you whenever I worked on the lines. I feel close now whenever I pick up the book, smile at how our minds met, our styles met or didn't quite meet— and how all is resolved in your exquisite watercolours. People go out of their way to tell me how much they like the book. They love being able to pick it up for ten minutes—find a morsel and move on. It is the modern world, Jill.

We leave on July 31—return September 29. It is too long to be away but neither of us quite grasped the spaces in between. However, I think we'll get some deep rest. I hope the alpine air brings healing to Ross's eye. It hardly stays open; the lid has no muscular control.[160] Otherwise he is in splendid spirits. I hope your journey to Australia went well. And I hope you and Jeanne have a wonderful journey to Tuscany.

Dear Jill, I thank God every day for friends like you—and specifically for you. You are unique in my life. Take very special care of your dear self.

Always,

Marion

---

[160] Ross was being treated for ptosis of the eyelid.

∞

September 2/99

Dear Jill,

Mary, Ann, and I are here in Landegg sitting on top of the highest hill over the Bodensee,[161] which is bordered by Austria, Germany, Switzerland. The air is purity itself. My health is glowing. I can walk like a twenty-year-old up and down the hills. Air has a profound effect on my age. When I return to the pollution of London, England on Sunday, I'll be seventy again.

This workshop has several different nationalities, but everyone helps everyone with languages and in real difficulties we rely on the profound power of Silence. It <u>works</u>—Sophia enters the cells. This is the academy that the Baha'is hope will one day be the center for the world university. Already we are surrounded by young people of many nationalities who are studying here and/or living here because they escaped from their homes to save their lives. Just to look into their faces jostles the neurotics out of their love affairs with their own neurosis. We three are all well; Ross is in England with dear Bruce, who is very ill; John Hamilton left yesterday to go to Zürich. Life is happening, and Death. Bruce's depression with the Parkinson diagnosis is worse than the disease itself—I think a profound part of it. He nursed a friend through it, and I see him looking at himself a few months hence. Still we go to Kew and have had a splendid time together. (Sorry about that paragraph, Jill. I have no more paper and I couldn't buy any cards here so I'm jamming everything together.)

Assisi[162] was fabulous. The heat opened my bones as they haven't been opened since Greece. The dialogue among speakers was excellent. Ross and I both flourished in the atmosphere that Michael Conforti created with his archetypal planes.

---

[161] Lake Constance.
[162] MW lectured at Jungian analyst Michael Conforti's Assisi Institute seminar. JM and Jeanne Shutes had attended the seminar in a previous year.

This is to send you dearest birthday wishes for your new year. To tell you and Jeanne how close you were to me in Assisi. How close you always are to me, dearest Jill.

Marion

∞

January 8, 2000

Dearest Jill,

That's the first time I've written "2000" without having to strike out '99. In spite of full concentration on the EVE, I am not finding the passover easy. It feels like a new person has to step into the new consciousness of the millennium. I'm sure my deepest sense of that is coming from having spent a week, including the EVE, with 250 young Baha'is. They have an intellectual grasp, but not the consciousness to go with it. It was a fierce, powerful week. On our return, the first two messages on our machine were of the deaths of two very close friends, one—Ross's lifetime soulmate—David McKee. Ross has been very ill ever since he received that message. Total shock! Altogether I'm feeling like this tired soul on the front of this card.

That cranky animas in the background is not helping either. He wants to get on with <u>Bone</u>. My deadline is Feb. 1. But my feminine self has to take in two immense losses and process what happened in Switzerland.

I'm sure you're going through rough waters too, Jill, having just returned from Australia. I spoke with Jeanne a couple of times before we left just to know you did go and arrived safely. I no longer take "arriving safely" for granted.

I'll bring <u>Bone</u> with me when I come rather than sending it. It will be in its most completed form then. Penguin doesn't expect me to have all the permissions before Feb. 1.

Did I tell you <u>Coming Home</u> was on <u>Good Living</u>'s[163] list for best Christmas presents?

I've decided I really would like to speak with Dr. Bob if that is possible while I am there come April. I have one more test here. The doctors' attitudes are basically defeatist. "What do you expect [after radiation]?"[164] "We'll do our best, you live with the consequences." Ross and I are doing a program in Palo Alto for Patty Flowers[165] on Feb. 3, arriving on Feb. 2, resting on Feb. 4, beginning the workshop on the 5th. I know that three days on the ocean without pressure would be a godsend for us, and Patty is willing to rent from Feb. 3 on. If Bob could speak with me, consult with me Feb 14th or 12th, that would be excellent. I'm trying to clarify my thinking on this, Jill. Is there really anything he can say to me in person that we can't discuss on the phone? Is there anything he can say without tests? Will he accept the … results from here? I know this doctor was not "satisfied." … I also know the [test][166]… weakens … desperately every time it is done. This was the third and by far the worst. Maybe he and I should speak on the phone before we go to California.

You must tell me what is the best time for us to talk. If we came to you and Jeanne on the 12th around noon would that work for you? We don't know yet what we'll do—except <u>rest</u> until [the workshop][167] begins on the 18th. If I do see Dr. Bob on 14 or 15, Ross & I will stay in a hotel, Jill. That would put too much burden on you and Jeanne. This sounds like a jumble but it will clarify as facts become more clear. I certainly didn't think I would be writing such a long letter.

Just to say I love you. I wished you blessings of the new Millennium from the top of the mountain over the Bodensee on the EVE. That was a powerful spot to be with all those young people (250) from all over the world watching their own country come in on CNN.

---

[163] Canadian magazine.
[164] Information generalized to preserve privacy.
[165] Patty Flowers was the administrator of BodySoul Rhythms for many years as well as being employed by UC Santa Cruz Continuing Education Division.
[166] Information generalized for the sake of privacy.
[167] Name of workshop is illegible in MW's letter.

You are part of my daily consciousness.

Blessings my dear, dear Jill.

Marion

∞

JM Notes

Over the years of Marion and Ross's visits, we grew our own group friendship around art and literature. Ross, Marion, Jeanne and I had been literature majors and professors, teachers or seminar leaders in literature (some still were). While Jeanne had studied art history at Wellesley, neither Ross nor I had formally studied art; however, it was a powerful magnet for us. Ross was a discerning, serious collector and critic of modern art; I had been making art all my life.

Marion and Ross asked Jeanne to introduce them to the extensive American Indian art, pottery, and carving she and Jill had collected in New Mexico. ©Mellick

The first time Ross came to the house, having seen the painting Marion had bought at one of my one-person shows and having seen the watercolor of Pajaro Dunes that I'd sent her, he asked to see my art. To say I was reluctant is an understatement. When they first visited us here, I had not yet been to their house. However, I did know he was a collector and critic. After I had been to their townhouse for Marion's honorary doctorate, I was even more reluctant to share my work when Ross asked.

Ross and Marion relax in the sitting room at Jeanne and Jill's. ©Mellick

At first I showed him some large pastels, large watercolors. He did not mince words. Yes, I "had it." But I was wasting "it." I was preoccupied with "the thing" or "things." He declared in his intense, caring, unsparing baritone that somehow conveyed advocacy in each clearly enunciated word that I was wasting my sense of color on *externals*. He challenged me to pay attention to color. Itself! He wanted to see what might come out of *me*. I listened and recognized the truth and depth of his comment—and had not the slightest idea of how I might effect that. I valued highly his attention, intensity, honesty—and felt utterly unable to conceptualize that leap. I had already spent a month at a juried workshop with Nancy Graves[168] in Santa Fe and felt deconstructed without any attendant reconstruction of my vision or capacities. It would take years in the ripening for her words, criticisms and teaching to reach my comprehension and essence. However, having grown up with a Cornish-Russian musician mother who would not insult my father's or my work in the arts by being "nice," I welcomed and felt nourished by Ross's blunt, straight talk and challenges.

---

[168] Nancy Graves (1939–95) was an American artist of international renown. A prolific cross-disciplinary artist, Graves developed a body of drawings, watercolors, sculptures, paintings, prints, and set designs.

I took Ross and Marion to the Cantor Art Museum at Stanford. We went to the top floor, where the contemporary, modern and postmodern artists were installed. Sam Francis's work was featured. Ross was either silent, totally receptive and absorbed, or exclaiming sotto voce as though someone had given him a mild electric shock or a priceless gift. At some point he slipped away for a while.

When Ross and Marion left our house, he handed Jeanne and me something heavy in a paper bag, along with a letter in an envelope. We opened it after they left. He had bought us Sam Francis's volume *Saturated Blue* and handwritten us a two-page letter.

February 16, 2000

Dear Jill and Jeanne:

First off, congratulations on twenty-four years together in this lovely house, all the more lovely for the way you both have lived in it, carving out careers from parts of it and coming together at a centre with a garden, a fire, many pots and a dimensional glass table that in my imagination swings open beneath and closes again, giving, receiving, a pot perfectly placed where I detect swivel. It's a table I'm not entirely sure about, where I think it ends it curves away like a much gentler version of Niagara Falls. Certainly I would never sit on it, though, since I have never been at a loss for a place to sit (with extra comforts for the back), the urge to perch there has never surfaced (except perhaps now when it is fortunately absent except in my mind).

Now this small gift has, as Jill will at once perceive, its place of origin in the newly renovated glorious campus museum, the money for which (a fortune!) appears to have been supplied by the Cantors, whoever they are (though I can see who they have become). Its most immediate place of origin is a room full of Sam Francis, vaguely a Jungian, clearly a first-rate painter. Even more immediate, of course (I think "of course"), is <u>Coming Home to Myself</u>, a full-out version of what got going there.

Having settled this about <u>Saturated Blue</u>, I feel that I haven't fully fleshed Jeanne, left with the <u>Sopranos</u> while we went to the museum to return later than either of us intended, I not knowing ahead what I was in for and reluctant to leave. In truth, I experience Jeanne more solidly in the house than Jill, more substantially present in some very essential way if the delights of Sam Francis indulging in mandalas is to be fully, happily allowed. Had Jeanne not been there precisely where and how she was, Sam Francis wouldn't be where he is, or where at least we found him. The word, I think, is balanced, and balance is what, for me, this house is finally about. The Sam Francis is equally for you both.

Much love,

Ross and Marion XX

∞

November 19/2000

Dearest Jill,

How delightful to hold you even for a moment! So thankful to see you looking so beautiful, so well, so fresh and vital with your new eyelids.[169] May your healing continue in every part of your dear body.

---

[169] To preserve eyesight, JM had ptosis surgery on both eyes; it was necessitated by severe Ehlers Danlos Syndrome.

Marion, Jill, and Povi, the miniature schnauzer, in the sitting room at Mellick/Shutes residence. ©Jeanne Shutes

Marion holds Povi, the miniature schnauzer, in the Shutes/Mellick sitting room in spring. ©Mellick

I was so happy to be with you and Jeanne even for such a short time. Magical memory with all the gold and burgundy of autumn so vibrant. And we three so happy to be together in the beloved familiar space.

A big eye opener on the way to San Fran. My image of Silicon Valley has always been Steinbeck's Salinas Valley (I now realize). We drove through there once & I assumed the young rich had taken over that whole area, renamed it slightly and were making their fortunes there. My driver drove me through Silicon Valley, explained Silicon and suddenly I saw a very different world of images that has been coming to me in the workshops. Brave new world!!!

Here is Tami's number[170]. . . .

---

[170] Tami Simon, founder of Sounds True.

She is a great woman to work with—solid, spiritually committed, sharp in her insights and relationship to the collective.

Darling Jill, I do love you. Marion.

Love to Jeanne.

Now off to the wharf ...

∞

July 10/01

Dearest Jill,

This is so lovely, it reminds me of you. I am missing you these days so will just drop in for a moment. I do hope you and Jeanne are well and all is going well. Ross and I are having age problems with the heat—hard to breathe, heavy feeling in chest, extreme fatigue. The air conditioner doesn't change that heaviness. For the first time Ross is recognizing his age and feeling sad that he cannot keep up with his friends—all of them are in their forties. A new phase!!

Basically we are both catching up on much-needed rest. We plan to go to England August 15 until the end of September. London is our spiritual home on this earth, so we look forward. Do hope all thrives for you, dear Jill.

I reread your book of poems the other day. I was moved to tears. Such a beautiful forever gift.

Always

Marion

∞

Aug 10/01

Dearest Jill,

Thank you for your beautiful <u>The Art of Dreaming</u>.[171] It is a very inviting book to look at and to feel. Congratulations. I hope you are happy with it. I know what it is to have to reshape a concept to the point where you really wonder if there is anything of the original left and, indeed, if there is any point in creating this new thing. Not a good feeling! Anyway, I'm sure it will find its place in the world.[172]

Thank you for taking the time to talk to me about the move[173] that is on … I've had several talks . . . to try to clarify. I think with some success. . . . This is being set up . . . for the future. I am finished in two years— that is clear. Anyway, this is not your problem, Jill. I do thank you for alerting me …. I've dealt with it as honestly as I can. I thank you also for talking to me about foundations. I'll phone . . . next week if I can.

As you know, I'm pulling myself, Ross and the house together for our departure next Wednesday. I tell you it is a big job in the heat. Anyway, my love to you and Jeanne. All these beans[174] are full of new life for you— Marion.

---

[171] MW wrote the foreword to *The Art of Dreaming*.
[172] JM's first book on dreams, *The Natural Artistry of Dreams*, underwent significant revisions for a new edition with a new name, *The Art of Dreaming*. The first included many quotations from cross-disciplinary writers; these were left out of the second, and the materials were revised for a new format.
[173] MW is referring to logistical changes to the BodySoul entity as it became established as a foundation.
[174] Letter written on a card with a photograph of buffalo beans from Kew Gardens shown on the front.

∞

August, 02

Darling Marion—

This carries retrospective thoughts for the 15th (I hope the nutritionist was helpful).

You, dearest one, are in my heart daily. I miss the particular pleasures of just <u>being</u> together. What a strange summer of wounding and healing it has been.

I hope that the weeks to come bring you more and more strength in all ways.

For us to accept all the bright and shadowed dimensions of each other in the love we hold is a rare gift: I hold it quietly and rejoice that such a gift makes us family of the heart.

I love you in the sloughs of despond and on the mountain tops of delight—

Jill

∞

July 29/03

Dearest Jill,

I'm sending birthday wishes early because a heavy cloud hanging over my heart tells me Ross and I will be flying to England very soon and I want to honour your birth. I want to honour your life and our lives together.

Although we are not in as close communication as we once were, I always know you are there, and I know you hold me in your consciousness as I hold you. I need your clear thinking in my world and depend on it, trust it and phone when I need to or just want to.

I chose these buffalo beans for you because your dear white buffalo sits always on my desk and, in times like these, sits always in my heart. Did you know Kew Gardens, one of my heart centers like ShaSha, has a Millennium seed bank with seeds buried deep in vaults within the ground, that would survive nuclear disaster to Earth? They boast of seeds of every plant (known) on the planet and they are still collecting. So, dear Jill, I send you buffalo beans from the archetypal in Kew and in me, beings that will survive any blast and renew themselves here or elsewhere.

I'm fighting hard, loving hard to keep my dear cells from identifying with my darling brother[175] in his dying. Dearest Jill, "All is as God o'er rules," as you very well know.

Blessings on your day

Marion

∞

Aug 18/03

Dear Jill,

This is going to be a bittersweet letter. We just heard from Bruce that his four lower lumbars are full of cancer. So Ross and I are putting ourselves together to go to England. His spirit has been magnificent. [Space on page where image is printed.]

---

[175] Bruce Boa, an actor, lived in England

I just couldn't write all over that beauty. I think the portion of the picture with the wind inspiring the raw material is the part that should have been on <u>Pregnant Virgin</u>. And Primavera should have been on the (hopefully) new one. But life is as it is.

Dear Jill, I know you and Jeanne sent birthday flowers. Ross and I went away to the children's cottage on Friday so I asked the florist to send another bouquet the end of this week. No problem. Then she discovered she had two bouquets for me. So because Ross and I are now on our way to England, we will call for the flowers to be delivered when we return. I hope that is OK with you and Jeanne. I'll need them when I come home. Thank you both so very much. Yes. My 75th was a big day, but things have moved so quickly. I'm just moving with it.

I just remembered you were with us when we got word to come to Fraser. Dear Jill, you are always here.

Marion

∞

August 26/03

Dearest Jill,

Tonight I love the almost-not-there quality of this picture. Just a quick note to let you know Ross and I have not gone to England yet are still on alert. Today I was going through the beautiful book you once gave me on handsome paper, exquisite cover and exquisite poems touching right into the core of our relationship. Tiny details that spoke everything in our knowing of each other.

How very rich that knowing has been, dear Jill! Both of us see and hear what others either miss or dare not see or hear. Thank you again for the books, the poems and also for the serpent ring.[176] I have taken time this summer to clear things that I will never use again. It has given me space to find treasures that are forever treasures and bring them into everyday life.

Dearest love—

Marion

∞

August 28/03

Dearest Jill & Jeanne,

The flowers—my birthday flowers—came this morning. This last week of my glorious birthday month. As I told you, I delayed them because Ross and I thought we were on our way to England, but my dear brother Bruce begged us not to come (too close to a death sentence, I think) so we have kept in phone contact (several times a day) and prayer. Ross, too, is finishing his book, so it is a concentrated time and important that we are here. The flowers bless us—white roses, stephanotis—and white busy Lizzie—a delicate exquisite piece on my desk.

Many, many thanks, my Dear Ones—it is indeed a threshold—75 years.

To you both, much love—

Marion

---

[176] JM had given MW a silver serpent ring she bought in Athens. It resembled one of the snakes on Asklepios's staff.

∞

JM Notes

In September of 2005, Marion came to stay with us. *Jung Journal: Culture and Psyche* had indicated strong interest in publishing a conversation between Marion and me on a topic of our choice. On a phone call before she arrived, I mentioned the possibility to Marion, and she was open to it. I asked if there was something about which she'd like to converse. She immediately responded that she trusted me to choose. Between then and her arrival weeks later, I pondered about a possible topic and got nowhere fast. However, I noticed that the words "water" and occasionally "blue" kept bobbing up in my awareness.

When we were ready one afternoon, we sat across the kitchen table and talked with a recorder on. Our conversation is transcribed in the letter to Ross that follows. It was published verbatim.

∞

October 15, 2005

Dear Ross:

Greetings! As Marion and I arranged this morning,[177] here is a copy of the transcribed interview, which I am sending as a simple email so you don't have to worry about whether your computer can read my attachment. It will doubtless lose some formatting so please tell Marion not to worry about that. I'll send it double-spaced so that you can print it out double-spaced to make it easier for her to make addenda and corrigendum and deletions.

Marion said you were interested in the tiny prints of some of the new artwork. I'm glad. Now please don't take a lot of your precious writing

---

[177] During a phone call.

time to write to me about them; it is enough, for me, that you know how much you've inspired and influenced me (for better or for worse and for which I assume all the responsibility!).

Please ask Marion to add a couple of sentences that link her getting married into this narrative. And please ask her the origin of any quotations from Arnold, Coleridge, and so forth, so that I can be lazy and not look them up. I know most of them like the back of my hand but if she has them close by, that would be helpful!

With love

Jill

"TO CROSS THE GREAT WATER"[178]
A CONVERSATION WITH MARION WOODMAN AND JILL MELLICK
SEPTEMBER 25, 2005

MW: So, Jill, what had you thought we might talk about?

JM: Well, Marion, when you asked me to be the one to choose the topic a while ago, the words "water" and "blue" kept coming up.

MW: *Water*, Jill?

JM: Water! So, because the word kept coming, I mused about the role of water—within and without—in our lives, yours and mine. So many bodies of water we've each crossed. Many times. "It furthers one to cross the great waters."

MW: I've *never* looked at that! I just think it's *extraordinary* that you picked on *water*! Of course, we're both familiar with how important water is in the unconscious. But how important water has been and is to me

---

[178] A phrase used frequently throughout the *I Ching: Book of Changes*, as translated by Hellmut Wilhem, Richard Wilhelm, et al.

physically in my life! And at an imaginative level! And as a pointer to where I wanted to go and where I've lived and how I've behaved. ... "Water, water, everywhere...."[179] I've *never thought* about this, about how *many* of my decisions were based on water, on whether there was space to see the horizon—even choosing where I was going to speak. If there was water, a beach—particularly in the wintertime, of course—if I could walk out under a night sky with that "eternal note of sadness"[180] roaring in, the sound of the waves. How many decisions I have made on the basis of whether there was water!

I tell you that until this moment, I've never really thought about Port Stanley, the town beside Lake Erie where I was born, never thought about my roots as being in the lake. I lived there for the first seven years of my life and the water was part of my life. We were down by the lake almost every day and in the wintertime, we walked along the beach where it was icy but invigorating. And fish were a daily part of our diet. We just took it all for granted.

I had an experience there of nearly drowning. I was sitting on the floor of the lake when my father found me and brought me back in.

After my family left Port Stanley, we had a cottage up on the heights and the lake[181] was always present in the summertime.

Much later, before Ross and I moved into our present condominium, our house in London [Ontario], although not truly "by" the water, actually had water behind it.[182] Ross used to walk along beside it to go to the university.

JM: Bridging the worlds.

MW: Bridging. Always bridging.

---

[179] Samuel Coleridge, in "The Rime of the Ancient Mariner."
[180] Matthew Arnold, in "Dover Beach."
[181] Lake Erie.
[182] The Thames River, London, Ontario.

So many decisions I've made have been based on water! Workshops for one. Pajaro Dunes where we used to lead BodySoul Rhythms intensives for years. Ross and I would go out on the beach and walk for two or three hours and watch the pelicans and the tiny birds that run right at the edge of the water. Now we go to Grand Bend[183] for the workshops—which, as you know from our time there, is beside the water.

Then of course I think of our cottage on the island.

I think of sitting at the desk, the table, looking out on the vast expanse of Georgian Bay. Getting up in the morning at four o'clock, watching the sun rise, sitting there just watching the sun gradually take over the sky, gradually take over the water, watching the loons turning upside down in the water, the ducks. As I would sit there, I would go out of consciousness into my own depths and let ideas float up. Being in the waters of my own unconscious, writing from that place. Putting the pen down and just looking

Sunset from ShaSha. ©Mellick

View from ShaSha of other islands in Georgian Bay. ©Mellick

---

[183] Located on Lake Huron, Ontario.

at it all again. Feeling it all come through, just letting that happen, letting the space take over, writing from there, and going with those rhythms. No fear whatsoever.

JM: Fear of—

MW: —of dying into archetypal space where I'd get lost and never come back. Because that, as you know, can happen, sometimes, with a writer.

I always thought about the *depth* of Georgian Bay and the container of stone that was each of those islands. It was a primal world. When

Marion's rocking chair in "Miranda" on ShaSha. ©Mellick

The expanse and depth of Georgian Bay changes its moods constantly. ©Mellick

Spaces for contemplation abound on ShaSha. ©Mellick

Triangular rock and driftwood on ShaSha. ©Mellick

you went into the woods behind the cabin, you were in primal space. Somebody must have walked there some time but you couldn't feel it. You were with the pink rock—the oldest rock in the world, I've been told. We had a friend who could shape rock. He created "rooms" on the island. Each room had its own identity. So the cottage was just a tiny point on the edge.

But *my* joy was in contact with the water. I loved the space. No—nothing, nothing interfering with that space. And ... ahhh!

Marion pauses before descending to a bench and outlook on ShaSha. ©Mellick

JM: I remember your pointing out the "great beyond" to me, the horizon line beyond the islands. We'd sit out at the end. What did you call it? Prophet's Point?

MW: Mt. Sinai! It was indeed "prophet's point"! It was a huge rock, on the highest point of the island. We had to climb up to the top. Hours we'd spend out there, by ourselves and with guests. At night we'd go there and be with the stars. You *were* in an eternal world. When I say that, I just feel the wash that goes through me. It's as if my body is empty of everything except that eternal rhythm. Right through me.

Marion examines unique shapes of driftwood with a retreatant. ©Mellick

We had all the special points on the island named. But we knew we were only perched there for a moment in eternity—and perched we were! There was nothing you could really hang on to. The word "perched" became very meaningful when I had a fall that landed me on the rocks below and I wasn't able to get off the rock. Then you realize the precariousness of the eternal. You are just a little tiny marker.

JM: And the journey across to the island was almost as important as being there.[184]

MW: Yes, it was. I suppose water for me is a bridge. It was a forty-minute journey in the boat. It was a ritual. We were leaving land. Ross and I were not sailors. We were not used to living in the wild. We bought the island

---

[184] Water taxis ferry from Parry Sound to different islands, not just to ShaSha.

when we were well into middle age. So for us, the journey across was a passover into a very different world that demanded different energies from us. Very exciting! We were like two kids exploring a world we didn't really know or understand but found terribly exciting.

Then, for several years, I invited analyst and therapist friends like you to come and help me with those weeklong intensive retreats for five women each summer. Do you remember how the crossing over was a ritual for them? For all of us. How we would drive all those hours to Parry Sound? And sing! Then we would get in the boat and begin that journey out into an eternal space we had inherited for a few seconds in eternity.

We were cut off from the mainland and there we did our work, which was often a mystical, mysterious world.

View of nearby island from ShaSha, late afternoon. ©Mellick

We had to be extremely careful getting off the island because that's where accidents happened. Taking "the treasure" home became very important because, in the flurry of getting ready to leave, there was often an accident if there wasn't recognition that we were in a transitional space.

Walkway to a jetty on ShaSha. ©Mellick

Wooden planks bridge rocks and a jetty at ShaSha. © Mellick

JM: Speaking of taking the treasure home, I remember we had to take the garbage on the boat with us! For literal reasons, of course, because of bears and so on, but to "cross the great waters" *with* the garbage seemed important metaphorically as well. To have it contained and disposed of responsibly.

The last time we all were there, I somehow knew we wouldn't be back. And I found myself singing as the boat made its way through the passages. I often sang Leonard Cohen's song, "Suzanne"—"she shows you where to look amid the garbage and the flowers." I would look at the women, the garbage and the flowers we were bringing.

MW: We took the essence, the treasure, and we also took what was no longer needed, took it away from the island to dispose of in a meaningful way.

JM: Did you go swimming in the summers in Georgian Bay?

MW: Oh yes. I'm not a good enough swimmer to dare to go out with two hundred feet below me, so I had what I called my "Bumblebee," which was a gorgeous yellow life jacket. I used to be out three or four hours a day in my "Bumble." I could do all sorts of things with my legs and arms with no fear. I wouldn't have dared go without it but I loved the water. I never really learned to swim. I think I might have been a good swimmer if I'd dared to take the Bumble off.

JM: So you both loved the water and feared it.

MW: I feared it. Absolutely. Always feared it. Let's say I have immense respect for it. The kids[185] always used to laugh at my Bumble—but I was confidant with it and I could handle myself with all the swimming motions and with no fear of drowning. I'm sure the fear was from that early, almost fatal accident.

JM: You spoke earlier about how you would go out of consciousness into your own depths and let ideas float up to consciousness for your books.

---

[185] The children of MW's brother Fraser Boa.

Your actual description reminds me of how you described your experience of your father's bringing you up from sitting on the bottom of the lake.

MW: That is true.

JM: The conscious masculine energy—

MW: Yes!

JM: —that brought you up.

MW: That brought me up, and brought me back into … life.

JM: Did you see *The Piano*?[186]

MW: Yes, I did. Oh, yes, I did, Jill! I not only saw it; I lived it! [laughs] Even as I sit here right now, I can feel it in my body.

JM: I think of the moment when the woman is finally escaping her husband's cruelty in the small boat. Her beloved piano, her only voice, falls overboard. The rope attached to the piano wraps round her boot and pulls her, too, overboard. There is an excruciating moment when she seems to be choosing whether to free herself or drown. She chooses life. The film, to my eye, is a myth about redemption of the feminine spirit— and true of actual women, as well—and about the sacrifices we each have to make to live our own lives. She had refused to give in to his cruelty, survived and escaped—but then she, herself, alone, had to choose life. That moment from the film came to me when you said, in your near drowning, that you were "sitting" on the bottom of the lake.

MW: I had given up. I was about three or four. I remember splashing around in the water trying to stay up. I knew my father was on the shore but couldn't get my feet onto the bottom. I can remember the fear but I also remember just thinking, just sort of giving up…and relaxing

---

[186] *The Piano*, written and directed by Jane Campion, is set in the mid-19th century. The film focuses on a Scottish woman, an elective mute, who, after an arranged marriage to a frontiersman, travels with her piano to a remote part of New Zealand with her young daughter.

into… "I can't win on this one." I was partially unconscious when my father got me.

I think, you know, there's something in me that measures, even now, whether I can win on this one or I can't, by which I mean whether I can move into life at a new level or perhaps not move into life at all. It's strange to say that, Jill, but that's the way it is.

JM: We don't have to include that comment in the final version, you know. At this point, this is all written in water, not stone!

MW: Well, that's the way I handled the cancer. It's the way I always seem to handle it: I may live and I may not. I'll do everything I can but if this is my time, this is my time.

JM: The way you've spoken about this kind of thing with me before has sounded less like an experience of equanimity than it sounds to me today. When you've spoken about incidents like this before, you've even smiled a little when you've said, "I might give up."

MW: I smile when I say "I might give up"?

JM: It hasn't sounded before as though your feelings were simply "Oh well, if it's my time, it's my time." It has sounded as though there's another place for you, a pull from another, perhaps archetypal world. Even today, you were talking earlier about the risk of "dying into archetypal space where I'd get lost and never come back." It sounds as though it's a beautiful place for you.

MW: Yes … It is. I am not afraid of it. I know it's a highly controversial place. I know that it's very much related to the Death Mother. And…I know you could say, "Well, once you start feeling yourself hooked in there, it's pretty hard to pull yourself through and out on the other side. And it is easier to surrender to death, if you're in that space. But so far I haven't hit that space and I still really, really try to stay on the side of life. But I'm well acquainted with the other side, not only through my own experience but through my experience with dying people. I think there is a place where … the fear has gone. And something totally *other* is on the other side.

JM: And you had that experience during that moment as a child?

MW: Yes. I did. Now I do remember, too, the comfort of knowing that my father was there and that he would take care of it. But I was unconscious enough that I just let go.

JM: I think of another important body of water in your life: the Zürichsee. And, given what we were talking about just now, I remember your telling me about seeing a man jump off a bridge into the lake and surface, much later, near you—to your great relief.

MW: I was down at the lake every day. My apartment was five minutes from the lake. So I could go down any time I wanted—and did.

The man on the bridge had to do with the marriage. I had been studying in Zürich for several months, and Ross had come to visit me from Canada. It was a critical time of growth in our marriage. We were beside the water and saw a man hurl himself off the bridge. The man was living out, in Ross's eyes, Ross's fear and conviction that the marriage was over, life was over, everything was finished.

I didn't identify with the man but I sure identified with what was happening to Ross. And that ran my blood cold. Those were terrible moments for both of us. And the *relief* I felt when that man came out of the water very, very close to us! That was a huge passover for Ross. It was a whole new relationship coming out of the water. Ross needs to say what he wants to say about that, too.

Then we went out and bought ourselves, for our new relationship, an ancient candlestick, and we took it home and burned a candle in it. That was saying a new relationship is wanted, is lit ...

JM: Fire out of the water.

MW: Spirit.

JM: I smile when I remember you told yourself, on being shocked at the size of an audience shortly after you published *Addiction to Perfection*,

"Marion, you should *never* have left the church basement in Port Stanley!" You had traveled a long way from the church basement by the time you got to Zürich. And it didn't it really begin when you did what all we Canadians and Australians did in those decades: we had to cross the great waters to go to what we thought of as the center of culture: Britain, Europe?

MW: While I went to university and completed my English Honors degree,[187] my world had been Wordsworth, Coleridge, Byron, Keats, Shelley, the Brontë women, George Eliot, Jane Austen. Virginia Woolf—very big. And William Blake—oh my goodness. London London London. My world was London. For four years. And before that, too, in childhood—Beatrix Potter.... And I loved poetry.

I wanted to be in England and see it and live it through my own body. Besides, I wanted to get away from all the old images. I didn't want to be a minister's daughter any more. I didn't want to be a schoolteacher any more. I didn't want to have any projections on me at all.

JM: You'd been teaching already.

MW: Oh, yes. I couldn't possibly have gone to England right after the Honors degree. I mean, I was just a frightened little girl when I left university. I couldn't have dealt with going to a foreign country at all. So I went to Ontario College of Education for the yearlong course that led to my teaching certificate.

That was my first venture into the world. But when I attempted to speak, I lost my voice completely. Only because my lesson plans were so excellent was I allowed to stay! I both was and am profoundly introverted. I know I look extroverted but I definitely am an introvert. That's why water is so important to me: it's just utterly in my *being*.

---

[187] An Honors (Honours) degree is a graduate degree equivalent to an American M.A, required for any student who wishes to pursue a higher degree. It is offered in universities following the British academic tradition. Both MW and JM completed Honours degrees in English Language and Literature.

JM: Water doesn't talk back, either!

MW: It doesn't!

JM: It doesn't ask anything of you.

MW: It doesn't. I'm just … there.

But to come out into the world, especially as a teacher at the beginning. … The image of Aquarius, the water carrier, is so important in my world. It's that new vision and new hope, the Aquarian splitting off from what it is into what may be.

There were these Grade Thirteen—big, big guys where I was teaching. I was trying to teach Wordsworth's "Michael." It was a poem that struck my heart profoundly—about a boy on the farm who wants to leave and go to London. His parents loved him so much. He brought "light to the sun and music to the wind." Michael promises his father they will make the sheepfold and then he will go and come back. And he did not come back. And he did not write letters. Old Michael used to walk "and never lifted up a single stone."

Well, all these young men were interested in who was getting the highest mark in their national exams. I couldn't deal with this. My heart would just break when I was putting this sacred material out to these guys who just wrote down everything I said and felt nothing. So that was part of the problem and the other part was that I was shy, very shy.

I eventually did learn to get my voice *out*. I was training with a teacher for three weeks who said, "I want you to go home and sleep. And relax. Then when you're completely relaxed, come back here and speak. There's a guy putting coal in that window over there. You have to learn about putting coal down the chute into the cellar, Miss Boa. When you learn that, you'll be able to speak."

Well, I went home and did exercises on my belly, particularly my lower belly. I knew that's what he was talking about and sure enough, when I relaxed, I could speak.

So then I taught for two years to get my permanent certificate, and I took a job in Northern Ontario, as far away as I could possibly get from everything I knew. I had to find some kind of strength in myself that was *me*—that was not trying to please the university professors, not trying to please my parents, not pleasing anybody. So this opportunity for a job came up in August—most unusual—so to Timmins I went. And when you got in there in the wintertime, you didn't get out.

JM: Not by the water!

MW: Not by the water. But they had a magnificent dance floor—on springs. You could dance all night and not hurt your knees. I learned to dance up there and to throw away all the images I had always lived with of myself and find something else inside. In that sense, I did cross the great water at that point.

I was afraid I might give up and stay in Timmins, so I resigned in January and got my ticket for crossing the great waters in June.

JM: And the name of the ship?

MW: The *Homeric*.

JM: Of course! Was it a Greek shipping line?

M.W: No, English. I'll never forget pulling out from the station in London [Ontario] for Montreal. In those days, you used to hold on to colored papers.

JM: Streamers. I had the same thing when I left Australia after I finished *my* English Honors degree and teaching for a year.

MW: Well, nobody came down to Montreal, so when I left London, I was gone. I was in a wiped-out state. I was not conscious from London to Montreal.

J.M: I got on the train, left everyone I loved. I was almost passing out.

MW: I was too, Jill.

JM: The train was an overnight journey from Brisbane to the port in Sydney—

MW: That's right, an overnight. Mine was overnight, too.

JM: And then I got on the ship the next day. Everyone sent flowers to the cabin.

MW: *Exactly!*

JM: And then the streamers.

MW: And then the streamers. And when those streamers broke, I was scared to death and ... *happy* as I'd never been happy before! Crossing the great water was immense. I had no idea what I was going to. And things were pretty difficult, actually, when I first arrived—simply because of fear. And I got a job at the time, but then I realized that there was no holiday time. I was over there to see England, not to work in *The Times* newspaper office! Besides, the pay was very low. So I thought I'd better go for teaching—good holidays. So I got a job at the East End. That was crossing the great water again. It was a world I had no idea how to deal with. Several times I ended up crying in front of the class. And the little girls I was teaching would say, "Oh, I didn't mean to make you cry, Miss! I didn't mean to make you cry." I learned to love those kids so much. I found a new person in myself. And then I met a woman and we put a rucksack on our backs and we went youth hosteling through Europe for five months. I'm sure you did the same thing, didn't you?

JM: The same thing. As soon as we graduated and earned enough money to travel to Europe, we left, usually for a year. It was a kind of graduation journey, an initiation and a return to the cultural birthplace before we got serious. Some stayed, of course. We sailed for six weeks to London.

MW: Six weeks on a ship! Oh, how fine!

JM: No, Marion, six *long* weeks! We even had an extra day sailing in the Pacific because we crossed the dateline. We also, of course, left the Southern Hemisphere for the first time in our lives. Our ship was Greek. I learned Greek dancing. My Timmins!

MW: How marvelous.

JM: Yes and no. I found shipboard life confining. The ocean was endless but, as an introvert, I disliked not being able to really get away. Of course, I'm sure you did the same thing as we: bought a berth in a cabin for four below deck because it was cheap. Everyone smoked, even in the cabins!

MW: We had a cabin below deck. I didn't want to spend my money either. We were ten days crossing. I was glad to get off the boat. Except I had learned to make the boat a safe container.

JM: It was a Bumble!

MW: It was a Bumble! Exactly, Jill! It protected me. I'd be out on the back of that ship every night.

JM: I, too—especially across the Atlantic when we hit a Force 8 gale. The ship lost a stabilizer, so it would stay at an angle for minutes at a time. Some people died. We weren't supposed to go on deck; it was too dangerous. But I needed time alone and fresh air, so I'd sneak out to the stern. The ship would be in the bottom of a swell. All I could see between the two decks was a wall of water. No horizon line. Just a wall of ocean. I loved it.

MW: And the water was black and the stars were shining and I was just *nothing* between stars and sea. I loved that feeling of going through eternal space.

JM: A *between* space. We were each between countries, between cultures, between selves, between sea and the sky.

MW: I was between everything. And no projections to hold me back. I was simply who I was in that body on the back of that ship. Of course, there was always someone who came along to talk, but neither of us was putting anything on. It was just stars and ocean.

That crossing time was essential. I went back and forth across the Atlantic in a ship three times during those years. I hated the airplane the first time I took it across to England. I profoundly resented … well, not being able to dance, for one thing—the ships had terrific music! Not getting to know people; not having the time to actually move inwardly from America to Europe.

JM: The ship gave us the time that the plane does not: to truly cross the great waters. In the plane, there's not much liminal time and space.

MW: No liminal space. And I live in liminal space a fair amount. I don't mind it—at all. I quite like liminal space! Because I *feel* partly in one world and partly in the other. I feel totally at home there.

It's like being a therapist or an analyst, Jill. You're in liminal space. And— you know this, of course, from your work as a therapist and your work with dreams, Jill—we're living with the archetypal world, which is the sea and the sky. As therapists, we're in that liminal space, hoping something will come through from the archetypal world. At the same time, we're trying to connect to the personal world of the dreamer. So I always think of working in my office as liminal space.

I used to have a daily ritual, if possible, of a long, hot bath. My back bothers me now so I don't do it. But I had all these lovely perfumes. And I would just lie in the water and dream what I was going to teach about, how I was going to teach it—and just let it come to me—it was in that bath that my body could completely relax and I wasn't even *in* my body. And all these ideas would come up through. And then I was speaking in various places and I would do the same thing—a long, hot bath. And I would just enjoy the total relaxation.

I also realize the damping down of my spirit because that's not available now.

The sea is very important in dreams, of course.

JM: In your dreams?

MW: I dream about water at least once a week. I dream of the sea. The new imagery comes up from the sea. Even my horses come up out of the sea. Mind you, they often have wings! But I think the sea in my dreams also has a lot to do with my own body. My body takes and releases water regularly. I have to have two sets of clothes of different sizes. It started when I went to Timmins, actually. I take on water particularly when I'm trying to bring something new in or having to hold, times when I'm really birthing something—like a pregnancy. Writing a book—I can put on around thirty pounds!

JM: Not from eating; from—

MW: —water. I just have had to accept that if I'm going to birth a book, I have to go through this period of taking on water. And I know it is not going to leave until the book is finished. And I find that ... upsetting, sometimes!

JM: To say the least!

MW: And I know now that is the way it is going to be.

JM: So it doesn't matter how you're sleeping or how you're eating or anything else external, it's purely a relationship between you and—

MW: —what's happening in my body. And so the dreams. ... It's like "The Ancient Mariner."[188] I feel I'm out there in a boat and the water snakes are all around me. I do have a lot of snake dreams: snakes coming out of water or being in water—the new life, the snake bite that puts you into new space. Like the chamber at Epidaurus.[189] I never used to know what all those images meant but they used to be in the dreams and I finally

---

[188] Samuel Coleridge, "The Rime of the Ancient Mariner."
[189] Epidaurus, on the Peloponessos in Greece, was an ancient complex of buildings dedicated to the healing god Asklepios. Each building was devoted to a different aspect of healing. The Tholos was a round marble building with an astronomically designed floor under which lived snakes. Those coming for healing to Epidaurus (the first known sanitorium) would spend a night or nights sleeping on benches around its walls until they had a healing dream.

figured out what they were about. Birth, new vision comes through the water, both inwardly and outwardly. And I certainly have always wanted to die beside water.

JM: Do I remember that water played a role in your decision to stop teaching and go to Zürich? Is that too personal to talk about here?

MW: Well ... well, there comes a time in life when you speak the truth. And I don't want to be too personal but let's just look at it. I'll tell you. The truth is that when I lost 100 pounds through anorexia, the water came on. And I thought God had really betrayed me. And my anger was limitless. I would step on the scales and I would have gained weight although I was not eating.

This was after I came back from Europe after those first two years. While I was in Europe, I was *beautifully* thin. I don't think the thinness was just in my imagination.

JM: No. I've seen the photographs.

MW: Yes, I think it was fine and I felt perfectly fine. But as soon as I got back to Canada the old images came back on and I started to put on weight.

JM: What does that mean to you: "the old images came back on"?

MW: Being responsible for other people; not having my freedom any more to live in the moment and be who I wanted to be, who I WAS in any moment. Being a good girl, being an ideal schoolteacher.

JM: The perfect colonial young woman—in the collective. And there was a lot expected of us as colonial good girls.

MW: Colonial good girls and—

JM: —a tremendous push to conform—

MW: —and I think a whole lot of mother complex in it. You know, as a teacher, taking care of the children, making sure that they felt the understanding that they didn't feel they had from their own mothers.

JM: But this was different, clearly, for you, from how it was when you were teaching in England.

MW: England I couldn't. ... I wasn't close enough to the children. The world that they were coming out of, the Cockney world after the war, was so horrific, that I couldn't really relate to it. And so they would come and they would touch me and roll their fingers down my skin and there was a huge communication between us but I couldn't take responsibility for their psyches because I couldn't understand how they thought.

JM: To use the water analogy, you didn't immerse, you weren't drowning in their lives, whereas when you went back to Canada, you were immersed again.

MW: I felt imprisoned. The weight I was carrying was prison bars. I remember I used to hold my hands on the edge of the blackboard behind me and I would think, "If I can just hold on to this hard enough, I won't put my fist through that window." I felt it was a prison when I first came home. And I didn't sign a contract.

JM: Why *did* you come home? Why did you cross the great waters again?

MW: *Good* question! I sure wondered that when I found myself on the boat in Liverpool. I remember thinking I was saying goodbye to freedom. But I also knew that I had to reconnect with what I had left behind. I had led a totally free life there for two years but I also would sometimes come in from a dance having had a fabulous time and cry for two hours and not understand why. So I knew there was another whole dimension there I had to deal with and so long as I was having this kind of joy and living my "new life," the depths of my soul were—I was going to say that they weren't being touched but they were being touched because I was being profoundly influenced by the Australian writer

Charles Morgan, *The Fountain* and *The River Line*.[190] I think it was his. It was made into a play. And you see I was living in the theater. In those days, you got in for practically nothing to sit in the gods.[191] And most Canadians have never heard of him but I have French friends who adored him. And his whole interest was in finding out who you were. I remember one of them was about letting a man out of prison. Who was he when he was out of prison?

JM: So here you were holding on to the blackboard trying to figure out who you might be if you were out of prison. ... So there was something about needing to go home to complete something.

MW: To release whatever was still in prison, yes. And interestingly enough, living in London, Ontario, where there was no wide sea to look at, the water came inside instead of outside. It went up and down a bit and did steady itself. It was always my thermostat: when my fingers and legs started to swell, I knew there was something really wrong and I had to go to bed. And often it got to the point where I couldn't teach on Fridays. And the dear principal would say, "Look, if you need an extra day to rest, accept it and go home and come back on Monday morning." Which I did. But then I thought this can't go on and that's when I decided to try to go to Zürich.

JM: What did the medical people have to say?

MW: Couldn't explain it.

We could refer to it in terms of fear. I wanted to find out who was or what was inside that fear and what was freedom to live your own life. That's what sent me to India. Now I didn't go over any water there, but a bath in a hotel in India would give me the peace I needed to keeping going the next day.

---

[190] Charles Langbridge Morgan (1894–1958) was a playwright and novelist. His maternal grandparents had immigrated to Australia from England, and his parents were married in Australia. He himself was born in England, in Kent. As a writer, he enjoyed enormous popularity during his lifetime, particularly in France.
[191] The highest level of theater seats. It is a British-originated term used in Commonwealth countries and Britain.

I connected with Dr. Bennet in England when I was on one of those sabbaticals with Ross and that was the beginning of getting out of the social structure that I couldn't deal with. And never could. Never.

JM: You mean the collective—

MW: Yes.

JM: The colonial expectations of what you were supposed to be.

MW: As a schoolteacher, as a university department head's wife, entertaining and so on. And all of it would have been all right if I had found the person inside that, but I was still looking for her.

JM: Well, you had had her and then she had to go underground.

MW: She went underground. Jill, my weight went up and down according to whether I was living underground or on top of the ground. It fluctuated sometimes fifty pounds. I just accepted that as best I could. But then I went to Dr. B[192] and all the time I was in analysis, I was crossing the great water. And the weight went right down again. I was normal size.

JM: Both in Canada and in England during the summers and the sabbatical, you were holding the paradox of your two lives; you could have both. You didn't have to sacrifice one or the other.

MW: No! I didn't have to sacrifice one for the other. I was embracing both.

JM: And the water enabled you to do it.

MW: Yes. And the other thing was that I went to Central Drama School when I was in England during one sabbatical year so my wild side got expressed in my acting.

JM: You could try her out!

---

[192] E.A. Bennet was an English physician, Jungian analyst, and close friend of C.G. Jung.

MW: And I *did*!

JM: Acting was your Bumble.

MW: It was my Bumble. And it wasn't that I wanted to be crazy or do a whole lot of stupid unlived life stuff. I just wanted to. ... I found out at Central Drama School that I had an incredible sense of humor, which I had not known. I mean, I discovered a person whom I never knew in myself anywhere—and I sure liked her. She would say what she thought. And she had huge capacity for emotion—no, feeling. And I could bring that into my acting. And, in fact, at Central Drama School, they said, "Your timing is born in you and your sense of humor with an audience is born in you and we'll make a character actress of you." It was a huge temptation. This was before I was working with Dr. Bennet, in 1963, and Ross had a sabbatical every seven years. I tell you I loved it. And again, my weight went right down again. There was no dieting. I was so happy and my weight just dropped. I was finding this person that I'd never found. We were working with poetry and with Shakespeare. I was so happy with that life. But then the sabbatical was over. I came home and let the kids do the acting and I'd do the directing at the high school. But eventually even that collapsed. And that's when I had to give up teaching.

JM: And it was the water retention that did it.

MW: It was. I decided that, having been with Dr. Bennet for a year and then the three summers following that, when I was teaching.

I had a dream before I left Dr. Bennet: "Turn your face towards Jerusalem and do not turn back." And I knew that Jerusalem was Zürich. So did he. That was really crossing the great waters: to go to Zürich and leave the safety of my home and teaching. I truly loved teaching school—I loved it and I didn't want to leave it but I had that dream in the June that I left Dr. Bennet. I said to God-—I know you're not supposed to make bargains— but I believed that the dream was divine and so I said, "If you give me two years, I will make enough money to go to Zürich. I'm not going to ask my husband for money because the whole thing might end in divorce!"

Well, having been in analysis with Dr. Bennet in England in the summer, I had a new sense of being. I had such a marvelous time teaching the next year. I didn't really want to go to Zürich any more and I didn't really want any more analysis either. I was happy. But in January of that year came the dream again, "Turn your face towards Jerusalem and do not turn back," and I thought, "I'm going to have to stay with my vow."

But I didn't do that. I handed in my resignation—and the kids cried. I handed it in at the end of January. By this time they were totally in love with creative drama. Anyway, I quietly walked toward May 31st, and that day the principal walked down the stairs and said, "Marion, shall I throw your resignation in the waste basket because we all know you're not going to leave." And I said to myself, Abraham didn't have to sacrifice Isaac. He was willing to do it but he didn't have to do it. Thank you Sophia! And I went home happy happy happy. This was the last day to hand in my resignation and I didn't have to do it. God was merciful after all. Anyway, that night, I went home to Ross and he was delighted.

I woke up at three o'clock and my fingers were like bear claws. Just absolutely swollen stiff and three times the size they should be. By 5 o'clock my feet were in the same condition. And I knew what was wrong: crossing the great waters. And I knew that I had to go.

JM: You had become a body of water.

MW: A body of water. So we went to the hospital and on the way Ross said, "Marion, I think we'd better call Bob[193] and tell him you won't come back." And I said "You'd better" and he did and we both knew it wasn't going to work our way.

JM: As Jung said, "What is not brought to consciousness comes to us as fate."

MW: I knew that my destiny was that direction to Zürich and there was no getting out of it. And I see, looking back, that each of these turning

---

[193] The principal of the school where Marion was teaching.

points was destiny: "You are going to go that way whether you want to or not." As dear old Dr. Bennet used to say, "You can either go like a pig squealing to the slaughter or you can muster as much grace and majesty as you can and *walk*." I was in the hospital for three days. I did go back to say goodbye to the kids and went to the last Morning Assembly. But I never did get back to the classroom.

No it was done, finished. Finished.

I mean I cannot *help* but accept destiny. Not once in my life. Ever. And I've hit these points in my life repeatedly. And every time, there is a crossing of the great water. It's immense to leave "this" behind and venture out into the totally unknown world.

JM: I'm not sure you've always had a Bumble!

MW: No, I haven't. I had no Bumble in India. That's for sure! I was in terror all the time. I was alone. I didn't understand what was happening to me and no way to get through on a telephone, no way to even mail a letter because I didn't understand that it had to be franked before I put it in the slot! So I was just sinking deeper and deeper into the great water of my imagination. Real sinking. And I thought I was just ... drowning.

JM: What do *you* mean by the "water of your imagination"? Not some unconscious sea of humanity in India but the water of your own imagination ... drowning.

MW: Well, not understanding that when I went out onto the street that I wasn't in the presence of evil or in danger of being killed necessarily but my imagination would think that the man who came up to me in the street and said that he knew that the Africans were the best lovers in the world but that Indians were second and I was supposed to understand that and ... or you know, seeing somebody, particularly a little child—and the faces of those children were so haunted—and they would take hold of my skirt and hold onto it all day so that the dress was all torn in the seams—and I would think "What am I supposed to do with this child?" It was just one unknown incident after another. Totally unprepared.

So my imagination would take hold of that fact and try to give me. ... Talk about a dream! A dream coming out of the sea! I was living a dream.

JM: So was it innocence? This fellow wants to take you off somewhere and—

MW: Oh no! I knew he was soliciting me. But how to get rid of him? Dare I go out on the street again? Is he going to be out on the street again? And feeling my body fill up with whatever it is you fill up with when you're terrified. At the same time, knowing I had to venture out. I couldn't stay in the hotel room all the time. I had to venture out.

Robert Johnson said, "The reason you got along in India, Marion, was because Indians are intuitives. And they recognized your intuition."

When I was at the end of my rope, some intuitive person would take hold of me and say, "I will take care of you. I will take care of you." And my intuition would say, "Great. You can trust this person. You can go with this person."

JM: Like your father plucking you from the bottom of the ocean?

MW: Yes. In that way.

JM: You knew he was there—that somehow you could trust somebody.

MW: I knew ... I had the sense that this person was trustworthy. I remember one day this woman came up to me out of midair and said, "Are you alone?" And the word "alone" hit me so hard that I collapsed in the street and I woke up in her hotel. She just took this bag of bones with her. An extraordinary thing to do. She got me into a cab and took me to her hotel and said "Look, I ..." She was American. And she said, "I will take you to the airport. You are in culture shock and you are not going to live if you stay here. *Go home now.* And I will pay the bill for it so you won't have to deal with this any longer." And I said, "That would be defeat and if I am defeated, I will have to come back. And I cannot go home. So let me go." So I said goodbye to her and thanked her very much and went back to my hotel room and got myself together again in a slightly different way.

But Jill, India was ... my life was before India and after India. I had to let go. I couldn't control *anything*. And my nature was to control. And up to that point in my life, I was trying to be in control. Even though I might look as though I was not.

JM: Looking as though you were spontaneous, but not.

MW: But in India I had to say there's nothing I can do. I will take what comes. And what came was incredible. You know my story about the Black Madonna? And the story about being taken off as the goddess in that sacred celebration?

What came was *knowing* that there was a presence taking care of me. I call her Sophia, that Black Madonna energy, that earth, that instinctual body that can care for you. And does care for you, whether you know it or not. And surrendering to destiny. And so that's why it was before India and after India.

Dear old Dr. Bennet—you know, every time I was over there, he would say, "Why did you go to India?" [laughs]

And finally I said to him, "You ask me that question every time I come. You must be getting senile!"

And he said, "I know, but you always give me a different answer! Think about that."

So India was crossing over to the feminine side of life and saying, "I will take what comes."

And that's also what got me to Zürich. And the waters always come up, as it were. And in my dreams, carried me to where I was going. To the next. And Zürich.

JM: The lake, the Zürichsee.

MW: The lake. Yes, the lake. I got myself beside the lake. I walked beside the lake every day, morning and night. And I loved the air of the lake, for one thing—as I love the air beside the ocean. But it's the freedom. There's nobody, nothing, no *thing* on one side of you. As you walk. And I guess it's, as I think about it, I guess it's the eternal on one side and the human on the other.

JM: In Australia, when I was growing up,[194] I used to walk on those long, unpeopled, soft, soft, white beaches. I would walk on the line where the wet and dry met—right along that line.

MW: That's where I walked, too.

JM: I *loved* to do that.

MW: That's *exactly* where I walked.

JM: I'm fascinated by "the space between." It's what I've painted so often. It's the line.

MW: It's the *line*!

JM: Again and again, I paint the line—where wet meets dry, where the sky meets sea or land. I never even noticed that was what I was doing until a curator of a group show I was in pointed out to me that it was in every painting! It was so central to me that I couldn't see it!

MW: I can remember at Pajaro Dunes the little birds danced right on the edge where the tide comes in and goes out. That's where I walk, *just* at that line. And feel caged in without it. When I didn't get the apartment by the sea in Toronto, I chose one on the seventeenth floor. So the sky became my sea.

JM: One way or the other, you needed space.

MW: Space and silence.

JM: Space inside you.

---

[194] In Southern Queensland in Australia, particularly on the Gold Coast and Stradbroke Island.

Pajaro Dunes Walk. Pastel on paper, 24 x 18. Jill Mellick. ©Mellick

MW: And silence. The immensity of that silence of the sky and the sea. I can't write without that kind of space. I don't do well. Much as I love my garden and much as I have fire, a lot of fire, in my dreams it's the water that is my ...

JM: Inspiration?

MW: Inspiration. It's what gives me space.

JM: For some reason, I find myself inwardly rewriting the Twenty-third Psalm as you're talking. Rewriting it using "space" as the beneficent other. "[Space] is my shepherd.... [It] leadeth me beside the still waters. [It] restoreth my soul..."

MW: Well, I say the Twenty-third Psalm about three times a day! Or sing it! I sing it. Always when I used to go out in the boat, when we used to ride the boat into Parry Sound, I would sit in the back of the boat and sing, "Under the hills around do I lift up my longing eyes"[195] or the

---

[195] John Campbell, Duke of Argyll, wrote the words to this hymn in 1877, based on Psalm 121.

Twenty-third Psalm. My two favorite hymns, which I sang as hard as I could all the way back!

I guess I feel "caged, cribbed, [and] confined,"[196] like Macbeth, when I cannot feel that space on at least one side of me.

JM: I have to live on a coast. My mother spent her pregnancy swimming in the Pacific Ocean daily;[197] I grew up by water; we spent every vacation at the beach.

MW: While I wasn't born on a coast, I was born on a lake. But it still turns out to be—

JM: —the eternal on one side and earth on the other.

MW: And without that, I ... I feel the same thing about my apartment in Toronto now. I really can't justify having it because I don't work there very much.

But to lose that sky? Is that the end of my writing? Hmm. Is that the end of my freedom? It's a very real question. It's not giving up the apartment that's the problem; it's giving up sky. That is my space.

JM: That is your creative space.

MW: That is my creative space.

JM: You *must* have felt the same thing about ShaSha.

MW: Oh yes! Looking out at that water, with the loons in the morning. ... That was where *Pregnant Virgin*[198] was born. And several others, too.

---

[196] William Shakespeare, *Macbeth*, Act III, Scene 4.
[197] JM's grandparents had a cottage, "Samarkand," right on the beach at the Gold Coast, south of Brisbane in southern Queensland. Vacations were spent there or on Stradbroke Island.
[198] Marion Woodman, *The Pregnant Virgin* (Inner City Books, 1985).

Well. I wonder how we're going to bring this conversation all together, to end it!

JM: Well ... for some reason, I want ... I don't know why but—I've trusted my intuition with this whole venture. I'm seeing a baptismal font.

MW: Oh, I had a great dream about the baptismal font once. Did I ever tell you?

JM: No. But I keep seeing a baptismal font and the father, your father. And your growing up with that baptismal water being part of your life. ... Perhaps it was because of the dream you're mentioning that I'm asking now about it.

MW: One of the last dreams I had in analysis.

JM: With Dr. Bennet or in Zürich?

MW: With Dr. Bennet. The world that I had with Dr. Bennet was totally different from the world I had in Zürich. ... It was my last analytic session with Dr. Bennet.

I was in my father's church in Forrest. It was the last church before I left home. I was in the front of the church and I all of a sudden had a *terrific* desire to run on the top of the pews. So I went out of the pulpit in great glee, jumped up on the pew, and ran the length of the church. The baptismal font was at the back of the church. I ran the length of the church on the top of the pews, an impossible thing to do but anyway, I *did* it in the dream, turned a *somersault* through the baptismal font, and landed in an old feather tick,[199] and it was a particular color of blue. And I knew I was *home.*

My interpretation of it was that I had left the church, free. And that in finding that freedom, I turned everything upside down in the baptismal font. The baptismal font still had meaning for me but it was ... *most*

---

[199] A feather tick is akin to a duvet or eiderdown, filled with feathers and held together by tightly woven fabric.

unconventional to turn a somersault and to land on this other side. But I was free.

JM: It furthered you to cross the great waters of the baptismal font.

MW: That's right. And crossing the great waters of the font gave me the strength to go free.[200]

∞

Easter Sunday '06

Dearest Jill,

The Angel of the resurrection is sounding loud in my soul this morning. Angel of Death and Life. Two years ago today my brother Bruce died; today the daffodils from our garden bloom on my desk. Spring is laboring to be born. Ross and I both had vicious flu picked up on the plane returning from England. We're both recognizing a new phase of life. New enough that I am giving up my apartment in Toronto—a huge decision because it has always been my place of writing. But I really have to close life down a little and those journeys alone are no longer safe for me. My left leg has a tendency to freeze and I cannot move when that happens. Radiation eventually catches up. Still, Life is good, even radiant.

Dearest love to you both—

Marion

---

[200] JM transcribed this conversation while flying over the Pacific to Kaua`i, a bridging place between her natal home in Australia and her Californian home. The next day she phoned MW in London, Ontario, and described the view of the Pacific. After she hung up, she noticed a guest had left in the kitchen a can of "Bumble Bee" tuna "In Water."

∞

Sept 30/06

Dearest Jill,

I didn't forget your birthday. Life has gone over the top of one a bit. I had a cataract operation, but glorious as color and line are for me now—truly I feel like a child waking up to a Brave New World, but I am seeing two Brave New Worlds. Very confounding!

Even as I look at this little bird and rejoice in its beauty, I burst into tears. Maybe my double sight is as much spiritual as physical. Our government is about to perform a genetic holocaust on our land and they may well do it. Alberta is already tearing their province apart from North to South to send it across the southern border. Each province has its own choice. It is heart-rending to see how power, corporation, money destroy. Our Prime Minister adores Bush. Enough, enough.

This is a totally dark day for me. I emptied my Toronto apartment yesterday. That is hard to accept but I can no longer go alone—and that was its purpose. Anyway, I do hope your new year brings you joy and whatever you need to fulfill your life at this point. Ross and I are in basic good health as I hope you and Jeanne are.

Blessings of your new year,

Love,

Marion

∞

JM Notes

October, 2006

Marion's and my next meeting in Palo Alto was thwarted.

Through a circuitous and, in the end, unrelated series of events, I underwent a series of tests.

The following Tuesday, three patients in a row cancelled—the first time in years we had time free during the work week. Jeanne and I drove to the de Young Museum to enjoy the hours between commitments. I parked underground. At that moment, my mobile rang. My primary care physician told me I had an aneurysm and that the neurosurgery department at Stanford would be in touch soon.

Seeing no reason to miss our few hours in the city, we walked over to the de Young. I must have been on more heightened alert than I realized; I remember the Ruth Asawa hanging in the stairwell, many of the Gee's Bend quilts, and ascending the Hamon observation tower. When we were wandering around the tower with its uninterrupted view of San Francisco, my mobile rang again. An Irish-American surgeon confirmed I had "a little balloon" and needed to come for further tests—as soon as possible. I forgave him his misplaced, if kind, euphemism, told Jeanne, and we continued our tour. Why waste a good outing?

I met Head of Neurosurgery at Stanford, Gary Steinberg, M.D., his handsome, Swiss, visiting Fellow, and his nurse. Jeanne took excellent notes as always. The surgeon slapped up images on a plate and showed me where the large, as yet unruptured aneurysm and a smaller mirror aneurysm were. Surgery was to be in a week. They were going to operate on the larger one only, the risk-benefit ratio of surgery for the smaller, resulting in wait-and-see. His parting words were "Walk carefully between now and then."

What ensued is engraved in me but mainly irrelevant here other than one non-event. I arrived at the hospital at 5 a.m. on Halloween to be met by skeletons and ghosts. Hours of surgery later, I spent days in ICU, then days on the neurosurgery ward. Marion planned to come down to Palo Alto from San Francisco to be with me the day I came home. However, I was taken back to the ER within hours, sent home yet again, overmedicated, then taken by ambulance a second time directly to a neurosurgery room. Marion's and my time together, which would have been so welcome, was not to be.

∞

February 3, 2007

Dearest Marion,

Uncanny! Your letter[201] to me arrived the *day* I left a message at your home. Patty gave me your mobile number in Santa Barbara but then I received your letter saying you dislike using a mobile so I'm writing.

I am so happy for you both that you are at Pacifica and off to Hawai'i! My beloved Hawai'i (It was on Kaua'i where I painted the watercolours for *Coming Home to Myself.*) Enjoy, enjoy, soak it in, dear heart. You deserve it, need it. I wish we could be together by the water as we were at Pajaro, Asilomar, ShaSha. So many years in each other's hearts.

I was sad but not surprised to hear that your energies sometimes do not match what you would want. You ask much of that dear body of yours. I stand amazed. However, you know better than anyone what nourishes you. I myself received flack from doctors and friends when I returned to my therapy office in December two weeks after the brain surgery. But it was part of my *own* healing to return to a vocation I love.

---

[201] This letter is missing.

I can't distill the last three months. I believe we spoke once after I missed seeing you the day you were coming to see me but I was rehospitalised. I don't remember well. November is a long parenthesis in eternity, at once a living hell and graced beyond description. Those endless days hovering between realities changed my soul's experience forever. I lived 30 years of inner work in 30 days. I shall be digesting them forever. Brain surgery is the fastest way *I've* encountered to pure soul! The suffering cuts away all except the bright light of pure consciousness and the pulsing of Self. Our white buffalo[202] has been with me every day. I'm returning him to you through Patty.[203] I'm loath to give him up but he wants to go home. I hope I shan't need him again soon! Thanks, thanks.

I can't remember if I told you: I discovered that large brain aneurysm through synchronicity, intuition and medical self-advocacy (strange to use it for me this time—and yes, Bob Mindelzun played a part!). I'd had odd symptoms last May for which I sought medical counsel. The docs did tests and gave me a rare diagnosis. I did research, fell upon and sent my tests to a Harvard lab that was doing research on it. Thought I could help by being a participant. They said I was misdiagnosed. This led to more tests at Stanford. The neurologist threw in an extra, unrelated test that just *happened* to show the aneurysm. The *original* symptoms turned out to be nothing significant and unrelated to the aneurysm (which was completely asymptomatic).

I've traveled so far, Marion—down, up, away, in. So much learnt and still being learnt—about synchronicity, intuition, trust, community, connection; about politics, power, gender bias, disenfranchisement, loss of identity, dependence, privilege, our medical system, hierarchy; about being a small dot in a large field filled with love and eyeless fate; about "what supports you when you find that you cannot support yourself,"[204] as Jung

[202] The Zuni buffalo fetish JM originally sent to MW went back and forth, depending on which of them needed it.

[203] Patty Flowers, administrator of MW's BodySoul Rhythms workshops. U.S.-Canada mail is strictly monitored; anything can be subject to customs, whether owned by the receiver, a gift or a purchase.

[204] Carl Jung: "The highest, most decisive experience is to be alone with one's own self. You must be alone to find out what supports you, when you find that you cannot support yourself. Only this experience can give you an indestructible foundation." *Psychology and Alchemy.*

said. Even with the finest personal and medical help I could have imagined, there were drastic foul-ups that caused me unnecessary and unspeakable suffering. I know now, too, what it is to offer one's rawness to strangers and to love them in the offering and their receiving. I'm absorbing shifts in every personal and professional relationship as well as in every belief. How a tissue-thin meeting with death can move things along. All has changed; nothing has; my life is more my own and less my own.

I've learnt, too, that I was living close to death for an unknown time. The aneurysm was not only big but complex, "nasty and about to rupture" (surgeon's words). We always live close to death, I know, but sometimes it's more in focus. Now the surgery is over, I am coming to terms with knowing I have that second, mirror aneurysm, currently small enough not to risk surgery; if it grows, however, it'll need brain surgery, too. The surgeon muttered, "You're too young for such fragile vessels." Thanks, doctor! So I'm not an ad for longevity!

My night nurse, Celestia, was half African American and half American Indian. A Black Madonna, beautiful, in her 30s, brilliant mind (went to MIT at 16), beautiful hands, long braids, three children she's home-schooling because she doesn't like the system—hence nursing at night. She sat still and present in the darkest hours of pain. She told me when we parted that it would take a season to heal. It has.

Now I find I'm ready in heart and soul (and body) to do a much deeper level of work with people. I haven't taken new referrals for a long time because my practice has been full. Some people have completed since my return to the office. I finally have hours free for the first time in a couple of years. I'm also opening up extra morning hours. Because I only want to work with people who truly want to do inner work, I am telling only you and a couple of professional friends. I'm keeping a low profile. I don't want a cascade of folk not willing to work at the depth I want to offer now.

So if you meet people you sense might be a good match, you're welcome to give out my name again. I'm open to phone consultation with those who could bring the dedication and containment needed for such a commitment. I do quite a lot of interstate and overseas consulting.

Strange how timing happens. After 17 years of silence, a month after my brain surgery I spent a day in December with my erstwhile fiancé (about whom I told you once). Although we went our separate ways, he in Australia, and I here, we walked arm in arm down a monochromatic "Japanese landscape" beach south of San Francisco—waves crashing, fog low to the sand, rain soaking us. We would not have been good life partners but have loved one another for forty years and do, still, just as much. We have stayed in each other's hearts and our relationship has grown and flourished, somehow, even though we have been apart all these years. There is no conflict in this for either of us, each long since committed to others (and in my case, as you know, including a soulmate). It just IS. It was an innocent, ethical, extraordinary day—no pretense, seduction, or acting on what is a truth held best, now, between souls— just open-hearted love and timelessness. My encounter with death and his own encounter left us a washed inner and outer beach on which we walked in timeless time for a few hours, free of history and context but faithful to our current lives, loves, and promises. Parting pulled at his heart and mine but was, in best Aussie fashion, understated.

It was good to talk with Patty yesterday. She was saying how very well the foundation is going, which is wonderful news. While I don't have money for donations at present, I have offered the foundation the remaining

Baker Beach, San Francisco, 2006. ©Mellick

original paintings from *Coming Home to Myself* for sale/auction/whatever to benefit them if they would like. I hope they might generate some funds and can't think of a nicer way to have these paintings' energy move on. Patty will bring, as I said, the buffalo to you and will also bring you a little book I put together during my recuperation; it has paintings and poems from my last show. I hope you enjoy it.

Dear Marion, I'm still here and so are you. I don't know all I've learnt or how long fate will give me to learn more, but I do know I love you. My love to dear Ross, too, with whom you are welcome to share this missal or not. Jeanne sends love. She, too, is restored and opening herself to new hours in her practice after our long, dark fall and winter, so spring is coming to our house.

J.

PS Don't respond, dear one. You are so good about letters but I want to be a friend who does *not* draw on your precious energies. I'm off to Australia from February 23 until March 9. (My mother is ill. My parents don't know and won't about the extent of my surgery. It would have worried them unduly and affected my mother's health. You and I can talk after that.)

With abiding love,

Jill

∞

February 3, 2007

Dear Patty,[205]

I was so pleased we could visit for a while earlier today. I have such a lovely sense of heartful, easy continuity with you these last twenty (!) years. I

---

[205] Patty Flowers, BodySoul Rhythms.

look forward to a walk on the beach. How nice that we can each be the excuse for the other to be at the beach and renewed by the ocean!

You were a dear friend to listen to part of my tale. I remember when someone told us about her cancer experience. At the time I could not imagine going through that with the peace of soul and heart she described. Now I know that peace is not something one brings to life but something life brings to one—as a grace. I feel blessed by the inner journey as well as extraordinary community love and support and the amazing good fortune to come through treacherous waters whole and richer. I look forward to sharing the gifts from this time in whatever ways my heart and soul now allow with those with whom I work. Perhaps one day I shall write about it; for now, it is enough that it can quietly inform my hours, both personal and professional.

During this time when I've not had energy to paint, I've been making art books. I want to send you one. I am going to send one along for you to give Marion, too, together with the little white bear she loaned me when I was ill. I'll send it all together. Marion is afraid to have me mail the bear over the border and you have given me a chance to return it. (It is one I originally gave to her during her first big surgery and which she mentions in *Bone*; we are currently sharing it between us when one of us needs healing energy.)

I look forward to receiving your materials from you. I have several people ready for . . . a BodySoul experience. . . .

At this point in my own journey, I want to commit my best vocational energy to people seriously interested in working with soul material. My recent initiation has brought me into a new cycle and I hope it can enrich what I bring to this work I love so much. . . .

So, until we meet on the beach, dear Patty, and thanking you in anticipation for your kindness in returning the little bear to Marion as well as taking the book down,

Love and blessings on your own continuing journey,

Jill

∞

February 19/07

Dearest Jill,

Happy Saint Valentine's Day to you. I know you will have gone and come back when you receive this, but before the MOMENT passes I want to say how thrilled, deeply thrilled, I was to receive your letter today telling me of your journey to a new part of yourself through the challenge of this illness. I understand exactly what you mean. I also understand why you have to make such radical changes in your practice. You have to radically shift position—or/and be shifted in your position and that opens a whole new world. I'm with you there. Cancer took me there. I hope things [go well] in Australia. My love and prayers are with you wherever you are.

Always,

Marion

∞

April 18/07[206]

Dearest Jill,

Yes, Hawaii was as sweet, feminine, fierce as any country I have ever loved. We had a wondrous time there traveling all over the big island[207] with our hosts in an excellent van. Its skies remain most with me. I always sat in the front seat and the sunsets seemed to be right inside the van, certainly inside me. Enjoy all the time you can there. It is unique.

---

[206] The letter from JM prior to this letter is missing.
[207] The Big Island is the island of Hawai'i itself.

I do understand "November is a long parenthesis in eternity—changed my soul's experience forever." I can understand "Brain surgery is the fastest way I've encountered to pure soul."[208] That all makes total sense to me, Jill, although I've not experienced brain surgery. I pray to God this second aneurysm will take a different course in your healing.

I know exactly how you feel about the shift in your practice. I will keep my eyes and heart open to someone ready to go to the depths you are offering. That is the only place which can now give you creative healing.

Wondrous what has happened between you and your old fiancé. What an incredible gift!

Thank you for the gift of your paintings to the foundation. Patty and I will find the right time and space to offer them.

Dear Jill, the little buffalo[209] is safely returned. He caused me considerable anxiety because I put him deep among my clothes when Patty returned him from you. My suitcase was lost on our return trip. For two weeks I called the airline every day. No sign of it. Finally they said, "No point in phoning any more. We'll settle for $600, $200 to you, about $400 towards your next trip." I was devastated because my little buffalo was in the case along with other treasures. One week after I had let it go (insofar as one can) an old man arrived here one night with my case. No idea where it had been but my guts came back into my body. Travelling is becoming impossible.

Much love to you, dearest Jill. I pray daily for your healing. The book you sent is utterly beautiful. Ross is in good shape in spite of a winter of profoundest work with the difference between "poetic faith" and "religious faith." It became an analysis of his life with Romanticism[210] and the Bahai

---

[208] This letter and many others from JM to MW are missing. MW is referring to one of them.
[209] MW is referring to the buffalo fetish that JM originally gave her during her cancer treatments. MW had sent it to JM after the craniotomy.
[210] Ross Woodman was a specialist in the Romantic poets in the English Department at the University of Western Ontario in London, Ontario. He was also a senior leader in the Baha'i faith in Canada.

faith. He is exhausted on every level, but the second book is now finished. My container is again clear.

Dearest love to you Jill and to Jeanne.

Marion

∞

May 3/07

Dearest Jill,

Life goes faster than I can go these days. I feel as if I am under the waves. A bit like these floating leaves suspended in water.[211] People see my creative days as numbered and I am constantly choosing between which film crews I will work with, which magazines etc. etc. Strange this should all happen when the physical energy that would once have loved it is basically gone.

Ross is suspended between finishing a new book and never giving his final voice to the world—it would be fascinating but dare one reveal the totality of the soul?

We are going to France next week. I will be working in Chartres Cathedral—huge gift! I've given myself over to the Black Madonna during the past four weeks—powerful! I do hope you and Jeanne are well, Jill— spring is new health.

Dearest love,

Marion

---

[211] On the front of the card was an image of floating leaves.

∞

5:30 AM
May 8/07

Dearest Jill,

In the midst of trying to get ready to go to Chartres, I came upon your "earth water sky."[212] I sat down and took time to read it and meditate on your pictures and the poetry that goes with each. I felt the anguish you felt, the questioning, the delight, the fear, the letting go—all in the words and the specific movement of clouds, water, color, earth—everything so beautifully and powerfully worded and painted. Truly, my heart was with yours every step of the way.

I know something of your experience first-hand and believe me, you measured it inch by anguished inch. Nothing too much—powerfully understated—the whole diurnal world included.

Thank you for sharing so deeply.

Love always,

Marion

∞

JM Notes

Many phone calls ensued between Marion and me from May to October of 2007, during which time Marion was hospitalized for cellulitis.

---

[212] MW is referring to the catalogue for a solo benefit art show JM held of pastel and watercolor landscapes. She printed and placed a short poem beside each painting; buyers took the poem when they purchased their artwork. The catalogue included a miniature of each painting together with its poem. Patty Flowers took the catalogue to MW.

∞

Oct 4/07

Dearest Jill,

I know my writing is off balance but I must drop you a note. The dire situation seems to have left my body. The staring white face has become more human, the eyes less terrified.

It was a ferocious time, Jill. I dreamed red—blood-red lobsters were tearing me to pieces (and each other) as my veins and arteries. The early morning the doctor came with four students and said, "I'm doing all in my power to save your life. Are you willing to do all in your power or shall I take you off life support?" Death as a reality had never occurred in this round to me (this was my second day in hospital). I just lay stunned.

Then I heard this almost child's voice filling the silence, "I'm in no hurry." Everyone laughed. She is the little beauty that says exactly what she means—flat out—courageous, slightly defiant, rambunctious (sp?). Absolutely honest. Everyone laughed. He said he'd leave the support connected but I had to realize my situation when blood poisoning takes over—cellulitis (sp?) it is now called. I'm just coming back from the door of Death now—by which I mean I feel as if I'm on the side of Life now, not alone in the dark corridor of Death. The paleness is becoming pink and I am able to walk with a walker down the hall here.

I've had to cancel all my work until at least after Christmas—and who knows when? I think God may be saying "Time for introversion, Marion" and that's OK too. Well, it has to be, but I do accept it if I know that it is now the direction. Ross has been magnificent. He took over the seminar I could not do.

Company came in and I am going to post this before anything else happens—the postbox outside the hospital.

I have to check in today.

Just to say Ross is finishing his book in the midst of all this. At 85 he has to keep going no matter what. And the book is a stunner.

Hope all is well with you, Jill, and your wonderful home and Jeanne. Autumn doesn't come here yet. First year I've ever seen green leaves at Thanksgiving (ours is this weekend).

Much love

Always,

Marion

∞

November 20/07

Dearest Jill,

Our weather has finally caught up with itself. This is a dark November day—raining, cold, threatening. Our golden and maroon leaves are literally just finished. Usually they are off the trees by mid or end of October. Because the sun is so low this time of year, I saw colour as I have never seen it before. Magnificent.

I'm sending you my antique ring of blossoms.[213] In this time of year, Bruce[214] and I used to shop in old London corners finding old women and old men selling wondrous old things like these blossoms. I loved those days—always before Christmas. I miss Bruce terribly this time of year. He adored the season and did everything possible for everyone he met to enjoy it too. Our home is already sporting some of his unique decorations.

Well, I'm getting stronger, but the hideous rash persists—glaring red. I have accepted that I must rest. Where that is going to end, I do not yet know. Ross and I have tickets to go to Pacifica in January, but I have no timetable of work this year. My nervous system is in a state of fear because

---

[213] On the top of the page, MW had placed a decal of a wreath of blossoms enclosing a spray of flowers in which the words "Purity" and "Ever true" were held.
[214] MW's younger brother.

I'm never sure whether I'm going to get across a room or not, or across an intersection, or what will happen if I do. Strange!!! Part of the problem now is the cold. It exacerbates the body fears. So it is, Jill.

This will be your first Christmas without your mother.[215] I'll be sending special thoughts your way. No doubt you will be going to your father.[216]

Ross had the cancer cells taken out of his nose last week. (I must throw this pen away). He is in good spirits but his poor face is still swollen and holding quite a few stitches. "Old age" is not for the weak of heart—that is for sure. He still goes on writing his book separating religious faith from poetic faith. In fact, he is putting himself through a very painful analysis. Having taught the poetry for a lifetime, he is looking at forty years in the classroom with the Bahai faith always in the background of his interpretation. The upheaval with the coming of Babrallah[217] in Persia was like the upheaval in Romanticism in Europe. Of course, that is the background for all that is going on there now. His courage and stamina are all magnificent. He seems to be a conduit. I'm doing my best to care for him. His 85th birthday is on Wednesday, November 28 (Blake's birthday).[218]

Dear Jill, my love and prayers are with you. Please give my love to Jeanne. I hope you have a splendid Christmas. I think too of your Dad whom I love from afar. And safe journeying if you are going home.

Our friendship is one of the precious things I continually give thanks for, especially at this time of year. Always.

Love

Marion

---

[215] JM flew to Australia in September 2007 to care for her mother during her two-week final hospitalization.
[216] MW did not recall that JM was bringing her father to California and that they would then go to Santa Fe, New Mexico, for Christmas. Two days after MW's letter, JM learned that she herself had advanced lobular breast cancer.
[217] Bahá'u'lláh (1817-92) was a Persian religious leader and founder of the Baha'i faith.
[218] William Blake, the visionary poet born on November 28, 1757, was one of the central figures of the Romantic movement, Ross Woodman's specialty.

∞

JM Notes

Marion found ways—often tough on her body—to continue teaching for some time. A diminution in written communication between Marion and me began around 2007. It was easier to call each other on the phone. Health matters occupied both of us. Marion's and my many telephone topics included finding ways around health limitations, and we each felt deep pain for the other's conditions.

Just as my body had instigated the circuitous path to the craniotomy, once again, it had been reporting a slight pain to my physician for four years. She assured me it was nothing and that any investigation would cost me out-of-pocket $4,000 to $5,000 and probably give a false positive. However, finally in November 2007, after sitting for two weeks with my mother as she died in September, my body simply said calmly, "Do it." The MRI and a biopsy showed advanced lobular cancer. I got my money back. I'd rather have been out of pocket. My father arrived for Christmas.

After my father flew home to Australia, I had surgery in January 2008 followed by six weeks of radiation. I was scheduled for chemotherapy. My body said, "No chemo." I was quietly disappointed in myself, in what I viewed as lack of courage; innumerable women had endured chemotherapy, and here I was balking.

However, I was and am graced with an oncologist[219] who listened and went out on a limb with a new genomics test soon to be FDA-approved for node-positive women. We were in our Kaua'i condominium taking a week's break before I began chemotherapy when my oncologist phoned me with the results. My cancer cell rate of growth fell at the lowest left end of the bell curve, indicating I would only lessen chance of recurrence by between two and four percent over ten years were I to undergo chemotherapy. Once again, my body was right. That night I bought a single Tahitian black pearl to thank my soul and bought shoes for the soles of the feet that had got me

[219] Juliet Kral, M.D.

this far. The sandals were elegant and understated from the front and outrageous from the side; they had dice for heels.

In June I started on long-term aromatase inhibitors. The year passed interminably slowly and at the speed of light.

∞

Dec 24/08

Dearest Jill,

The world is still asleep. Many parents will be lying in bed wondering what their children will do when they sneak down and see the decorated tree and presents and Santa has come and gone. Christmas was total magic for me as a child—even when I knew Santa didn't really have reindeer. It will be a quiet day here. Ross and I are alone for the first time. Ice and cold are treacherous this year—dreadful storms of snow covered with ice—dangerous so we are alone and it is good to enter into the great gift—seriously.

It has been a rough six months for me. The cellulitis (which I hoped would be clear within a year) after its first appearance [September 2007] has not cleared. It is very disabling—in fact it is at its worst a blood stream that is poisoned. Mine came from an eye infection [after surgery] which got into the bloodstream a year ago August. Anyway, I do go on although I am cutting back radically on speaking and teaching. I want to be with Ross and bring my own soul together.

Terrible weakness is the main symptom.

Ross is finishing his "last" book. I think it is his best. But what an anguish he has been through writing it. He and I are thinking of writing one together. That would be a real test of where life has taken us together. And not taken us together!!

I do hope you are well, Jill. I think of you daily and send up a prayer. Are you giving yourself to painting and creativity? I try to imagine what your home now looks like since your renovations. Beautiful Japanese!?

Our friendship is very important to me, Jill. My health and concern for Ross are making me much more introverted but I am here & I do love you & feel you close many times.

Love to Jeanne. Love to your dear self. The best in 09.

Marion

∞

January 25 (Sorry, Jill. I have to cut this.)[220]

Dear Jill,

I imagine you both having a joyous time in Hawaii. I love that island. There is no other like it in the world. Oh enjoy!

Our snowstorms are happening such as we have never experienced before. People could drive no farther—couldn't see, stopped, and literally froze to death in their cars—were not found until morning. A fierce winter here! We had our home relined with foam to hold the heat. It has worked, but our heating bill will be impressive. It was worth it.

Ross is writing another book—he up there, I down here. You know the layout of our apartment. We meet in the middle. Every day I love this place more.

Now I'm going to have trouble finding an envelope for this shape. This card was just to say hello out of this blizzard. We're here and safe. Much love to you both—

Marion

---

[220] MW had cut and used blank parts of a card that had been sent to her. She didn't note the year, but it would have been after 2012.

∞

JM Notes

After Marion's incorrect diagnosis of a cancer recurrence and her treatment for cellulitis, she endured another serious condition. At her request, I arranged a consultation for her at Stanford. She and Ross came together and stayed nearby as usual. The experience was traumatic for her. I realized what had happened when she described it. I had never encountered a teaching hospital before I was hospitalized at Stanford in 2006. I had felt (and was) objectified by drifts of bone-tired, brave, impartial young physicians staring not at me but at a set of symptoms while their particular medical God cross-questioned them and me, examined, and demonstrated. I intellectually understood that learning on the job has to start somewhere. I was just unprepared for it to start with me. I didn't learn until much later that I could legally (politely, if possible) refuse their presence if I was not up to being the Lesson of the Day—which I later did when situations were too unbearable to role-play being a model patient.

No one at Stanford Hospital told Marion she had the legal right to refuse to allow interns to be present. She would have used a word from a title of her books to describe her experience: "ravaged."

Surgery was eventually successfully undertaken in Canada; she loathed the radical changes required in routines and commitments. Her friend and mine, Eleanora Woloy, frequently flew up to be with her.

Much later, it took another inner illness to ruthlessly, slowly take her away from the work that was her passion and the participants she loved. Ross cared for her as long as he could until the journey required multiple hands.

Because I cannot reconstruct this period of our connection accurately without rifling through date books and journal entries—not possible with Stage IV cancer and a fused neck—I am moving to our next documented exchange. I stayed in touch with Eleanora, who was flying up frequently at Ross's request and who clued me in as to what was welcome and appropriate.

∞

Email, June 19, 2011

Dear Ross,

I think of you and Marion daily. So does Jeanne. I think as much about you as I do about Marion. Your role is exquisitely difficult, intimate, impossible, irreplaceable, chosen, and lonely.[221] At least this is what I imagine.

I leave for Australia for two weeks tonight. When I'm back, I'll send you the promised photographs of my new work. I'll send it separately some time in case it intrigues you. I send it because your words, long ago and so clearly enunciated in our sitting room, have resonated within ever since.

As you advised, I'm sending Marion postcards without reference to anything that might upset her. I stay in closer touch now with Eleanora,[222] who, I know, is in constant touch with you.

Loving greetings to you, dear Ross.

Jill

∞

Email, August 9, 2011

Dear Jill:

Here I am! Thank you for persisting. I am, well, in and out of it. I—dare I confess it—finished another book. It's my very strange way of remaining

---

[221] MW's health had worsened. Ross was caring for her at home.
[222] Eleanora Woloy, close friend of MW and Ross Woodman, also JM's close friend and a ShaSha facilitator.

sane. I find it on one level impossible to witness Marion in this condition without going in there with her and staying there with her. It seems to take all my intelligence and will to keep out. I am succeeding, but it is a strange mode of success. I think I am doing it for both of us. I am almost persuaded if she could read it she would say yes, that's what I think, that's the book I would like to write with you. But that's also my way of comforting myself, knowing that comfort is not what this, for either of us, is about. Not that I know what it's about. But I go on writing as if I did. So yes, you did get through on email, yes this is me replying, yes I do look forward to hearing from you, knowing or almost knowing that the one I need to hear from cannot respond except . . . .

Much love,

Ross

∞

Email, August 14, 2011

Dear Ross,

I'm glad we're in touch. I've always valued our link both distinct from and in relationship to Marion. It is a sad tipping of the scales of irony that our writing is only now active now that Marion is so ill.

Your role is impossible in this latest turn of the ruthless wheel. So much attention goes on the "patient;" so little on the carer. You are denied multiply, too, because one wants to share one's experience with the other whose illness is creating one's experience but one cannot. Too, there are more and more helpers around so less privacy. The rhythms are gone. At least that's what Jeanne and I have found at such times—although thus far we've been blessed with a return to (lesser) health.

Thank God for your writing: a steady lover who continues to meet you in your front study overlooking the park.

I've been in contact with Eleanora recently as well as with you; you each gave me a clear, sad picture of how things are with Marion. ...

So I'm sure you can imagine that I was taken off guard when I phoned you from Kaua'i about two weeks ago—just to speak with *you* to see how things were for *you*—and Marion answered.

You and Eleanora have advised me not to try to have a conversation with Marion ... because she is upset afterwards for hours; Eleanora also said she just says hello to Marion, who usually just hands the phone to you after a couple of sentences; she said she also sends short love notes with virtually no content so the latter is what I've been doing.

When Marion answered, I tried to do likewise. But Marion *initiated* a rather long ... conversation with me. Does this happen often, Ross? I made sure I made *no* reference to anything [upsetting] and *no* reference to things [that could lead to perilous waters by association]. In short, despite her talking, I was careful not to mention or respond with anything that might lead her down a path that would cause her (and therefore you) anxiety and distress later as you had described happens.

Having had Marion really let down at our house and our having seen each other through some pretty dark medical hours, I am not unaware of (at least, I like to think so) when Marion is having to put up a good front. During this recent phone call I couldn't hear that effort. She asked about Jeanne, my father, his remarriage, etc.

She said again she wanted to see me, that with me, unlike most, she doesn't have to keep up a front because we've been and have seen each other through so much medically. Her reiterating this was sad and tricky for me; as I told you I think, I'd promised her in a phone call early in the year (when she *sounded* fine and before I knew what was going on with her) that when I came to see cousins nearby (to make it sound lighter, more casual), I'd be happy to drop by for an hour if she liked but only if she felt fine about canceling last minute if she were not well enough that particular day. She was very happy about that and urged me to come because she said she felt free to be herself around me or just to sleep. However, I said all this before I knew how ill she is. Now, I know from you and Eleanora it could cause you and her anguish. . . . So in this phone call I just said I'd have to see and moved it away from the topic. Your wisdom, please? You're the one who's there, who knows how it really is.

Ross, I'm also curious and concerned about any fallout from my recent conversation with her—for you or for her—careful as I was to avoid anything other than flowers and neutral things from my end. Do you remember there being any? This was about two weeks ago.

I would like to know what the writing that is keeping you sane is focused on if you're inclined to tell me; otherwise, I shall be patient and wait for it to emerge in the publishing world.

For me, the long journey through the miasmic world of emergency brain surgery ('06), midwifing my mother in her last days (a joyful, numinous experience) in '07, my intuition leading to the diagnosis of advanced breast cancer ('07-'08), Jeanne's nearly dying twice, and . . . were enough to occupy my psyche for a couple of decades. However, I seem to be coming up for air now. My writing has changed and my art has changed (with your voice still reverberating in my head, challenging me). Later, I shall send you some small pictures of the new artwork. I think I am finally working from the inside out. It only took 63 years.

I shall be thinking of you as well as Marion on her birthday, look forward to hearing from you as and when the spirit takes and time and energy permit, and I send my love,

Jill

PS This email is scatty but I have technical oddities besieging me on the computer and wanted to get this off as soon as possible before something else goes wrong!

∞

August 15, 2011 (Marion's birthday)
From Marion to Jill

Jill, I just realized I won't be around at your birthday time,[223] so let me send your birthday greetings now. I'm sure you take stock at this time of year as I do.

In my treasures, I hold our relationship—unique. I had to really search for that word.

Your clarity, your vision, your presence in the moment is very important in my life. I have those three in me but I can become clouded by too much softness, indecision, fearful. Even the sound of your voice can constitute that [unfinished]

∞

Email, September 1, 2011

Dear Ross,

Now it's my turn to be uncertain. Did you receive my last email? No need to reply in detail if you're immersed, Ross. Just want to know that it reached you and a little uneasy in case it bothered you somehow. ...

I dreamt of Marion last weekend. She'd written a final book. I saw a page: it contained an abstract. Bold, brushwork gesture in black sumi-e ink, done with broad brush, quickly, brushwork flying off the page with certainty—like Kazuo Tanahashi's[224] contemporary work. Beside it were

---

[223] JM's birthday is August 29.
[224] Kazuaki Tanahashi is a contemporary Japanese calligraphy and brush master (https://www.brushmind.net).

a few printed words by Marion related to the brushwork. They said something like "It is. Now" or "Just to be." The meaning behind the koan-like words was "All is now: just being."

(Just went online and looked up Tanahashi's recent work; right there on his gallery website was a painting entitled "Miracles of each moment.")

I'm sure the dream has much to offer me. I wonder, too, because I sometimes unconsciously pick up things in the larger field, whether it might not resonate with changes in Marion and their effect on you.

Loving greetings

Jill

∞

Email, September 14, 2011

Dear Jill:

Thank you for your powerful dream. I know you are getting ready for your new exhibition and if this dream is related to it—as I feel sure it must be—then it will be a very powerful show. Ideally, of course, each painting is the miracle of a moment and if you are drawing inspiration from Kazuo Tanahashi you are certainly where you need to be.

Jill, abstraction in its truest sense is now where life is bringing you. Do not in your painting waste any time turning back to representation. That is gone. What now remains waiting in you is the abstract, bold brushwork gesture in black sumi-e ink done with a broad brush, quickly, brush work flying off the page with certainty. Such a stroke is what Blake described as a "Pulsation of the Artery." In this "Pulsation" he explains "the Poet's Work is Done." All the great works of Eternity, he goes on, are "concievd" (Blake's spelling) in this "Pulsation." The danger lies in the gap between conception and execution.

Between them falls the Shadow. I just read your dream to Marion. She showed me her jewellery which she had just cleaned. "Were you talking to Jill?" she asked. Then she was gone. Was it her ghost? This is the way the days now unfold. . . .

Much love,

Ross

∞

Email, September 9, 2011

Dear Ross,

How much your email to me conveys not only your care in receiving mine but the sanctuary in which your sanity takes refuge at present. These words from Blake are pulsing in *me* now. Thank you for them and for your reflections on what you sense is the inevitable path for Jill—abstraction. I've never been able to dive into abstraction before; but after aneurysm, cancer, mother's death, Jeanne's two close brushes with death and so forth, things are pared in the spirit. "Bone," Marion would call it.

My art has become verbs, not nouns ... wrapping, breaking, tearing, mending, placing, replacing, redeeming the discarded, burning, tying ... and informed by soul and intuition only and to which I am wordlessly accountable for better or for worse—mostly for worse but it's the experience that is important now, not the outcome.

Your thumbnail of Marion is unflinching in its starkness and love. The experience of holding the tension between the opposites never had anything on what you are doing at present. I simply cannot fathom what you must have to draw on in yourself.

There's no need to comment, unless the spirit moves you, on the art "things" I sent. Have no idea what to call them. Far better images of them will appear, together with quite a lot of the others, in the next issue of *Culture and Psyche* (the old *Jung Library Journal*), in which the conversation between Marion and me appeared and in which I've published a few articles and poetry. I'll send you a copy.

I am doing an inventory of my mother's 80-year music collection (shipped over!). I have (love this metaphor) a young Oberlin Conservatory student in my garage listing 600 pieces of music from all genres; as a break, he sits down and composes on my mother's high-end electronic piano with thousands of voices and orchestral sounds. It is out in the garage, too (the grand is in my studio in the back). So I come in from being away to a fury of creation sitting calmly on the piano bench. He is infused with the muse and knows his calling—at twenty-one. I'm a little in love with his presence and gifts … wonderful young animus figure in between semesters of brilliance.

Enough. You either need to be tending chaos in the rest of the house or in the act of creation in your study far more than reading my emails.

With love—and finding a quiet, unsought wellspring in our occasional connection,

Jill

∞

JM Notes

After floods in my native Australia at the end of 2010 and the tsunami in Japan in March of 2011, I dreamt of a no-ren[225] hanging in the ether. It was faded indigo; the ends of the two pieces of material that constituted the no-ren were in tatters from the weather. The image stayed with me. Eventually, I decided to see if it might prove a departure

---

[225] A no-ren is a thin curtain, divided vertically, marking the entrance and exit for everything from a noodle shop to an art gallery or a sacred area. Usually, it is decorated with a sumi-e brush design.

point for … for something. Something came. Then something more. Each felt like the prototype for a multimedia series. I had no idea whether they were *something* or just something, but I did know they originated in my inner world. I emailed images to Ross with resigned objectivity and trepidation.

∞

Email, September 20, 2011

First of a very few selections from Japan Dreaming series. Sending as separate emails so they don't overwhelm your computer!

Japan Dreaming I
Antique Japanese accounting book material, bark paper, pastel. ©Mellick

Japan Dreaming 7
Watercolour paper, watercolor, cheesecloth, natural indigo and ochre pigments. ©Mellick

Japan Dreaming 17
Wood, raffia, paper rope, antique Japanese paper, sandpaper. ©Mellick

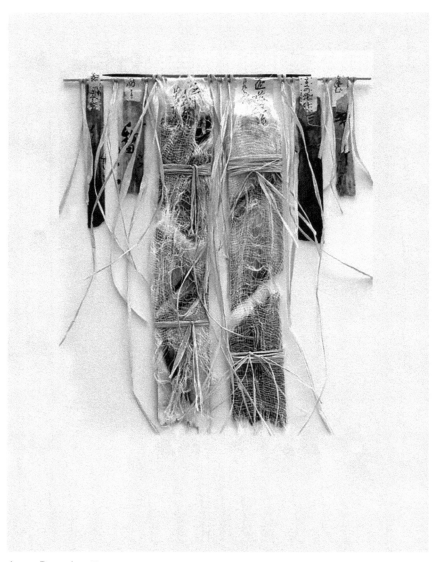

Japan Dreaming 19
Wood, cloth, raffia, pastel, burnt sticks, pastel. ©Mellick

This one is pretty big. Perhaps 18 x 30…. temporarily laid on two pieces
of large board …

∞

Email, Sep 20, 2011

Dear Jill:

I see what is taking its place. It is certainly the strongest I have seen by you. Glorious to know you are where you are. How hard it is get there.

Some lives are so far ahead of the living of them that the only way of living them is by way of art. Only that way can we catch up. Otherwise we know we have been left behind to inhabit what has been taken away from us. This you have reached out to and claimed in the only way it can be claimed. I certainly recognize what you are doing—what is being done in you and to you.

As for that 21-year-old animus in the garage—keep him there!

When is your exhibition? There was a recent show here in London. I do short reviews of them. I enclose one.

Much love,

Ross

∞

Email, September 29[226]

Dear Ross,

Each day I drive myself slightly crazy because I see your unanswered email and want to respond—want, not should. But the quality of what you offer me makes me want to respond with relative articulateness and often it's not possible.

---

[226] September 29, 2011.

However, let me just thank you very much for your honesty and for taking the time to look at and respond to my work. I really trust you not to be "nice" about my art. That is an inestimable gift. From what you say, I sense you are saying "Good beginning Jill. Not there yet. You have a long long long way to go but at least you've begun finally."

Oddly, these beginnings are attracting interest, which is encouraging in another way. But no, they are not part of the Spring 2012 show. In that show, I'm farewelling my love affair with landscape. It's called "Power of Place." The one AFTER that with the Japanese group will be called "Water Wind Breath: Japan Dreaming" (or perhaps I'll leave off the subtitle). "Water wind breath" is the translation of *po-wa-ha* in Tewa Indian. It is the spirit that flows through everything; the closest word for creativity and art the Tewa people have.

Your review of the show floored me. I know you're brilliant but this awed me some, frankly. I'll never forget walking around the MoMA in SFO with you and Marion and having my eyes opened by you. I looked in detail at the London show after reading your review.

Ross, do you know anyone who either is a conservator of art or a restorer? I am in touch with the Jung family about *The Red Book*[227] and its MAKING. No one, no one is looking at the art MAKING involved in the book—just taking it for granted. I am interested in the effect of the art on the maker over the 16 years he did it. No one can even tell me whether he prepared his own pigments in binding solution (which would be a naturally alchemical thing to do) or whether he bought pigments. I'm sure a restorer could at least tell me what was available in Switzerland at the time in terms of paint—or look at the repros of the RB and see whether the colours used there are commercial or derived purely from mineral and synthesised mineral pigment. Also what kind of brush was used.

---

[227] *The Red Book* is a large, handmade manuscript in which Carl Jung painted and recorded in calligraphy his inner visions. Jung's descendants eventually deposited the book in a bank vault; Jung had not specified what to do with it in his will. It later became clear that typed copies of the writing had been made during his lifetime, and a facsimile of the manuscript was published by W.W. Norton in 2009. JM saw the original at the Rubin Museum in New York and began inquiries into its making. This led to research with Jung's descendants and eventually the 2018 publication of her book *The Red Book Hours: Discovering C.G. Jung's Art Mediums & Creative Process* by Scheidegger & Speiss.

Don't worry if someone doesn't come to mind easily.

I send my loving greetings to you both and hope each of you are able to receive them; in other words, I hope there are some clear moments in the miasma today.

Jill

∞

November 20, 2011

Dear Jill

Is "Japan Dreaming 19" available? Could it be shipped? What is happening with this work? I think it is hugely wonderful stuff. Even if I did nothing more than write about it. Life here, of course, is very difficult even with full-time assistance. But I find what you are doing—or I think you are doing—hauntingly beautiful.

Much love,

Ross

∞

JM Notes
November 2011

On a phone call with Ross, he gave his opinion of my recent art pieces— at length. I cannot possibly remember what he said; it made my artist's heart sing so.

"You've *done* it! This is *magnificent!*." He didn't stop for about ten minutes. He was having what a close friend of Ross's called one of his "archetypal fits," and I was amazed at his comments. I was unable to take them in. They were another Qumran for me; as soon as his comments were exposed to my air, they crumbled into illegible fragments.

Finally, we hung up. All I knew was that someone I respected more than any other I knew in the field, who told the truth and whom I loved, had said, "Yes … Yes yes *yes*." My long climb up Everest was worth it just to hear his response.

Each construction would become the modern equivalent of a woodblock for a limited print.

I told him that yes "Japan Dreaming 19" was available, that I wanted him to have an A/P[228] and that I would not accept payment. His praise was payment enough.

When he received it, he framed it, floating its large size.

The thought of my strange experiment keeping company with art by makers whose work I'd only seen in musea with awe moved me greatly. Knowing how careful Marion and Ross were with the use of space in their exquisite two-storey townhouse with its white carpets and walls, my artistic journey had been worth it regardless of whether the rest of the pieces ever saw the light of day or ever sold. I only ever have written and painted so that I might touch another and/or be worthy of a valued other's respect. I've never written or painted for popularity. Ross gave me that respect. He deserved the first fruit. My painting was hanging out with the Rietveld chair I loved so much in the white-carpeted hall, with Curnoe and Molinari, with Northwestern alabaster, minimalist, First People carvings in the sitting room. That was more than enough for me.

---

[228] A/P is an Artist's Proof. In a print series, up to ten percent might be artist's proofs. As each of these series were limited to 30, I only had three A/Ps. A/Ps are more valuable than the early prints in the series.

∞

Email, December 5, 2011

Dear Jill:

Here is another review[229] of a recent show by another London artist, which may suggest why I was stirred by your recent work.

Love,

Ross

[Review not included.]

∞

Email, December 19, 2011

Dear Ross,

Greetings from Kaua'i where Jeanne and I are INTROVERTING for two and a half weeks. I'm finding some more in "the series" coming forth—I can't "make" them; I have to follow them.

Your words to me about "Japan Dreaming 19" continue to shake quietly in my bones. I wish the hell I'd written down what you said because they speak so deeply to me yet elude conscious repetition. Still, the meaning of what you said is in my marrow, thank you.

---

[229] Review not included here.

I hope you have, by now, received the copy of the journal *Culture and Psyche* with a selection from the series (including yours) in it as well as on the front and back covers. Did it arrive safely?

I have acted on all advice you gave me about the series, by the way. I don't take that kind of wise counsel from an expert and friend for granted!

If you can stand it, Ross, I have two other things I would like to ask you. Not as complex as our last discussion.

Firstly, do you know the name of an art restorer?

I am writing an article on what Jung's experience of painting *The Red Book* might have been. Everyone is focused on the content and the meaning and what a good artist he was; but no one is talking about the fact that the man spent SIXTEEN YEARS of his life painting the thing! THAT has an effect on one as you and I both know. One does not engage in such a prolonged and dedicated creative activity without the activity itself becoming a spiritual act.

I've been in touch with Jung's grandsons, each of whom has treated my ideas about this with surprising interest and respect; they have said that nothing is known about how Jung worked or his materials.

I have basic questions such as whether Jung made his own pigments or bought commercial; it makes a huge difference to his experience of painting—an alchemical difference apart from a technical one. Not even Sonu Shamdasani[230] knows anything (I've written to him) about the materials themselves, let alone Jung's habits. So, as my final piece of research before I write what will now be more of an imagined experience than a reported one, I'd like to get in touch with an art historian/restorer who would be familiar with what materials were available in Zürich during the years that Jung was painting. Someone who could even look at the high-resolution reproductions in *The Red Book* itself and take a guestimate at what he might have used. I have, for example, pretty much determined that the inks Jung used for the calligraphy would have come

---

[230] Sonu Shamdasani is the editor of the published version of *The Red Book*.

from a particular French ink maker. That's easy. The gouache/tempera question is a whole other thing.

The second question: might you know a graduate student or post-grad who is both familiar with journals that publish fiction and who might be interested in earning money by the hour submitting some of my stories. One doesn't use an agent for such ventures because short stories make an agent no money. However, I have no physical energy for doing the submissions myself. Post brain surgery and post cancer, I must set priorities on my use of my energies. So I need someone who knows what journals publish what fiction, what preferences and requirements are, and who might be good at submitting for me. Any thoughts? I'd like to give first refusal to someone who is known to and respected by someone like you.

If you have no thoughts about possible people for either of these ventures, that's fine. Don't even worry about replying. I am so *keenly* aware of the chaos of your days—and nights. However, do let me know whether you at least received this email; after our last experiences, I don't trust they are coming through to you.

With love, as always, and hoping that perhaps we might see each other, even if briefly for a cup of tea in London, this coming year.

Jill

∞

Email, December 27, 2011

Dear Jill:

Lucky you and Jeanne in such a beautiful introverting place. I am here so nearly out of everything that I am no help even to myself, let alone Marion. Little Marion (niece) went to England for Christmas. ... So we are here more or less alone. I think it was essential for her to go. What is here is mightily difficult. She'll be back in the new year.

I got the copy of *Culture and Psyche* which was a great help. They are beautiful pieces[231] and carry their own account of the ruins in a way that I had not seen before. What is particularly powerful is the life that remains in ruins as a mysterious transformation of them. It's like those sonnets of Shakespeare that address a love affair long over, yet living on as a sonnet to the last syllable of recorded time.[232]

"The Tempest" is the fullest sense of that. It begins with a shipwreck that magically restores life by finally taking him to his death. "This rough magic I here abjure. As you from crimes would pardon'd be,/ Let your indulgence set me free." He is addressing his audience, acknowledging its applause (indulgence). Born into a Catholic family in a Protestant England where the active practice of Catholicism (eucharist, etc.) is punishable by death, Shakespeare may be conducting a series of undercover, highly disguised Masses in his plays, particularly "The Tempest."

Something as remote as that is at work in these works of yours.

I don't know anyone who can help with your work on Jung. I doubt that he mixed his own pigments. He worked alone after supper, very few people knowing what he was doing. I never see students but I will ask my editor—if under the pressure of what goes on here I do see him—I see almost nothing—and yet I have still some secret inner life which I cannot share with Marion… but no more of that.

Much love,

Ross

---

[231] Several of the "Japan Dreaming" series were included in *Culture and Psyche*; one was chosen for the cover and one for the back cover of the journal.

[232] Ross was referring to "Macbeth," Act V, Scene 5, Macbeth's soliloquy.

∞

Email, January 22, 2012

Dear Ross,

For heaven's sake, this email from you written on December 27 *just* arrived in my mail box! How very strange!

Thank you for it. I love getting emails from you. Some of what you wrote in December I now know from our more recent phone conversation. However, I didn't, obviously, have your comments on Shakespeare, which enrich my views of things studied in depth long ago. Thank you for those.

I ordered your latest book. It just arrived and yesterday joined what I hope will be good friends for it beside my bed—a lovely selection of new and old friends. I move forward slowly in my reading of them. I seem to be so driven to bring order to the past (archiving my mother's musical legacy is a task that gives new meaning to "infinite"), my patients, medical stuff and my health, making art and writing; so sitting down during the day and just reading is nigh impossible. So instead I keep my book mates by the bed, begin to make love with one, then promptly fall asleep. So it takes me inordinate time to get through a book. But it is THERE, your book, with some elegant friends, and I look forward to glimpses of you, your perspectives, and insights in the same way I am nourished and stirred by them when we speak.

Certainly the title of your recent book could well be a title for a book you are living at home at present. ... But enough: even if you were to entertain writing about it, even to friends, you are too busy *living* it ... enduring it.)... Last time we spoke you said that, because of my training and experience, I did seem to comprehend some of how it is for you. It might be odd but I do think of this as a privilege: to be one of those willing to accompany you at times, only if wanted and however I can, on this dreadful, unspeakable journey.

Your words—about my recent explorations in the realm of the wordless in these...*things* I'm making—continue to be a central source of encouragement to go further. Where on earth I'm going to sell them is beyond me but I'll leave that for another day.

With love to you, dear Ross,

Jill

∞

Email, April 24, 2012

Dear Ross,

So glad I reached you and we could talk a little. I have your new book, you know, and it sits happily along with other promises of immersion beside my bed for reading (it's quite a pile!). Thank you for mentioning the new Sonu book. I ordered it, received it, and have reviewed it. It's beautifully put together ... the concept of it fits perfectly with the RB[233]: the seamless interweaving of word and image in the true spirit of the medieval manuscript.

I keep meaning to tell you that the certificate I sent you is a working copy of one, not a final. So if you are showing it to the Gibson,[234] please let them know this is not the Final Authority. It is a work in progress, like all of this—but will give them an accurate idea of the printing process at least.

Must be up and off with the dog to the groomers.

Nice to be able to just send you a little note like this.

Love

Jill

PS Beirut wants 27 of the pieces![235] Oy! Large investment. I would like to move away from calling them ALL Japan Dreaming because clearly this

---

[233] *The Red Book.*
[234] Gibson Gallery in London, Ontario.
[235] Galerie Pièce Unique in Beirut invited JM to have a one-woman show.

form is leading me, not the original inspiration. Do you have any thoughts on what to call different suites? I'm terrible at naming things (except for my landscapes for some reason).

∞

Email, April 26, 2012

Dear Ross,

This note is written in haste but always with heart.

I have to prepare materials pronto to send to Beirut for marketing the show. (Hits my shadow—can't *stand* self-promotion but *some* "buzz" and press releases are necessary if this show is to fly).

Could I invite you to write a short, quotable para about the series? You see things in them no one else does and you express it with breathtaking elegance. I'd like to send a quote/brief review from you—along with the other information.

I suppose it would need some kind of identifying information underneath, e.g. your name, your place in the art world (e.g. collector ... critic for____ or whatever one puts on these things—this is all new to me) and your title and so on to give the quote heft.

The gallery marketing person would like information by the end of May if possible but as late as the end of June would probably work.

If you are so swamped internally and/or externally that you can't even think of doing this, don't even contemplate replying. You sounded so present *and* so tired the other day.

With love and appreciation for even thinking about it,

Jill

∞

Email, June 28, 2012

Dearest Ross,

I've not heard from you in response to my last couple of emails so I'm concerned about you—and Marion too. The well-being of one affects the other's. I did leave you a phone message before I went off to Oz (translation: Australia as she is known by the locals).

Before I waffle further, please just let me know you received this and how you each are.

With love as always,

Jill

∞

Email, July 17, 2012

Dear Jill:

I all too quickly lose track and when I see 150 messages am bewildered. Knowing what I fear may be happening I withdraw further and attend to something else. Duration is now the issue. I am still arranging affairs here. Marion remains in and out, like me. We have ample help, thank God. Bought the third-floor apartment as a further retreat. … Explanations! Explanations!

Much love,

Ross

∞

Photograph of a Canadian lake[236]
MW to JM
This is what Ross and I are going to in two weeks' time. Every night from our window!

∞

May 23[237]

Have spent the afternoon together on our back porch. Glorious sunshine! Now I feel quite exhausted. But good. Ross and I have hit a good balance between leisure and work. I don't know if I'll get things together to write another book. I'm thinking of editing my own journal and seeing how that feels in terms of putting it out either while I live or after I die. That's a narrow line. Only I can make those decisions. Well, maybe that's not true. Maybe someone more objective could do a better job.

Well, dear Jill, much, much love. Blessings to Jeanne. I hold you in my prayers. So many times we had together were so rich—I miss that with my friends. Ross and I have it together—but male/female is different.

Dearest love—

Marion

---

[236] MW wrote on the back of a photograph and sent it as a postcard.
[237] MW did not note the year, but given the content, it would have been after 2008.

∞

May 23[238]

Dear Jill,

The 24th of May is "the Queen's Birthday" which we still celebrate in Canada—the Queen was originally Queen Victoria who died almost a century ago.[239] However people really go on a rampage with government if their first visit to their cottage in the year is taken away. So we have a long week-end every month of summer. I hope you are both well. Am still in trouble but the pain is lessening and I can safely move in the house. It has been a very hard winter for Ross and me. We are looking forward to a gentle Spring and Summer. He has been a magnificent nurse when I was in need of just plain love.

∞

From Marion: [undated card of Japanese ukio-e woodblock with 2007 printed on it.[240] She chose a page from an old calendar of Japanese prints.]

I've learned to look at Japanese art through your eyes, Jill. Not enough. But at least able to see it richly.

Love

M.

---

[238] MW did not note the year, but it would have been after 2012.
[239] MW's early dementia might be sensed here, or the fact that she was writing to a fellow member of the Commonwealth might not have been in her awareness. The Queen's birthday is celebrated in all Commonwealth countries.
[240] No date was written, but to judge from MW's capacity to write and the delivery mode, she sent this well into her dementia.

∞

January 26[241]

Dear Jeanne and Jill,

Blessings of the new year. The snow here is still piled higher than our heads. And cold. There comes an event where it doesn't feel natural anymore. Cut off from nature and the whole outer world. Ross and I are OK, both working. And are enduring. (Sorry about the wreck of this card but I love to think of summer heat and our garden.)

Ross is writing a splendid book. We help each other.
Love your [writing illegible] card.

Love you both

Marion

∞

JM Notes
Sunday, March 16, 2014

I called Ross. Despite all indications to the contrary, he had been determined to care for Marion at home but finally had to accept that he was no longer able to give her the care she needed. It nearly cost him his soul to acknowledge this and to act on that knowledge. He visited her daily. However, this did not allay either his or Marion's distress at the change that her condition had necessitated.

---

[241] No year was written by MW.

A few weeks into Marion's change in care, I called Ross on a Sunday afternoon—evening in his time zone. We spoke as though we had been speaking all afternoon and were just continuing. We spoke for about an hour. He was in torment. Ross spoke intensely and with angst about the situation. I recalled Marion's saying she would rather be dead than in a compromised state and dependent. She and I had shared that wish early in our friendship. However, it was neither needed nor kind to share this comment, made long ago, with Ross. Life had taken them both far beyond that. What had inevitably happened was that things had become medically unaddressable in a home environment.

I was glad to be able to draw on experience of working with people and their families who needed to be in residential care. I could tell him that it would take Marion about six weeks—possibly longer—to become used to a new environment and that time would take on a different meaning. I also told him, and meant it, that he had great courage to do what he had had to do as the person Marion loved most in the world—especially when she was the one he loved most in the world.

Somewhere during his eloquent, heart-rending *cri de coeur*, I reflected that in my experience of working with family members, *no-one* ever thought he or she had put a loved one into a higher-care environment at the "right' time. There *was* no right time. Family were convinced that they had done it either too early or too late. There was no magic day when it became clear, either in the present or retrospectively.

Ross listened to my words as though he were in quicksand and I, holding out a stick. However, I knew nothing could really stay steady in his perspective. While my experience and his greater understanding of her condition might help, his pain would not lessen. Marion's lodestar poet, Emily Dickinson, best described his state; I could not:

There is a pain — so utter —
It swallows substance up —
Then covers the Abyss with Trance —
So Memory can step
Around — across — opon [sic] it —

As One within a Swoon —
Goes safely — where an open eye —
Would drop Him — Bone by Bone —[242]

He told me of his daily visits, how painful they were; he felt he had betrayed her trust and that, as her illnesses progressed, there would be nothing for them to share.

Then grace dropped in on us. The field between Ross and me at that moment opened us to it because I have no idea what made me say what I did. Were I to be grateful for only one thing about my advanced studies in English Literature—also Ross's field for over forty years—it would be this: I heard my voice say with conviction that startled, "Ross! It's under our noses! *Poetry's* what brought you together. *Poetry's* your life. *Poetry's* been your life together. *Poetry's* what's going to *keep* you together. Read Marion *poetry!* She *needs* it. And she needs it from *you!*"

"By God, girl! You're right! You're right! *Poetry!*"

Ross's entire mood changed. He was spilling over with excitement. The language of love that had brought them together, poetry, was what would keep them together. Ross sounded like someone who had just been released from solitary confinement on death row in a high-security prison and was walking free, someone who was feeling the sun on his face for the first time in years, who could feel and smell the earth, who could see colors again. The joy in his voice was full-throated, palpable. He couldn't wait to walk the next day to share poetry with his beloved Marion.

We both felt it. We each hung up changed. I heard that he and Marion had a good visit the next day.

That Thursday night, Ross died in his sleep.

---

[242] Fr#515 in: Franklin, R. W., ed. *The Poems of Emily Dickinson: Reading Edition* (The Belknap Press, 1999).

∞

March 2014

Dearest Marion,

. . .You are in my heart all the time. I know your world has changed. You have to be in the hospital now and Ross's time on earth has ended. But *nothing* separates you from you and nothing separates you from Ross. The love you and Ross have for each other is strong and endures all changes, even death.

My love for you and your love for me is steady and strong, too.

When I talked with Ross recently he missed you at home so much, but the doctor told him that you need to be in the hospital to get the help you need to feel better. Ross said he loved coming to see you every day.

He and you have always met in poetry and imagination. You can still meet with him there. That place of "poetic faith" Ross used to describe is where you and he lived and loved together. It still exists.

Because Ross died, he cannot visit you for lunch but you can visit Ross in your heart, dear Marion; Ross loved and loves you. Even on the day Ross passed away, I dreamt that he told me of his love for you. Everything changes. But true love does not change.

Shakespeare said it better than I. You know this sonnet well:

Let me not to the marriage of true minds
Admit impediments. Love is not love
Which alters when it alteration finds,
Or bends with the remover to remove.
O no, it is an ever-fixèd mark.
That looks on tempests and is never shaken;
It is the star to every wand'ring bark,
Whose worth's unknown, although his height be taken.

Love's not Time's fool, though rosy lips and cheeks.
Within his bending sickle's compass come:
Love alters not with his brief hours and weeks,
But bears it out even to the edge of doom.
If this be error and upon me prov'd,
I never writ, nor no man ever lov'd.[243]

Soon Spring will come. You will see green from your window. It comes whether we are sad or happy. Our Spring here has already come. All our tulips are out. All our hyacinths are blooming. All our irises are blooming! I shall write again soon.

I send you love, dearest Marion.

Jill. Jeanne sends love too.

∞

JM Notes
May 2015

Wanting to be with Marion once more, to say my own farewell to her—in a way I'd been unable to do with two other cherished people in my life— I flew to Toronto in 2015 during tulip time. I was prepared for anything. However, I was unprepared (especially for an Australian used to big distances) about how much territory Ontario covered! I planned to stay with one cousin in Toronto, visit cousins I'd not met in Ottawa, and visit Marion in London. I achieved this—and learned a lot about the vastness of Ontario in the process.

Marion Boa, Marion's niece, was her companion and full-time advocate at the time. She kindly advised me how to get from my hotel (where I had a long swim) to the facility. She was warmth and sensitive observation itself. She spoke of her pleasure in seeing more of the

---

[243] William Shakespeare, Sonnet 116.

"Auntie" she'd loved before Marion became so in demand. She explained that they were looking forward to being able to move Auntie to an even better facility before long.

I recognized the feel, the preternatural stillness of some of the patients in wheelchairs, and also the efficiency of nurses and nursing station, as I followed "Little Marion" (as Marion had been in the habit of calling her niece) to Marion's room. Marion had her bed, a window, a small desk and chair, a comfortable seat, and seemed relaxed. I was prepared for anything, from her medical ravages rendering her unable to recognize me to her being unresponsive. I'd encountered everything in the years I'd consulted to an assisted living facility.

What I was not prepared for was someone whose soul was in excellent health and who welcomed the Jill she knew.

She recognized me at once, and with delight. We spent no time on idle chatter. My professional experience had led me to understand how much personality depended on memory. However, what I now recognized with Marion was something new: memory can fade after trauma, serious chronic illness, and loss but it can also leave the personality and soul intact and steady. We spoke—Marion to Jill, Jill to Marion—as we had always spoken: we spoke of inner matters important to each of us. Her stamina for being with and conversing with me surprised me.

We were overjoyed to be together. And we were together far longer than I had expected. We sat and talked and laughed alone in her room for more than two hours, close by one another, holding hands, gazing at each other.

We dropped deep into matters of heart and soul. Despite all she had gone through and was still going through, she remembered surprising and particular aspects of my past and present history. More important, her steadiness of *essence*, of *soul*, was unbroken—and her knowledge of *my essence, my soul,* was intact. We spoke as we had always spoken: from the deepest place in each of us. Nothing had changed. We relished in, delighted in being physically together again. The love between us was as strong, as intense, as joyful as it always had been. Her love for me was undiminished, as was mine for her.

We still were.

What follows I have excerpted and edited from journal notes of this final meeting in person. (I'm fated with a poor memory for facts and good recall for conversation; it's helped in my vocation.)

This does not represent a continuous or complete conversation, just what I noted later. We were together about two and a half hours.

Something about which Marion and I were speaking made me think of Archibald Macleish's "Ars Poetica." I pulled out my phone, found it, and read parts for us. "'A poem should be palpable and mute / As a globed fruit....A poem should be wordless/as the flight of birds.... A poem should be equal to / Not true. // For all the history of grief / An empty doorway and a maple leaf....'"

"Just give me the last two lines you read," Marion asked.

"'For all the history of grief / An empty doorway and a maple leaf.'"

"That's right. Exactly."

"I've never really *taken* that part *in* before," I mused. "'For all the history of grief / An empty doorway and a maple leaf.'"

"Terrific," said Marion, as we sat quietly.

I entered the silence at the edge. "Sometimes poetry's the only thing that—"

"—satisfies." Marion completed my sentence.

"That's why I wanted to see your work in poetic prose in *Coming Home to Myself.*"

"I'm getting ready to write again," Marion said. "I've got two worlds going; one stops and the other goes ahead. It's quite simple. I notice 'This is a new idea.' It expands into vocabulary and I get as close as I can to the meaning. Then I work around the place and I think 'I'll just try that again.'"

"So there's the daily world and the eternal world that's moving through your psyche forming ideas and words."

"Yes. I try to let it be and not try to hammer it into shape."

"You don't try to make it '*mean...*'"I added, referring to the last line in Macleish's poem.

"Yes, that's right. Though it's hard."

"It *is* hard, Like waiting on a birth. I don't know if you've felt this or if all people who write, paint, compose—whatever—feel that if it doesn't come or if I don't like what has come, it's never going to come again. One feels, 'I've lost it. I've lost it forever.'"

"That energy wants to destroy what the ego is trying to produce. For me, anyway, the ego is my standing point. And usually it speaks up and says, 'This is what it is.' But sometimes it doesn't and that's a different story..." She did not elaborate.

"That other voice says, 'Well, you've lost it. You can't do it any more.' It's that 'Don't *be*' voice, isn't it?" I commented. "It's the one you used to talk about: the crocodile lies still under the water; then if you move even a *little* bit, it snaps its jaws to kill."

"*Exactly.*"...

... Marion sat, looked at her hands and over at her desk. "I see something that's supposed to be 'so great.' And *I* don't see...It's a *show-off* thing! It's not the real stuff. But I don't worry any more. I just think, 'Well, that's that—but I want the *real.*'"

"One doesn't have time for the rest," I added.

"At *my* age, you don't have time to fiddle around!"

"That's crone energy, isn't it, Marion."

"That's crone."

"It's 'Don't bother me.' energy."

"And at this age, I need that. I've got to be able to stand on my own knowing. And not play around with it." She looked at something in the unknown, then at me. We let being together without speaking hold us.

"Marion, there's a Japanese concept: *ma*—'space' is a simplistic translation—it's multilayered. I'm learning to live by it slowly. It's hard. It's easy to fill up space—I should do art, write, play the piano, do one more consultation, call family, friends… I should, should, should. I try to remember *ma*. It's the space in Japanese temples, gardens, paintings. It isn't *empty*. It's the present in potentia, unfolding." I stopped. I didn't know how to express it better.

"And you walk in there and you know," Marion said, picking up where I left off. "Something comes and hits you or does something, but you know that you've *got* to move into it. What comes through that door comes through and you work with it. That's it. When I don't, my body tells me. And you know what? It's not putting up with any nonsense any more. It just knocks me flat if I don't pay attention to it. That's one thing about old age that I like."

"Just before I left, I received a card from a woman who consults with me—she went to one of your workshops a long time ago. She didn't know I was coming to see you. She said, 'I was reminded recently of being at Marion's workshop at Pajaro Dunes. I went for a walk on the beach one day and stood and watched the little birds. The waves would come in and out, and the birds would race in and get all their food before the next wave came." She said, 'It's the space between where one gets fed.' It's the space between."

"And I think of all those years when I was traveling so much. I'd get a red something in my dreams. It would say 'Stop!' And I did."…

… I could see Marion was tiring yet wanted to prolong the visit. "You know what I was thinking? One of the things we could do, given we want to be together but don't have energy for doing much, is to listen to music or just be silent—meditate together."

"Yes, I can do that," she replied and added, "We'll both do it."

"And we also know we only have the present..." I said quietly....

... She took my right hand. "Your hand is so cold!"

"My hands run cold."

"It really is *cold*!"

"Well, I have this hand too!" We laughed. She took my other hand, too.

"That ring! Woo! And it complements the other." I was wearing two sapphire and diamond rings.

"Yes. But this one is special. It has stones from grandmothers—put together."

"May I put it on?"

"Please."

"Oh! What a *beautiful* ring!" She turned her still slim fingers so the afternoon light caught the facets of the old, mine-cut sapphires and diamonds.

"It has a lot of love in it." I commented as she gazed into it.

"Sure does.... Wow. I *really* like that ring!"
.
"So do I. This one's beautiful but it doesn't have the same feeling."

"If I get into a certain mood, there's something in the vault.... I used to go down and get it. It's a ring with a sapphire too..."

Marion gave me back the ring and looked up at me again.

"And your pearls!" she exclaimed. I was wearing a pearl necklace over forty years old.

"A gift decades ago. I usually wear them. Pearls and I—" I realized I need say nothing about pearls. Pearls were highly significant to both Marion and me. Years ago, we had included her dream of losing her pearls, her feminine essence, and having them returned to her in *Coming Home to Myself.*

"*Beautiful* string!" Marion exclaimed. "I can see from here. They have *your* oils in them now after all this time. They're *your* pearls."…

…Marion was tiring. I texted her niece on my mobile phone. She came to the room to ease the parting, arriving cheerfully and showing Marion and me things on her iPad. We all agreed that Marion and I could "visit" courtesy of FaceTime on the iPad when the time was good, which would be Marion's niece's choice.

We hugged a long hug and kissed each other. Her cool cheek was as soft as always.

I walked back to the hotel alone.

∞

While Marion was in full-time care, her niece Marion Boa came daily to keep her company and go together for walks in the nearby park. Marion lived for almost three years after I visited her. Thanks to Marion B, Marion and I did speak on FaceTime; we were still Marion and Jill. When her health deteriorated further, we were no longer able to do that.

Marion Boa stayed in regular contact with me. She sent me photos of Marion smiling, walking, delighting in spring walks in the park, raising her arms up in delight at the coming of spring, sitting contentedly in front of a Madonna in the park, relaxing on a bench. She was walking remarkably well. (She also had a walker and Marion B. to accompany her). Her physical strength improved, in fact. I sent her photographs and short emails through Marion B.

In December 2016, I was diagnosed with metastatic breast cancer in neck, spine, and hips. Fusion of neck vertebrae in January 2017 was followed by radiation and permanent chemotherapy. Soul mate Jeanne died in December 2017, two weeks after seeing me sign the contract with Scheidegger & Spiess to publish *The Red Book Hours: Discovering C.G. Jung's Art Mediums & Creative Process*—a research project that had taken eight years since we first saw the original *Red Book* at the Rubin Museum in New York City. It was Jeanne who had introduced me to Carl Jung's work in 1972.

Somehow—with superb help—I prepared the manuscript for publication over the next months.

On July 9, 2018, Marion died.

Marion Boa and I stayed in touch afterwards.

In November 2018, *The Red Book Hours* entered the world—on the same day that *The Art of C.G. Jung* (prepared by the Foundation of the Works of C.G. Jung and to which I had contributed a chapter) entered the world. Thomas Fischer, Ph.D., Director of the Foundation, told me both books awaited him on the doorstep of his office the same morning. I wished I could share it with Jeanne. I wished I could share it with Marion.

Ross and Marion's bequests were handled by Jean Peacock, longtime friend and secretary, and Joel Faflak, Ross's collaborator and friend. What Marion and Ross each had chosen for me arrived halfway between Marion's birthday on August 15 and mine on August 29. Ross had chosen a painting. Marion had chosen a delicate pendant—a circle of pearls and rubies. In the Victorian era, a pendant or brooch of this style symbolized deep friendship. Pearls were symbolically highly significant in both

Marion bequeathed this pearl, ruby, and gold pendant to Jill. In the Victorian era, these pendants were given within deep, abiding friendships. ©Mellick

Marion's and my inner and outer lives as I said. In *Coming Home to Myself,* we even referred to her dream of losing her pearls, and in one of her letters, she mentions deep concern at being unable to find her pearls.

Rubies, of course, are linked to the heart. The two circles formed by the pearls and by the rubies symbolize friendship, wholeness, the Self, timelessness, eternity. I wear the pendant often.

The painting Ross intended for me was the one I had given him, which had met with his explosive approval and which he had wanted to buy but I had sent to him. He had told me he had spoken to the Gibson Gallery in London, Ontario, (where a room was named after him) about holding a show for me. In the complicated task of distributing bequests, that painting ended up with someone in Canada. I'm glad it's still up there somehow and that I have no idea where. The watercolor I had given Marion of Pajaro Dunes did come home to me.

A memorial in Marion's honor was held January 19–20, 2019, at Pacifica Graduate Institute, which had regularly hosted Marion and Ross for months at a time. Health and treatment made it impossible for me to hold the fire ceremony I had promised Marion in Canada or even at Pacifica. However, I held it with the assistance of friend Sherry Cassedy, intimate both with yogic rituals and Marion's work.

We held the fire ceremony in the studio. Its skylight spreads filtered light from three giant deodar cedars over ten stories high; they started life in one-gallon pots planted by Jeanne decades earlier. It was the room we had given to Marion for writing and quiet when she stayed with us, the room in which she and I had worked joyfully, honestly, exactingly on *Coming Home to Myself*, the room in which we had revised Marion's words and my music for "Emily Dickinson and the Demon Lover," the room in which I've written my books, played the grand, painted. Only creative things have happened in this room.

I gathered the ashes. Sherry took them to Pacifica and stood in for me. Participants were planting a rose in Marion's honor. Sherry explained *homa*[244] and Marion's request that I hold it at her funeral. She asked those present to chant "Svaha"[245] as she placed the ashes in the earth with the rose. Then she spoke for me: "Marion, as you asked, the fire ceremony has been done. Now we each shall tend our own pots and keep our separate flames alight—the same, yet not the same."

Only later did I realize the ceremony enacted the last line of T.S. Eliot's *Four Quartets*,[246] from which Marion frequently quoted, "And the fire and the rose are one."

---

[244] A ceremony held at transitions. It originated thousands of years ago in Hindu tradition. It symbolizes the release of the old and embrace of the new.It is often performed at sunrise, births, holy days, blessings, and deaths. The fire is lit in a copper pot using cow dung and ghee; participants offer herbs, rice and mantras to the fire. *Svaha* is chanted each time an offering is made.

[245] In Sanskrit *svaha* connotes "So be it. I bless and commit this to its fate, now forever changed."

[246] From the last section of T.S. Eliot's *Four Quartets*, "Little Gidding."

∞

Postscript

I sent a draft of this manuscript to my editor and completed revisions on July 9, 2021, which I later realized was the third anniversary of Marion's death.

Later, I chose images for the manuscript. The night I finished choosing them, I dreamed Marion was alive, frail, and in Canada. I was delighted and decided to visit her.

Perhaps I'm wrong; perhaps the arc of certain friendships—the arc of certain relationships— does not end with the death of one. Rainbows are not, in fact, arcs; they're circles—but they are only visible as such from above.

Acknowledgments

Peter Cassini, M.D. skilled, gifted, generous, experienced neurologist, has kept my rare disorders balanced on the head of a pin day and night; his dedication, discernment, openness, love of profession, and capacity to cut through the kudzu vines of symptoms with which I present him give me quality of life.

Joel Faflak, Ph.D., Professor of English, University of Western Ontario, and one of Marion and Ross's patient, superb executors, provided helpful information about Ross Woodman's art collection.

Edith Gelles, Ph.D., author and Senior Scholar at the Clayman Institute for Gender Studies, provided wise guidance about the ethics and responsibilities of writing biography—particularly when it includes oneself—and gave me faith in my capacity to write this.

Mary Hamilton, graduate of the National Ballet School of Canada, M.Ed., a former professor at the University of Western Ontario, where she taught modern dance, improvisation, and choreography, created and led, with Marion and Ann Skinner, BodySoul Rhythms. She gave me her warm blessing on anything I wrote and any image I included. It felt timely that she sent her consent from Colenso, her family island in Georgian Bay.

Juliet Kral, M.D., gifted, experienced, skilled, dedicated, and loving oncologist and person, has kept me alive against poor odds since 2008. Her always current, far-ranging knowledge, coupled with empathy and respect, is rare.

Jennifer Maxon, Director of OPUS Archives, Pacifica Graduate Institute, Santa Barbara, reviewed Marion's archives for me. OPUS is still archiving my work—slowed, of course, by COVID restrictions. She and her associates have been kind, sensitive, and exemplary in their treatment of Marion's and my archives and of our friendship.

Hugh Milstein, President of DigitalFusion, once again brought his artistic and technical gifts to the imagery in this book. He made the hundreds of images in *The Red Book Hours* sing. He did the same for those I include here.

Megan O'Grady Greene, with her wide range of skills and degrees, had already organized my materials for OPUS archives, including the correspondence between Marion and me. This made the writing of this manuscript possible. She was, too, the American production manager of *The Red Book Hours*.

Ellen Questel, Ph.D., beloved sister-friend and distant cousin, believes in and heartens me in rich times and lean.

Paula Reeves, Ph.D., clinician, author, facilitator at ShaSha and later leader in BodySoul Rhythms training, kindly gave me carte blanche to include what I wish in this manuscript.

Phyllis Selving, patient, kind editor, was as careful with this manuscript as she was with the tome that preceded it: *The Red Book Hours: Discovering C.G. Jung's Art Materials and Creative Process.* Her quiet respect for what I do coupled with her knowledge of grammar and punctuation are rarities I value and respect.

Ann Skinner, Head of Voice Emerita at Canada's Stratford Shakespeare Festival, former Head of Voice at the National Theatre School of Canada, and creator and leader of BodySoul Rhythms with Marion and Mary Hamilton, gave me generous, unconditional blessing on anything I said and any image I used.

Eleanora Woloy, M.D., was the first to cast eyes on this manuscript. A deeply private person and one of Marion's closest friends, she gave the manuscript time, love, and attention—twice of her own volition. She gave it her unconditional blessing and made one small, important suggestion, which I made without question. My trust in her preservation of Marion's privacy and mine allayed my residual concerns about sharing any of this material, already heavily edited for privacy, with a larger readership. She was surprised when I asked if I could include her in the dedication. Our bi-coastal friendship has always let us dive into the depths independent of time and distance.

No manuscript is written in a vacuum. My days move among water workouts; chemotherapy; multiple outpatient surgeries; medical appointments; family and friends; consultations with my patients and consultees; writing, painting and playing the piano when physically possible; home health care; tending the aesthetics of garden and house; maintaining quiet order; and returns to our second home in Kaua'i. Most of my days have been spent in this haven since 2016 and the demise of my immune system. Several quietly help me live my fullest here and make my passions and medical commitments possible; they include Maria Castillo, Jofresina Delatorre, Nynke van den Berg, and Lastenia Tejada. They are the embodiment of values that Marion held and I hold. They grace my days.

Above all, my family, extended family, and friends, visible and invisible, are nonpareil. Their love permeates me from near and far.

CPSIA information can be obtained
at www.ICGtesting.com
Printed in the USA
BVHW020058251121
622346BV00029B/1165